PICTURING RESEARCH

Picturing Research

Drawing as Visual Methodology

Edited by

Linda Theron
North-West University, South Africa

Claudia Mitchell
McGill University, Canada & University of KwaZulu-Natal, South Africa

Ann Smith
University of the Witwatersrand, South Africa & McGill University, Canada

and

Jean Stuart
University of KwaZulu-Natal, South Africa

SENSE PUBLISHERS
ROTTERDAM / BOSTON / TAIPEI

A C.I.P. record for this book is available from the Library of Congress.

ISBN 978-94-6091-595-6 (paperback)
ISBN 978-94-6091-597-0 (hardback)
ISBN 978-94-6091-596-3 (e-book)

Published by: Sense Publishers,
P.O. Box 21858, 3001 AW Rotterdam, The Netherlands
www.sensepublishers.com

The contents of this book were blind peer-reviewed, pre-print.

Printed on acid-free paper

As members of a team of researchers involved in piloting a module titled "Being a Teacher in the Context of the HIV and AIDS Pandemic", we came into contact with many dedicated teacher educators and teachers in South Africa who were keen to use participatory methods in their classrooms. We dedicate this book to the people who continually inspire us to do this kind of work.

TABLE OF CONTENTS

ACKNOWLEDGEMENTS

The bigger picture of *Picturing Research: Drawings as Visual Methodology* includes the international symposium titled "Every Voice Counts: Critical Partnerships for Teacher Education and Rural Communities" that was convened by Naydene de Lange through the Centre for Visual Methodologies for Social Change at the University of KwaZulu-Natal from February 27–28, 2009. At this symposium, Mathabo Khau presented some of her work on teachers' sexual identities and Linda Theron presented some of her findings on teachers' perceptions of the HIV&AIDS pandemic. Both these presentations foregrounded drawings as a data collection method and also as powerful data. During teatime Claudia Mitchell suggested, "You know, we should do a book on drawings." And so the idea of our book, *Picturing Research*, was born. Although there was immediate and collective editorial enthusiasm, Linda, Jean, and (later) Ann would like to gratefully acknowledge Claudia's zest for inspiring new projects, for championing methodologies that encourage social change, and for mentoring fledgling researchers (even towards publishing books)!

Picturing Research would have remained a dream for us as editors (and authors) without the contributions of all of the authors. We applaud them not only for their scholarly contributions but also for their use of participatory methodologies (such as the use of drawing) and for their commitment to the idea of research as social change. In the same breath, we wish to thank their respective participants for their willingness to draw and for their generosity in allowing their drawings (or photographs of their drawings) to be made public.

Although we are writing this set of acknowledgements as a team, Linda, Claudia, and Jean wish to acknowledge the significance of having Ann join the editorial team. Furthermore, we are very thankful for her co-authorship of Chapters 1, 2, and 11; for her thorough and incisive editing of all the chapters in this volume; and for her endless patience as a mentor and scholar. We are indebted to Heleneze van Zyl who assisted with the initial editing of the reference lists. We are particularly grateful to John Murray for his assiduous formatting of each chapter, for his keen eye for detail, and especially for his rigour in getting this manuscript into its final form.

We wish to thank the reviewers who conducted blind reviews of the individual chapters: Johan Botha (NWU); Kate Cockroft (Wits); Naydene de Lange (NMMU), Elzette Fritz (UJ); Mary Grosser (NWU), Louise Hall (UKZN); Sally Hobden (UKZN); Sipho Kwatubana (NWU); Rob Pattman (UKZN); Teresa Strong-Wilson (McGill); Di Wilmot (Rhodes); Lesley Wood (NMMU); and Kyung-Hwa Yang (McGill). We are appreciative of their perceptive comments and their selfless commitment to enhancing the quality of this book.

Finally, we thank Michel Lokhorst of Sense Publishers for his interest in and support for this project.

Linda Theron, Claudia Mitchell, Ann Smith, and Jean Stuart

LIST OF FIGURES

PICTURING RESEARCH: AN INTRODUCTION

Claudia Mitchell, Linda Theron, Ann Smith, and Jean Stuart

AUTOBIOGRAPHY OF THE QUESTION

We begin this book with a section that offers something of what Jane Miller (1995) describes as the 'autobiography of the question' or, in this case, the autobiography of the question of method. With an increased recognition of the importance of the positioning of the researcher, the place of reflexivity in qualitative work, and the emergence of work in autoethnography (Ellis, 2004) and self-study (Pithouse, Mitchell, & Moletsane, 2009), we think it is useful to 'draw ourselves' into the research. And in similar vein to Kathleen Pithouse's exploration in the third chapter of the issue of 'starting with ourselves', here we each offer a short 'how did we get here' illustration of our work with drawings—how did we each come to be using drawings and compiling a book called *Picturing Research*? We think it is an important question because none of us started out using drawings as method in our research, and so our accounts may help others to think about the evolving nature of ideas and the dynamic aspect of knowledge production, as well as the significance of method itself. We also offer these short accounts because they are primarily (though not exclusively) located in the southern African context. An impetus for writing the book in the first place was an awareness of the absence of work in an area of methodology that seemed so appropriate to the southern African context. Ardra Cole and Gary Knowles (2008) in their own reflections on how they came to be working in arts-based research cited the work of the artist Martha Rosler: "[If you want to] bring conscious concrete knowledge to your work ... you had better locate yourself pretty concretely in it" (p. 55). By exploring our own work with drawings historically, geographically, and culturally, we hope that other researchers will similarly embark upon autobiographies of the method.

Claudia Mitchell

My own experience of using drawings in research dates back to the early 1990s when Sandra Weber and I were first working together on studies of teacher identity. It was a bit accidental, really. We had just been thinking about using visual data when one of us, I don't remember who, noticed in the *Montreal Gazette* that a local visual artist had put out a call for entries to a competition for school children to draw their teachers, with the prize for the best drawing being a life-size cloth rendition, made by the artist, of the teacher in the drawing. Intrigued by such a call, we contacted the artist and asked her what she was going to do with the drawings when she was finished with them. "Why, you can have them," she said

L. Theron et al. (eds.), Picturing Research: Drawing as Visual Methodology, 1–16.

once she learned of our interest in teacher identity. And that was the beginning. It led to our working with collections of children's drawings and then later to asking beginning teachers to also draw teachers. The project with beginning teachers became the subject of an entire book titled *'That's Funny, You Don't Look Like a Teacher': Interrogating Images and Identity in Popular Culture* (Weber & Mitchell, 1995); several chapters in a follow-up book called *Reinventing Ourselves as Teachers: Beyond Nostalgia* (Mitchell & Weber, 1999); and several articles and other book chapters (Weber & Mitchell, 1996; Mitchell & Weber, 1996). But more than this, the draw-your-teacher contest led me into a career of using drawings along with other visual data—ranging from coming across yet another drawing competition (this one called "Let Every Child Learn", sponsored by the South African Post Office, and held right after the first democratic elections in South Africa in 1994) to the later use of drawings in a number of my own research projects in Rwanda, Ethiopia, and other parts of South Africa.

What I like about drawings, as method, is their simplicity. All you need is paper and a pencil or pen. But if there is simplicity in collecting the data, there is complexity in the interpretive process. Does one ask for captions? Does one use the drawing as a type of elicitation? What do the drawings really mean? One of my favourite drawings was created in the "Let Every Child Learn" competition. Very simply, it depicts a teacher with a group of children and shows a drawing on a chart. But the caption in Afrikaans suggests so much more: "Wie weet wat dit beteken?" ("Who knows what this means?")—showing in and of itself the interpretive possibilities in drawings.

What I also like about drawings is their tangibility, their concreteness. We can lay out 50 or 100 drawings and look at them and touch them. We can scan them and look at them on the computer screen. Everyone can have an interpretation. They seem to me the perfect prompt to elicit even more data. Why does a person read a drawing in a particular way?

But more than this, I like the immediacy of drawings and their potential to move audiences. In some work in Rwanda on developing a policy on violence against women and children, I spent time with young people in all regions of the country. They brainstormed, they performed through role-playing, and they drew pictures. It was their drawings that I shared with policy makers. The drawing "Baby" (see Figure 1.1) highlights the significance of unwanted pregnancy, which is often the result of sexual violence. The person who drew this picture was showing the tragedy and the waste of two lives—the baby in the toilet and the desperate young mother. When I showed this image in a larger-than-life format in a PowerPoint presentation to policy makers, I could see that it was difficult for them to look away. The image "haunts" as Susan Sontag (2003) would have said.

Figure 1.1. "Baby".

There are challenges, though. I think psychology still has a huge grip on interpreting drawings. Do drawings reveal deep dark secrets? We are used to thinking of drawings, especially those done by children, as being particularly revealing, and we might worry that if we are not trained psychologists, we should not be asking children to draw. Perchance, we will evoke pain and trauma that we are not equipped to handle. But then we run that risk when we conduct interviews. Perhaps, adult participants will think that we are treating them like children. Perhaps, they will not take it all seriously and perhaps we will destroy the researcher-researched relationship. Can we 'read in' too much? Do we see a drawing, for example, of an AK-47 as the child's real expression of violence, or does he simply like to draw AK-47s? I have always valued the participation of other readers in the interpretive process. When I worked with the several thousand drawings from the "Let Every Child Learn" competition, I invited a group of beginning teachers from The University of the Witwatersrand (Wits) to join me in the process (Mitchell, 2004). This taught me something about the richness of the images, their amenability to interpretation, which included the ways in which they evoked childhood memories.

Another challenge is the question 'But is it art or is it research?' Does the use of drawings fall into the category of arts-based or arts-informed research? Interestingly, there are many examples of how children's drawings are positioned as artworks represented in art exhibitions and even in coffee-table books. Drawings

3

done by adults rarely fall into the category of coffee-table books. How does this problematise ideas about childhood and where we place children? Also, then, what does this say about the creative images of adults?

And the questions go on ...

Linda Theron

Recently, I had a meeting with a team of experienced researchers in North West province, South Africa. We have been doing participatory, enabling research together for the last 5 or so years in a project called Resilient Educators (REds). In this project, we work with educators who are challenged by the daunting realities of being a teacher in the age of AIDS. One of the ways that we have generated data in our project has been through drawings. In the recent meeting as we were talking about how we would write up the findings emerging from the data, I noticed that my peers had become a bit uncomfortable. "You use the drawings," they said, "because you're the psychologist and so have the right to interpret them. We're not psychologists." Their response saddened me, and it dawned on me (again) how misunderstood drawings are as a way of generating data.

Yes, I am an educational psychologist, so my earliest use of drawings was with children and adolescents who had come into my practice for one reason or another. Drawings were a wonderful tool! With shy children, drawings often broke the ice. With boisterous youngsters, drawings regularly stilled them and encouraged them to reflect and gain a different perspective on complex issues in their lives. When my clients were troubled by something that seemed very overwhelming, it helped to concretise the issue as a drawing. Most often, the process of drawing reduced the issue to something that could be labelled, described, or defined. On the whole, this made the issue manageable. My experience of the power and magic of drawings in my practice inspired me to use drawings as a data generation tool. When I first collected drawings (as part of REds), I wasn't aware of the mushrooming use of drawings as a research method; I was just convinced that drawings were a super-effective way of encouraging people to express what they were thinking or feeling or longing for, or even what they had experienced—the good and the bad.

When we were trained as educational psychologists in the use of drawings as projective techniques, our professor (Elsabé Roets) became suddenly serious: "Never, ever assume you know what your clients' drawings mean ... you are not the expert on their perceptions or feelings or thoughts. Your clients are the experts. So, ask!" She then proceeded to show us a drawing made by a young boy: He was sitting all alone in a garden, hunched over, chin in his hands. In the background, his father was playing with his brother, and his mother was working alone in the kitchen. She asked us to analyse the drawing. We had nothing to go on, except the contents of the drawing. Of course, our analyses were wild—and dead wrong. The little boy had offered the following explanation:

> I'm an athlete. I'm training very hard to be in the school team and so in my
> picture I've just been for a run. I'm sitting there in the garden because I'm

getting my breath back. My dad and brother had been waiting for me and cheered me when they saw me round our street's corner. I'll go and play with them in a moment, like we always do. My mom is making a special supper so that I will have enough stamina to keep running. She likes doing things like that for us. (L. Theron, therapy session, 2007)

The lesson was powerful. Partly because of this lesson, and partly because I believe in a participatory research approach, I engaged participants collaboratively in making meaning of what they'd drawn when I began to use drawings as research method. When participants are engaged in interpreting the messages that their drawings were intended to convey, the use and interpretation of the drawing moves beyond the enclave of psychologists. Then, drawings become a compelling means to collaborative research. This was what my fellow researchers had not yet grasped that day. This is part of my motivation for this book—to broadcast the message that drawings are an accessible data generation process as long as they are embedded in an ethical, participant-researcher collaboration.

Although I have explained how I came to be convinced of the power of drawings and how I believe drawings should be used in my practice and in research contexts, I have not yet explained how I came to use drawings as a research method. The impetus was quite simple really: I was stuck. In the piloting of REds with educators who were not first-language English speakers, I was at a loss as to how to measure their perception of the HIV&AIDS pandemic. Most rating scales used English that was too complex. My participants' English was not at the level that we could engage in deep, unstructured interviews about how they perceived the pandemic. I was wary of using an interpreter. In the midst of trying to find a solution, I had a scheduled appointment with a child whom I was seeing for therapy. She was grappling with accepting her parents' divorce. As part of what we did that day, I asked her to draw her dad as an animal and then her mom as one. She drew a terrapin and then a little bird. When we put the drawings side by side, she started laughing: "But, of course, they had to get divorced: a terrapin and a kiewiet (type of bird) can't possibly live together." Her drawing-generated insight was the start of her healing. It was also my eureka moment—I knew what I was going to use to gauge educator perception.

I have used drawings with many other participants, too, such as street children (see Chapter 8 in this volume), orphans participating in my SANPAD-funded project to understand more about their lives and their resilience, youth participating in the ICURA-funded Pathways to Resilience project as an expression of the ecological resources nurturing their resilience, and resilient youth as a means of illustrating the role that teachers played in their resilience. I encourage my postgraduate students to include drawings in their research, as well. My belief in the power of drawings to communicate complex messages in simple but rich ways has been reinforced every time I have presented on drawing-related research at conferences or used drawings in my teaching. I love the fact that drawings are lasting artefacts that can be used to give voice to participant messages. I love also that even though drawings 'speak up', each viewer must make personal meaning of what is being communicated.

The preceding discussion does not mean that drawing as research methodology is without challenge. There are procedural, ethical, and interpretive challenges that cannot be gainsaid. Nevertheless, none of these challenges can corrode the rich, persuasive evidence embedded in the apparent simplicity of drawings.

Jean Stuart

My becoming sensitised to the rich potential of incorporating drawings into research began with an entertainment-education intervention in an under-resourced high school in South Africa. As a master's student constrained by lack of funds, I handed out large sheets of white paper and coloured pencils and asked the children to draw their own drug awareness posters. Spread out across the bleak room, the huge class was effortlessly engaged and their enjoyment as they drew was palpable. Together, we displayed the posters on the wall and each child placed secret and justified votes in a shoebox to indicate which poster he or she considered would be most effective in reducing drug abuse. The display was viewed next by the Teenagers Against Drug Abuse Committee at the school and finally by an older group of volunteering pupils with records of ill-discipline related to substance abuse. Focus group discussions after the drawing display yielded rich dialogue and data as pupils talked with animation about the relevance of the posters.

Shortly after this, I read with fascination of the work of Wetton and McWhirter (1998), who used story and drawing to access children's knowledge of drugs, and realised how much insight into participants' perspectives could be gained when drawings were incorporated into health-related research. It is for that reason that I went on to ask preservice teachers to represent their own points of view on HIV and AIDS with simple drawings. Thus began our exploration "From Our Frames: Exploring Arts-Based Approaches for Addressing HIV and AIDS with Preservice Teachers" (Stuart, 2006).

Foregrounding such perspectives was also my purpose in asking teachers and healthcare workers in a rural KwaZulu-Natal project to draw how they saw each other as professionals (see Chapter 13 in this volume). What intrigued me, though, was the disjunction between what each group politely said about the other groups and what hidden prejudices emerged in their drawings and in their discussion of these drawings. And time and time again, I have noticed how participants look at and discuss the issues depicted in their drawings with less inhibition than they do in conventional interviews.

Later, as a teacher and lecturer I realised more fully how drawings can contribute to self-study since they enable their creators to freeze and study their memories, aspirations, or thoughts. Inspired by Mitchell and Weber's (1999) method for enhancing student's recall of teachers and Haarhoff's (1998) use of drawing to recall spaces of significance, I encourage all students in my undergraduate creative writing course to step back into childhood by asking them each to draw a place they valued as a child and to indicate in the drawing some sensory memories of that place. The focused buzz of chatter that always accompanies the invitation to students to share memories with those around them, and the passionate writing that follows, bears testimony to the power of drawings for self-study.

More recently, I have been using drawings with students who are working to anchor and apply theory. For example, in picturing theory in the honours module "Critical Awareness of Language and Media" at the University of KwaZulu-Natal, our students working with Fairclough's (1995) Framework for Critical Discourse Analysis diagram (p. 59) have created drawings to understand his theoretical approach and to identify and propose solutions to discourses and social and cultural practices that promote violence in schools.

Working with drawings usually presents ethical challenges but also opens up opportunities. It is always intriguing and humbling to see the creativity of others as they work with drawings and to learn from these participants. This is why I welcomed the opportunity to write alongside others who work with drawings.

Ann Smith

I come to be working on a book on drawings through what a group of my colleagues at a national discussion held at Nelson Mandela Metropolitan University on the theme "Can Art Stop AIDS?" termed an interest in the hand-made (drawings, collage, tapestry, paper making) as opposed to the digital (photography, video, and social media) and performance (dance, forum theatre, and other forms of drama).[i]

I run my own business—an educational and corporate training consultancy called Creating Action Spaces Together cc—and I have been employed as an academic since 1979 in one way or another—ranging from the tenured to the part-time—at the University of the Witwatersrand, where I am currently a part-time contract lecturer at the Wits Business School (WBS). In early 2003, I had a very bright young woman—let's call her Thembi—in my Communication Skills class (which is part of a regular course in management called the New Managers' Programme [NMP]) that is offered to the public five times a year at WBS. It draws mostly businesspeople who have been promoted recently to, and those who are being groomed for, junior management positions. By 2007, Thembi had been promoted to a senior position in the Human Resources department of her company. She contracted me to run a Business Communication and Presentation Skills course for senior managers.

Now, whereas the academic NMP course at WBS has to be fairly rigidly structured, I had free rein with these corporate participants, and I decided to use, for my opening session, a visual arts-based teaching methodology that I had first employed in an academic setting. This corporate group was made up of 8 men and 3 women who were all within the age range of 34 to 49 years. I could tell that most of them were not too happy to be in the course, and this became even more apparent as I set out my piles of coloured tissue paper, unpatterned coloured wrapping paper, A4-sized pieces of heavy construction paper, and six or seven pairs of scissors and as many glue sticks on the highly polished boardroom table.

7

The participants were polite—even if only just)—and I caught the odd comment about "kids' stuff" and "nursery school activities".

I began this course by introducing myself by name only, without even a word about what I hoped to accomplish, never mind anything about my qualifications or academic affiliation. All I said to them was to "use these materials in any way you like to create a picture of a moment of perfect understanding of any communication transmitted to you in your life". In response to their near total incredulity and incomprehension of what I wanted them to do, I explained that they needed to think of any occasion in their lives when they had really understood a message transmitted to them. I encouraged them to think about a verbal message or a written one, one that was part of a movie, a song, or an advertisement perhaps or one that had been conveyed by body language or by the way someone was dressed. I told them that this process was called 'making a collage' and that the picture or collage they made could be realistic in its portrayal of the actual event or could be representational of how they felt then, or both. I gave them no special instructions, and I made only one stipulation: No religious experiences could be depicted.

The more they thought about the task the more anxious these women and men became. I suggested that they just try to do it and said reassuringly that there were no correct or incorrect responses. Gradually, the tension began to evaporate as these businesspeople got down to completing the task. They spoke very little and then only to ask a colleague to pass over a particular piece of paper, a glue stick, or a pair of scissors. Some participants chose to use the scissors and others chose to tear the paper; others did both. Once the process was under way, I negotiated a time limit with them and withdrew to a corner of the room, pretending to do my own work while covertly observing them.

When the time was up, I invited anyone who wanted to do so to stand up and explain her or his collage to the group. I was thrilled to discover that every single one of them wanted to do this. Here, I will describe only one presentation. A young woman had used yellow construction paper on which she had stuck an oval of crumpled black tissue paper. On top of this, she had depicted an obviously pregnant learner sitting on a chair in a classroom. Next to her was the figure of a teacher extending a comforting hand. The young female participant explained that the black paper showed her despair at falling pregnant towards the middle of her matric year. She believed then that her life was over; all her hopes and dreams of a successful future gone. However, the teacher that she had drawn had told her that she could stay on at school and write the exam even if she was pregnant. The moment of perfect communication, the participant said, had been her teacher's announcement that being pregnant had to do with her belly and not her brain. The yellow paper represented the sunlight that surrounded her black despair when she heard her teacher's words and understood perfectly the implications of the message she was hearing. (Incidentally, this young woman told me afterwards that this was the first time she had ever told anyone about her teenage pregnancy. She also told me that her child was 19 years old—2 years older than she had been that day.)

The success of the course as a whole had much to do with this opening activity, I think. In a discussion of the collage-making process, the participants said that at first the very idea of working with paper and glue at their age and stage of professional life was unacceptable. They all admitted thinking that I must be "crazy", "out of my mind", "seriously weird", and, much worse, "unprofessional", to expect this. They admitted, though, that as their ideas started to take shape on the construction paper, they became excited and eager to "do this properly and well". Many participants spoke about having been given the opportunity to say "important things without using words" while "playing with paper and glue" and that this had been a very liberating experience. Throughout the rest of the 4-day course, the participants kept referring back to the opening collage activity to help them articulate answers to questions that seemingly had nothing to do with it. For example, when I asked them to consider why it is so important to profile an audience before making a verbal presentation, one woman replied by saying that if you had to depict an audience in a collage, you would need to make sure that each member of the audience was portrayed differently.

The initial response of these corporate participants to the collage activity was similar to that of the academics with whom I worked in Trinidad and Tobago during a workshop on educational leadership in 2005. I read in their faces that they were appalled that I would even consider asking them to do such a childish thing as making a collage! It seemed not to matter that I was asking them to depict a moment of perfect leadership in their lives: What mattered was that it seemed to them so inappropriate to ask adults to do something like this. But they, too, came round to seeing it as a very valuable way of conveying an experience in a completely wordless picture. It was from this workshop that I learned to exclude any representation of religious experience in the collage-making process: It is impossible to discuss such experience neutrally in a group of people all of whom are not necessarily like-minded.

And that's how I came to be working with the hand-made.

OVERVIEW OF THE BOOK

Picturing Research draws on community-based and participatory research from a wide variety of contexts, most of them in South Africa, although various chapters include work from Rwanda, Lesotho, and work with immigrant populations in Canada and studies carried out in the context of global issues of displacement. Given the high rates of HIV and AIDS in sub-Saharan Africa, it should not be surprising that many of the chapters take up concerns such as the preparation of teachers and community healthcare workers to cope better with the challenges of living, caring, and teaching in the age of AIDS and the experiences of orphans and vulnerable children.

The book is divided into two main sections: "The Drawing's the Thing: Critical Issues in the Use of Drawings in Social Science Research" and "Illustrations From Practice: Drawing From Research". When we first started thinking of the organisation of the book, we had imagined that it would divide up simply into 'working with children' and 'working with adults'. However, when we began to assemble the various chapters, we realised that the child-adult split did not actually represent either the chapters themselves or our approach to the whole area of drawing. Rather, we began to see that in fact there were a number of critical issues—some of which might pertain to children, some to adults, and some to both—and we saw examples of projects and genres of drawing that seem to cut across age divisions.

The Drawing's the Thing: Critical Issues in the Use of Drawings in Social Science Research

In Chapter 2, "Drawings as Research Method", methodology itself is addressed. Claudia Mitchell, Linda Theron, Jean Stuart, Ann Smith and Zachariah Campbell consider the ways in which various research approaches converge to form a framework for looking at drawing in research: arts-based methodologies, participatory visual research methodologies, and textual approaches to research. The chapter draws on examples of both the 'doing' and the interpretation.

Following from this, in her chapter "Picturing the Self: Drawing as a Method for Self-Study", Kathleen Pithouse considers three different published examples of drawing as a method for self-study to identify some strategies for, and features of, this research method. Her discussion explores the nature and value of self-study drawing as a social research method as well as some potential challenges of using such a method.

Linda Theron, Jean Stuart, and Claudia Mitchell in their chapter "A Positive, African Ethical Approach to Collecting and Interpreting Drawings: Some Considerations" approach work with drawing in the context of ethics. Calling on the work of Mertens (2009) and others, they consider the transformative nature of research. In seeking to bring about social change, they advocate alternative data collection methods (like drawing) that give easier voice to marginalised groups or groups that struggle to express themselves in English. Ethical rigour and allegiance to Positive Ethics (Bush, 2010), which are aligned with African Ethics (Murove, 2009), are central to this approach. Thus, this chapter outlines a positive ethical process of (1) collecting and (2) interpreting drawings that promotes beneficence, respect, and justice. It also introduces suggestions for strategies that encourage the enablement of research participants through the very findings generated by their drawings.

In her chapter "Visualising Justice: The Politics of Working With Children's Drawings", Lara Bober considers the relationship between children's drawings and processes of redress and reconciliation. In the context of war, children's drawings can be powerful documents that help to bring perpetrators of human rights violations to justice, as demonstrated in the case of drawings submitted as evidence of war crimes to the International Criminal Court in proceedings against Sudanese officials. The Cambodian League for the Promotion and Defense of Human Rights has included children's drawings to document prison conditions for women and their children. Children's drawings and poems were submitted to the Australian Human Rights Commission's National Inquiry into Children in Immigration Detention that was tabled in Parliament on May 13, 2004. There are many political, colonial, and post-colonial perspectives from which to consider the visual production of children, and it is important to recognise that adults have used children's art to promote their own ideological positions and causes. The chapter considers how the implementation of International Human Rights Law is strengthened when children's voices are included in institutionalised processes of redress and reconciliation. By exhibiting children's drawings of conflict at art galleries, universities, and other public venues, this chapter questions how these sites might allow for other forms of redress and reconciliation.

Then Monica Mak, in "The Visual Ethics of Using Children's Drawings in the Documentary *Unwanted Images*", focuses on the visually ethical approach taken by researchers to create a discursive space wherein young people, through their illustrations used in a documentary video context, can freely express their views on gender-based violence in South Africa. This chapter shows how these drawings serve as a secure, comfortable environment for young people's creative expression. It also reveals how process (i.e., the act of drawing) and product (i.e., the video born of the drawings) are equally significant since each carries a specific reflexive benefit.

Finally, Katie MacEntee and Claudia Mitchell take the idea of children's collections back to the producers themselves (as well as other audiences) in their chapter "Lost and Found in Translation: Participatory Analysis and Working With Collections of Drawings". How do we understand data collection and data analysis in reference to children's drawings? Who has the potential to interpret and be moved by these images? And what is the impact of this project? In this chapter, three archives of children's drawings are presented as potential data for research into children's voice and experience during times of hardship and duress. The authors introduce participatory analysis as a methodological concern when researchers are working with the visual texts and discuss the possible clash between conventional aesthetics on the one hand and the agenda of research-as-social-change on the other, which arises when participant-produced art is exhibited. This type of research demands a critical analysis of how participatory, arts-based research fully mines 'collections' of drawings, particularly those elicited during fieldwork with participants.

Illustrations from Practice: Drawing from Research

The second section of *Picturing Research* brings together a series of case studies that exemplify the various ways that researchers are using drawing with child and adult participants. This section starts with Macalane Malindi and Linda Theron's chapter "Drawing on Strengths: Images of Ecological Contributions to Male Street Youth Resilience" in which they present drawings made by street children that depict the contributing factors to their resilience. Recently, researchers have begun to suggest that some children follow atypical developmental pathways and that in some instances these atypical pathways are trajectories of resilience. This holds true for street children. Despite this budding understanding, it is difficult to engage street children (who typically have low literacy levels) in quantitative research designs. As an alternative, the authors asked 20 street youth (identified as resilient by impartial, knowledgeable parties like NGOs or welfare workers) to make drawings of what they believed nurtured their resilience. Using current understandings of resilience as a reciprocal, ecologically embedded process, the authors interpret their rich symbols to illustrate which ecological resources nurture street children.

In her chapter "Teacher Sexuality Depicted: Exploring Women Teachers' Positioning within Sexuality Education Classrooms through Drawings", Mathabo Khau uses drawings to explore how women teachers position themselves as women and as teachers in order to understand how the two identities of womanhood and teacherhood influence and shape each other in being and becoming a sexuality education woman teacher. The author argues that women teachers choose to perform normative womanhood scripts at the expense of teacherhood, thereby creating impossibilities for effective facilitation of sexuality education, especially within rural contexts. This chapter provides important information on how the female teacher's body, female sexuality, and contextual gender dynamics are implicated in the effectiveness of sexuality education programs, such that these issues can be incorporated in the planning of programs that will curb further spread of HIV infections among the youth.

Continuing with the idea of having teachers draw, Linda van Laren, in her chapter "Drawing in and on Mathematics to Promote HIV&AIDS Preservice Teacher Education", is interested in drawing in relation to integrating HIV&AIDS education into mathematics education. In South Africa, the assessment standards listed in the National Curriculum Statement Grades 0–9 (South African National Department of Education, 2002) across all eight learning areas provide many opportunities for such integration. There are many interpretations of what integration/inclusion and mainstreaming might mean and include in relation to HIV&AIDS education. There are also numerous levels of integration. Integration ensures that learners' experience the learning areas as being linked and related to each other. Furthermore, integration is required to support and expand the learners' opportunities to attain skills, acquire knowledge, and develop attitudes and values that stretch across the curriculum. This chapter focuses on drawing strategies that can be used to assist preservice teachers to get started by exploring their beliefs about integrating HIV&AIDS education into the Mathematics Learning Area so as to help them overcome any initial uncertainties about integration. Encouraging preservice teachers to explore their own hand-drawn metaphors of how they believe that integration of HIV&AIDS education is achievable paves the way for integrated action in the school classroom situation.

In their chapter "Reading Across and Back: Thoughts on Working with (Re-Visited) Drawing Collections", Jean Stuart and Ann Smith consider possible further uses of the drawings produced in two projects—From Our Frames and Youth as Knowledge Producers—that were implemented at the University of KwaZulu-Natal (UKZN) to explore ways in which arts-based approaches can contribute to teacher education and development. Although the projects were different, each began with offering participants the same prompt—'*Draw a picture that represents your view of HIV and AIDS'*—which was followed by an invitation to write an explanation of the resulting drawing. The authors suggest here that the lessons learned in implementing these projects could result in further teacher development if the collections of drawings on how preservice teachers and teenaged school children respectively viewed HIV and AIDS were brought together and revisited by the researchers and participants. Stuart and Smith offer alternative interpretations, based on an 'outsider' semiotic and content analysis, of some of these pictures and consider the validity and possible usefulness of considering with the participants what they said their pictures represented in the light of these 'new' interpretations.

Liesel Ebersöhn, Ronél Ferreira, and Bathsheba Mbongwe, in "How Teacher-Researcher Teams See Their Role in Participatory Research", describe the use of drawings in exploring how teacher-researchers view their role in participatory research. Whereas Gaventa's (2006) theory of power provides a theoretical lens, the authors adopt a feminist metatheoretical stance and are guided by a participatory methodological position in exploring this phenomenon. The authors generated visual data with purposefully selected teachers (n=20; 2 males, 18 females) in a longitudinal participatory reflection and action project, as part of the Supportive Teachers Assets and Resilience (STAR) project. This project focuses on the role of teachers in promoting resilience in schools and involves partnerships with teachers in three provinces in South Africa. During a seminar focusing on partnerships between teachers and researchers, teachers worked in six school-based teams to create drawings portraying their views of being participants in the STAR project. The authors used Gaventa's 'power cube' to establish how these themes relate to dimensions of power. They found that the dynamics of power in a participatory project could be influenced by the three dimensions of power, as experienced by teacher-participants.

In their chapter "Learning Together: Teachers and Community Healthcare Workers Draw Each Other", Naydene de Lange, Claudia Mitchell, and Jean Stuart expand the use of drawings into working beyond education. The authors describe a study that took place in Vulindlela, a rural district in the lower foothills of the Southern Drakensberg, a district ravaged by the HIV&AIDS pandemic. In one area of the district, a vibrant clinic addresses the health issues of the surrounding community as best it can. Adjacent to the clinic lies the ever-expanding Centre for the AIDS Programme of Research in South Africa (CAPRISA) that is committed to finding a medical solution to the pandemic, not only for the world's benefit but to help this particular community. The many schools in the area are an indication of the large number of young people living in the community, all eager to learn and to make progress in life. However, these same youth are also most affected by the pandemic, compelling the clinic with their community healthcare workers and the schools with their educators to intervene in their lives. Yet, often, these healthcare workers and teachers work at cross purposes or without knowledge of what the other does. Considering this scenario, the authors were interested to find out how participatory methodologies could bring together the various sectors and partners working in the area of gender, youth, and HIV prevention and care in one community. Their focus was on the local context and the ways in which members of local groups within the same community and working with the same youth see their own work in AIDS prevention and treatment: their interface with the policies and procedures that drive their practices; the tensions, challenges, and barriers to service delivery; and their lived experience of their own needs and the needs of youth within the community they serve. With this in mind, the authors asked teachers and community healthcare workers to draw each other. Using the drawings and discussions about their perceptions of each other, the research team was in a better position to develop a 'research as intervention' strategy in this particular rural community.

Eliza Govender and Senyata Reddy express their conviction in their chapter "Drawing the Bigger Picture: Giving Voice to HIV-Positive Children" that assisting HIV-positive children through awareness, treatment, and support still remains a challenge in South Africa. UNICEF reports confirm that 280,000 South African children were living with HIV in 2007. Growing statistics emphasise the crucial need for new and innovative approaches to HIV&AIDS education for children infected by HIV and AIDS in order to raise greater awareness of how these children might be helped to cope with the exigencies of treatment literacy and treatment adherence. This chapter explores drawing as an art form and as a form of participatory Entertainment Education (EE) in the context of knowledge production, knowledge exchange, and knowledge transference as vital to increasing treatment literacy and treatment adherence in HIV-positive children. The focus is on the use of drawings in a project called Hi Virus that was carried out with children from KwaZulu-Natal who are infected by HIV or AIDS. As the authors highlight, the project demonstrated that drawing can be used as a tool to both entertain and educate children in a participatory manner in order to stimulate a greater awareness of the vital role of treatment adherence, to empower them to problematise this issue, and to forge ahead to come up with their own strategies to improve their treatment adherence through an increased critical consciousness of the need to do so and of the benefits of keeping to a regular schedule of pill taking.

In the final two chapters in *Picturing Research*, the respective authors consider other genres of drawings: cartooning and storyboarding. Catherine Ann Cameron and Linda Theron, in their chapter "With Pictures and Words I Can Show You: Cartoons Portray Resilient Migrant Teenagers' Journeys", consider that it can be challenging for young research participants to share the essence of their lived experience so that researchers can gain deeper understanding, transform gained appreciation into theoretical and practical knowledge, and transfer it back to stakeholder communities. In the authors' international, ecological research with resilient adolescents in transition, they use a variety of visual methods iteratively, including sequenced interviews, a filmed '*day in the life*' of participants, and photo-elicitation. Each method enhances understanding of the teenagers' perceptions. One participant volunteered cartoons she had drawn of her journey as an immigrant to Canada from Mexico, affording yet another vantage point for exploring her resilience-enhancing experiences. The authors invited her to choose other experiences to cartoon, and she chose to depict (and subsequently comment on) her experience of becoming a young woman in the Mormon Church and her aspirations for becoming multilingual. Another of their participants was a boy in Thailand who had migrated from Bangkok to the north of his country. He cartooned the routines of his everyday life. The analyses of what value-added information they gained from these examples of youth expression are the subject of Cameron and Theron's chapter. Like Hui (2009), who promoted cartooning techniques as mechanisms for creative expression, the authors have evidence that cartoons and discussions of them provide valuable insights that enrich the exploration of youth resilience. The utility of cartooning as a research methodology is confirmed.

Picturing Research ends with a chapter by Claudia Mitchell, Naydene de Lange, and Relebohile Moletsane on the use of drawings in a storyboarding project in Rwanda. Titled "Before the Cameras Roll: Drawing a Storyboard to Address Gendered Poverty", the chapter looks at how the use of drawing in storyboarding draws on the video-making process. The authors' idea of community-based participatory video uses the process of 'making a video in a day' through the No-Editing-Required (N-E-R) approach. In such an approach, community participants go from identifying which issues are important in their lives and choosing a topic to focus on for a video to planning out a short video (through the use of storyboarding) and shooting and screening it—all in one session. Drawing out the images in a storyboard is just one piece of the process. As the authors describe it here, the storyboarding process can also be visual text in and of itself. The authors describe the somewhat serendipitous discovery of the storyboard as a specific visual text (visual data), and they describe its use in a participatory visual methodologies workshop with a group of 60 adults in Kigali. The authors conclude the chapter with discussion of how researchers might incorporate the storyboard into the repertoire of visual data possibilities.

NOTE

[i] The NRF national discussion was titled "Can Art Stop AIDS? Exploring the Impact of Visual and Arts-Based Participatory Methodologies Used in HIV and AIDS Education and Intervention Research" and was held at Nelson Mandela Metropolitan University in Port Elizabeth, South Africa, on September 15, 2010.

REFERENCES

Bush, S. S. (2010). Legal and ethical considerations in rehabilitation and health assessment. In E. Mpofu & T. Oakland (Eds.), *Assessment in rehabilitation and health* (pp. 22–36). Upper Saddle River, NJ: Pearson.
Cole, A. L., & Knowles, J. G. (2008). Arts-informed research. In J. G. Knowles & A. L. Cole (Eds.), *Handbook of the arts in qualitative research: Perspectives, methodologies, examples, and issues* (pp. 55–70). London, England: Sage.
Ellis, C. (2004). *The ethnographic I: A methodological novel about autoethnography.* Walnut Creek, CA: AltaMira Press.
Fairclough, N. (1995). *Media discourse.* London, England: E. Arnold.

Gaventa, J. (2006). Finding the spaces for change: A power analysis. *IDS Bulletin, 37*(6), 23–33. doi:10.1111/j.1759-5436.2006.tb00320.x.

Haarhoff, D. (1998). The writer's voice: A workbook for writers in Africa. Johannesburg, South Africa: Zebra Press.

Hui, J. (2009, October). *Shanghai Daily: Travel collage. Graphic memoir on Pacific Canada and diaspora.* Paper presented at the annual meeting of the Canadian Asian Studies Association, Vancouver, BC.

Mertens, D. M. (2009). *Transformative research and evaluation.* New York, NY: Guilford Press.

Miller, J. (1995). Trick or treat? The autobiography of the question. *English Quarterly, 27*(3), 22–26.

Mitchell, C. (2004). Just who do we think we are? Memory work and self-study with beginning teachers. In R. Balfour, T. Buthelezi, & C. Mitchell (Eds.), *Teacher development at the centre of change* (pp. 45–54). Durban, South Africa: KwaZulu-Natal Department of Education.

Mitchell, C., & Weber, S. J. (1996). He draws/she draws: Texts of interrogation. *Textual Studies in Canada, 7,* 133–142.

Mitchell, C., & Weber, S. (1999). *Reinventing ourselves as teachers: Beyond nostalgia.* London, England: Falmer Press. doi:10.4324/9780203454497.

Murove, M. F. (Ed.). (2009). *African ethics. An anthology of comparative and applied ethics.* Scottsville, South Africa: University of KwaZulu-Natal Press.

Pithouse, K., Mitchell, C., & Moletsane, R. (2009). Introduction. In K. Pithouse, C. Mitchell, & R. Moletsane (Eds.), *Making connections: Self-study and social action* (pp. 1–9). New York, NY: Peter Lang.

Sontag, S. (2003). *Regarding the pain of others.* New York, NY: Farrar, Straus and Giroux.

South African National Department of Education. (2002). *Revised National Curriculum Statement Grades R-9 (Schools).* Pretoria, South Africa: Author. Retrieved from www.info.gov.za.

Stuart, J. (2006). *From our Frames: Exploring visual arts-based approaches for addressing HIV and AIDS with pre-service teachers* (Doctoral dissertation, University of KwaZulu-Natal, Durban, South Africa). Retrieved from http://hdl.handle.net/10413/858

Weber, S., & Mitchell, C. (1995). *'That's funny, you don't look like a teacher': Interrogating images and identity in popular culture.* London, England: Falmer Press. doi:10.4324/9780203453568.

Weber, S., & Mitchell, C. (1996). Drawing ourselves into teaching: Studying the images that shape and distort teacher education. *Teaching and Teacher Education, 12*(3), 303–313. doi:10.1016/0742-051X(95)00040-Q.

Wetton, N., & McWhirter, J. (1998). Images and curriculum development in health education. In J. Prosser (Ed.), *Image-based research: A sourcebook for qualitative researchers* (pp. 263–283). London, England: RoutledgeFalmer.

SECTION ONE

THE DRAWING'S THE THING:
CRITICAL ISSUES IN THE USE OF DRAWINGS
IN SOCIAL RESEARCH

DRAWINGS AS RESEARCH METHOD

Claudia Mitchell, Linda Theron, Jean Stuart, Ann Smith and Zachariah Campbell

INTRODUCTION

The use of drawings in social research is located within several broad yet overlapping areas of contemporary study. These include arts-based or arts-informed research (Knowles & Cole, 2008), participatory visual methodologies (De Lange, Mitchell, & Stuart, 2007; Rose, 2001), textual approaches in visual studies in the social sciences (Mitchell, 2011), as well as the use of drawings in psychology. For a number of decades—possibly from as early as 1935 (MacGregor, Currie, & Wetton, 1998)—psychologists and researchers have engaged children and adults in activities using varied forms of a 'draw-and-write' or 'draw-and-talk' technique that have facilitated the rich exploration of children's and adults' reflections, perceptions, and views on multiple topics and phenomena (Backett-Milburn & McKie, 1999; Furth, 1988; Guillemin, 2004; MacGregor et al., 1998; Mair & Kierans, 2007). Drawings have long been used by psychologists to measure cognitive development (Goodenough, 1926) and as a projective technique (with adults as well as with children) to explore conscious and unconscious issues and experiences. In a very real sense, drawings make parts of the self and/or levels of development *visible*.

Working with the visual is far from simple, and there are competing theories of practice about how best to use drawings and other visual texts in social research. Within the art-making community, some will argue that the art or visual text speaks for itself and that the drawing, collage, or performance exists precisely because the idea is not easily expressed in words. As Weber (2008) observed, "Images can be used to capture the ineffable .... Some things just need to be shown, not merely stated. Artistic images can help us access those elusive hard-to-put-into-words aspects of knowledge that might otherwise remain hidden or ignored" (p. 44). As researchers in the area of arts-based methodologies highlight, meaning-making through the arts is full of complexity and the artistic products are themselves texts to be read and interpreted by their producer and their audiences, including researchers. At the same time, the use of drawing as a research method typically involves more than just engaging participants in making drawings, followed by the researcher's analysis of these artefacts. When drawing is used as a research method, it often entails participants' drawing and talking or drawing and writing (Backett-Milburn & McKie, 1999; Guillemin, 2004; MacGregor et al., 1998; Mair & Kierans, 2007) about the meaning embedded in their drawing. The drawer's context (both present and past) colours what is drawn, how it is drawn,

L. Theron et al. (eds.), Picturing Research: Drawing as Visual Methodology, 19–36.

and what the drawing represents. As such, drawing as a research tool is often complemented by verbal research methods (Guillemin, 2004) that encourage collaborative meaning-making that allows the drawer to give voice to what the drawing was intended to convey. This collaboration is vital precisely because the drawing is produced by a specific individual in a particular space and time. This understanding of drawing (i.e., drawing as a participatory research method that relies on researcher-participant collaboration to make meaning of the drawing) forms the focus of *Picturing Research* although, as we point out in this chapter and elsewhere in the book, the richness of visual arts-based methodologies (as modes of inquiry, of representation, of dissemination, of transformation) means that we need to avoid thinking of drawings as a monolithic visual methodology. But why focus on drawings? Notwithstanding the ease (all you need is a pencil and paper) and the low-tech aspects (no need for digital cameras or even electricity), the benefits of the uses of drawings, as the various chapters in this volume attest, are many and include the active engagement of children (MacGregor et al., 1998) and adults (Guillemin, 2004; Stuart, 2007; Theron, 2008) and visible proof of research findings. Burke and Prosser (2008) talked about the ways in which drawings and other visual methods, especially when these are used with children, are really a stimulus for communication, and they argue that using the visual—especially drawings—with children is particularly critical in getting at their inner world: "Children have the ability to capture feelings and emotions through drawings and paintings while lacking an equally expressive written or spoken language" (p. 414). This same point was made by Robin Goodman in one of the opening essays to *The Day Our World Changed: Children's Art of 9/11* when he wrote:

> Special x-ray cameras for examining what children saw and felt on September 11, 2001, don't exist. The art in this collection, created in the first four months after 9/11 does, however, provide a snapshot of children's raw and immediate reactions. A private corner of the children's world of uncensored memories, thoughts and feelings is explored here in their drawings and paintings. (p. 14)

We believe that the use of drawings is also appropriate for getting at the memories, thoughts, and feelings of adults—and that sometimes it is that quick request to 'Draw. Quickly, just draw. Draw the first thing you think of.' that captures something that is not easily put into words.

SOME METHODOLOGICAL FRAMEWORKS: ON WORKING
WITH THE HAND-MADE

Our use of the term 'hand-made' hearkens back to the national discussion on the role of the arts in addressing HIV and AIDS that was held at Nelson Mandela Metropolitan University in September 2010 (see also Chapter 1). There, the group of assembled researchers, artists, and arts practitioners struggled to form groups for discussion purposes based on the particular arts-focus. In the end, the emergence of three broad (but, of course, overlapping) categories emerged: the Digital,

Performance, and the Hand-Made. Into the last category fell collage, paper making, tapestry, doll making, quilt making, and drawing. The issues around working with these various texts are many but perhaps the question that we are most frequently asked is one like this: "Help! If I use this work in my research, what do I do with the data?" To answer that question, researchers need, we believe, to locate their work within a methodological community (or communities); this is crucial. As noted above, there are several communities that we see as being particularly relevant, although we note that there are overlaps between and amongst these communities—arts-based or arts-informed qualitative research, participatory visual methodologies, and textual approaches within visual studies. Here, we offer a brief overview of each, and also direct the reader to more extensive descriptions and discussions of this work.

Arts-Based Methodologies

The use of the arts (drawing, collage, drama, dance, photography, and video to name only some of the modes) in qualitative research brings together researchers and artist-practitioners working in such areas as image-based research (Weber, 2008), arts-informed research (Knowles & Cole, 2008), and a/r/tography (Springgay, 2008). Shaun McNiff (2008) offered a useful definition of the domain of arts-based research:

> [It] can be defined as the systematic use of the artistic process, the actual making of artistic expression in all of the different forms of the arts, as a primary way of understanding and examining experience by both researchers and the people that they involve in their studies. (p. 29)

For McNiff and others working in the area of arts-based research, there is a distinction between studies that focus on the process of artistic expression itself (and hence consider the participation of the artist, the genres of expression, the audience, and the impact of the work) and those that use drawing, collage, performance, and other artistic modes as more conventional forms of verbal data.

Participatory Visual Research Methodologies (PVRM)

This body of work focuses on the use of the visual (photography, video, digital storytelling, drawings) as a participatory methodology and is often regarded as one aspect of community-based research. This area, informed by the study of the visual in the work of such researchers as Marcus Banks (2001), Sarah Pink (2001), and Gillian Rose (2001), combines a focus on the producer and production process and the ways in which producers/participants can be engaged in informing the study of (and, sometimes, the analysis of) issues that are critical to them. PVRM is increasingly used as a critical approach to intervention research in such areas as health, education, community development, and social work and is seen as a way of empowering community members to identify social issues and also to imagine solutions to these. As with arts-based research, the visual in PVRM can serve as a mode of inquiry, a mode of representation, a mode of dissemination, and a mode of transformation.

Textual Research in the Social Sciences

Although not entirely separate from either arts-based research or PVRM, textual research offers a set of analytical reading strategies that may be applied to visual and other artistic texts as well as to the study of objects, to things, to what Daniel Miller called 'stuff' (2010), to documents, and even to the self-as-text. Working across a variety of disciplinary areas including cultural studies, literary studies, archaeology, anthropology, sociology, and art history, textual studies re-frames what counts as data, how it can be read, and where. How can a school playground, a shopping mall, a toilet, a UNICEF document, and, in this case, a drawing, be read? As argued elsewhere (Mitchell, 2011), this does not mean that there is no place for the producer's voice (see previous section) but rather that there is space for more contextualised readings. How is the drawing read, for example, when it is displayed in a classroom, as part of a community-exhibition in a public space, or on a billboard display promoting a campaign on children and peace-building? Buchli and Lucas (2000), as archaeologists studying material culture, wrote about a child's drawing uncovered as an artefact left behind in an abandoned British council flat. In their analysis, they attempt to piece together a story of abandonment through the close reading of various texts, including documents, the spread of children's toys, and a drawing.

Critically, as researchers who are interested in the transformative potential of research suggest (see, for example, Boydell, 2009), the engagement of participants may go well beyond 'data collection', thus signalling a value-added component to the work in terms of therapeutic potential but also a cautionary in relation to what drawings may stir up. Although this book is not specifically framed within an art-as-therapy approach, we need to remember that much of the arts-based literature of Cole and MacIntrye (2008), Conrad (2006), and Gray and Sindig (2002) highlights the potential for a research space to also be a space of healing. In work in the area of PVRM, there is often reference to empowerment, engagement, ownership, and agency—all aspects of work with drawings that suggest an afterlife to the research.

ALL ABOUT METHOD

In this section of the chapter, we focus more on the actual 'doing' in social research involving drawings. We include attention to data collection, to working with the drawings, and, finally, we remind the reader of the positioning of the researchers—ourselves—in visual studies.

Part 1: Pointers to Using Drawings in Visual Research

We start by noting that there is not a single, prescriptive approach to using drawing as a data generation tool. In some studies, participants were invited to make simple line drawings individually (e.g., Guillemin, 2004; Stuart, 2007); in others, participants were invited to produce metaphoric or symbolic drawings individually (Theron, 2008); and in still others, participants produced group-generated symbolic drawings (see Chapters 12 and 14). More recently, researchers have adapted the 'draw-and-write/-talk' technique to include story-boarding (see Chapter 16) and cartooning (see Chapter 15). Nevertheless, even as it is apparent that drawings lend themselves to flexibility as a data-generation tool, there are a number of preferred ways of engaging participants in the making of drawings, particularly if ethical and participatory ideals are to be upheld. The following points offer some recommendations in this regard, based on our experience of using drawings as data generation tools.

A reassuring invitation to draw. Not all participants are confident about their talent for drawing, even when they are willing to draw. For this reason, when we are inviting participants to draw, the invitation needs to reassure them that the focus is on the content of their drawing, and not on the quality of it as a drawing. Researchers need to emphasise this when they first broach the possibility of a participant's engaging in a study that will entail making a drawing (or drawings). Researchers need to repeat this assurance in the letter of information, on the consent form, and again when the drawing activity commences. The importance of setting participants' minds at rest about the lack of emphasis on artistic talent is independent of the type of drawing that participants are invited to make (e.g., an individual simple line drawing, a group-generated drawing, a cartoon, a metaphoric drawing).

A choice of drawing tools. Drawing tools really depend on the demographics of the invited participants. If, for example, the participants are suburban children from a well-resourced primary school, paper and coloured pencils will be familiar apparatus. If, however, the participants are adult villagers from a remote, rural area, these tools could invoke anxiety. In this latter context, drawing on the ground (using sticks or sharpish objects) might be more appropriate.

Ideally, participants need a choice of culturally and contextually congruent drawing paraphernalia (e.g., coloured pencil crayons, lead pencils, felt-tipped markers). Some participants prefer more 'artistic' media, such as pastels or chalk. Regardless of the medium chosen, in our experience, colour facilitates richer expression and often affords participants a greater sense of satisfaction, both with regard to the process of creating the drawing and the completed product.

The type and size of paper will be influenced, in part, by the anticipated dissemination process: If participants' drawings will (with their permission) form part of a public display, then larger and more durable paper (e.g., thin cardboard) might be more feasible. However, some participants are intimidated by poster-size pieces of paper, so participant comfort should be factored in. Overall, it might be best to provide participants with a choice of paper.

A leisurely pace. When data generation includes the visual, researchers need to respect the maxim of 'going slowly, taking time' (Galvaan, 2007, p. 156). Participants who agree to participate in drawing activities preferably need the time to engage with the researcher prior to drawing. We recommend (as does Guillemin, 2004) that researchers spend at least one session getting to know research participants before engaging them in a drawing activity: Participants are often more comfortable with drawing when the researcher is more familiar to them.

Think about what helps you to be strong / cope well with your life. Draw something in the space below that will show / illustrate what helps you to be strong / cope well with your life. Remember, how well you draw is not important.

Figure 2.1. Example of a written prompt that stimulated the drawing of a South African soccer player.

When some rapport has been established, and participants have been reminded that the quality of their drawing is not important, the drawing activity (already agreed on in a prior ethical procedure—see Chapters 4 and 6) can be initiated. Although researchers have been known not to provide a specific instruction, prompt, or drawing brief, many do (Carlson, Alan Sroufe, & Egeland, 2004). In our experience, a specific prompt provides structure and contributes to richer data generation. It is often preferable to give both a verbal and written prompt (see Figure 2.1) and then to allow participants the opportunity to process the prompt and visualise their responses. "Going slowly, taking time" (Galvaan, 2007, p. 156) applies to the drawing activity too: Participants need enough time to visualise and to draw—making the drawing is contingent on a process of reflection and of finding a way to express this pictorially.

The leisureliness of the pace will understandably be influenced by the prompt. If, for example, participants are asked to produce a group-generated symbolic drawing or visual metaphor, this would probably take longer than meeting a request for an individually produced simple line drawing. If participants are asked to produce a series of drawings (as in a storyboard or cartoon), this could probably translate into a number of hours of reflection and drawing, which could mean that researchers should provide participants with the prompt and the drawing materials and return at an agreed time to collect the completed drawings.

A shared analysis.   When psychologists use drawings to make human experience, perception, or emotion visible, a clinical analysis of the drawing alone is never sufficient. To make meaning out of what they are seeing, more astute psychologists engage their clients in a participatory manner and ask them to collaborate in the process of analysing and understanding the drawing. In other words, a clinical analysis of the drawing itself (the visible) is insufficient to provide deep understanding. In a very similar manner, drawing as a research method is more than just engaging participants in making drawings, followed by researcher-based analysis of these artefacts. When drawing is used as a research method, it entails participants' drawing and talking (or writing) (Backett-Milburn & McKie, 1999; Guillemin, 2004; MacGregor et al., 1998; Mair & Kierans, 2007) about the meaning embedded in their drawing. This collaboration is vital precisely because no visual product can be neutral: The drawing is produced by a specific individual in a particular space and time (Rose, 2001). The drawer's context (both present and past) must colour what is drawn, how it is drawn, and what the drawing represents. As such, drawing as a research tool must be complemented by verbal research methods (Guillemin, 2004) that encourage collaborative meaning-making and allow the drawer to give voice to what the drawing was intended to convey. When the analysis is shared in this way, valid knowledge production occurs. In other words, once the drawing is completed, it is vital to ask the participant to describe and interpret the image. This needs to include what the drawing is illustrating (i.e., what the drawing means), and, if colour was used, what meaning the participant attaches to the colour. It can also be useful to ask the participant to comment on the spatial organisation of the drawing (Guillemin, 2004). This interpretive description can be done verbally (and audio-recorded) or in writing. In our experience, verbal explanations are best provided out of earshot of other participants so as to prevent one participant from influencing another. We have also learned that when written explanations are provided, it is a good idea to read these in the participant's presence to ensure mutual understanding.

A discussion of what the drawing means, and/or clarification of the explanation, often prompts further relevant data generation. These data add to the emerging understanding of the phenomenon in question. For example, the 16-year-old boy who drew the picture in Figure 2.1 explained his drawing as follows: "I want to play soccer when I am big. I want to have money. I want to play for the national soccer team, for South Africa." This explanation (and the subsequent conversation) helped the researchers to understand that the street youth who made this drawing believed that soccer and playing for a national team meant having enough money and a better life. Only once the participant was invited to interpret his drawing, did the deeper meaning of soccer as an opportunity for a better future and a chance to dream become apparent. The chapters in this book often refer to how participants helped researchers make sense of the drawings (see Chapters 8 and 11, for example) and, in many instances, how this shared analysis encouraged richer researcher understanding of the phenomenon in question (see Chapter 15, for example). When drawings are group-generated, the clarification of the drawing could also be group-generated (see Chapter 12 for an example of this).

The preceding collaborative process informs the analysis of the drawings as collective. So, when the researcher then engages in a process of analysis (e.g., content analysis, thematic analysis) of all the drawings generated in a research project, this collective analysis encompasses both the drawn contents *and* the participants' interpretations of their drawings. Once the researcher has identified patterns and themes emerging from the collective drawings and the participants' interpretations, the researcher needs to return to the participants and ask their opinions on the emergent findings. In other words, the shared analysis occurs in the initial interpretation of the drawing and again in the analysis of the collective drawings. In this way, the participants are acknowledged as knowledge producers and respected as the experts that they are (Mertens, 2009).

A civic dissemination. The old sayings 'a picture is worth a thousand words' and 'a picture tells a story' foreground the power of drawings. Drawings are veridical, and are often easily comprehensible advocates. They broadcast pressing social messages in irrefutable ways. They give voice to the traditionally voiceless (see Figure 2.2, for example), encourage expression, and demand attention. For all these reasons, drawings are ideal dissemination tools: They can be displayed as collages, as individual posters, as themed exhibitions; they can be reproduced on banners, t-shirts, shopping bags or turned into screen-savers. Regardless of how they are used, their use makes knowledge accessible. More importantly, using drawings (with the participants' permission) as a means of making study findings known facilitates public dissemination at community level. 'Research as social change' (Kretzmann & McKnight, 1993) is subsequently potentiated.

Scared and don't know
what to do.

Figure 2.2. Drawing by a female, rural teacher indicating how the HIV&AIDS pandemic has incapacitated her as a teacher.

As noted in Chapter 4, a civic dissemination necessitates participant participation: Participants need to be sure that they want their drawings made public; they need to lead the process of deciding which drawings are displayed, where they are exhibited, and the form such an exhibition should take. In this way, participants continue to express ownership of their drawings, even if these drawings are no longer in their personal possession. Finally, if a decision is made to archive the drawings in a public space, following their use in some form of unrestricted dissemination, participants need to sanction this, particularly since it implies the potential for public use over which participants will have no control. Another possibility, as is taken up in Chapter 7, is the idea of a restricted site where the drawings are seen and explored only by the participants and research team.

To illustrate the above suggestions, we refer to the study "Resilient Educators (REds)" conducted by Theron, Geyer, Strydom, and Delport (2008). In this study, the researchers wanted to understand whether participation in the REds program (an intervention aimed at encouraging educators challenged by the HIV&AIDS pandemic to function resiliently) enabled educators to adapt positively to the challenges of the HIV&AIDS pandemic. One of the ways in which the researchers set about determining this was to ask participants to make specific pre- and post-

REds symbolic drawings. The researchers implemented the recommendations described above, as summarised here in Table 2.1.

Table 2.1. REds: A case study

Recommendation	Application in REds
1. A reassuring invitation to draw	Teachers who volunteered to participate in REds knew from the outset that they would be asked to draw, as part of the REds pre- and post-testing. The researchers emphasised that although teachers were invited to draw, they had the right not to draw. If teachers chose to draw, how well they drew (or not) was unimportant because the researchers were interested in what would be drawn—the researchers made this clear during the consent process and again just before teachers made drawings. This reassurance was repeated in the written prompt printed on the pages given to teachers to draw on: 'Draw in the space below (remember: it is not about how well you draw but about what you draw).' The researchers did not provide erasers in an attempt to discourage participants from trying to produce 'perfect' drawings.
2. A choice of drawing tools	Participants were handed blank A4 pages and a variety of coloured pencils. In some instances, participants were also offered felt-tipped markers. What the participants chose to draw with was entirely up to them.
3. A leisurely pace	REds researchers asked participants to sit comfortably and visualise how the HIV&AIDS pandemic had affected them. Participants were asked not to sit too close to one another. The researchers did not rush this stage of the process and allowed participants to reflect quietly and independently. Participants were then asked to draw what came to mind. The following specific prompt was given: *When you think of how the pandemic has affected you, what symbol comes to mind? Draw your symbol in the space below.*

Figure 2.3. Example of pre-REds drawing by a female REds participant from QwaQwa. The drawing was made with a thin black felt-tipped marker.

4. A shared analysis	Participants were asked to make meaning of their drawings by writing a couple of sentences on a second sheet. Researchers made this request verbally and repeated it in writing at the top of the second sheet: *Write 2–3 sentences in this space that explain your symbol.* The REds participant wrote the following in explanation of Figure 2.3 above:

Due to high death rate as a result of HIV/AIDS pandemic thousands and thousands of children are left orphaned as a result of this pandemic. Many children are left with no one to look after them, they end up begging for food in the streets. They become our (teachers) problem. They affect me.

Alternatively, participants were asked to complete the following sentences:

My symbol is …

I chose this symbol because …

What my drawing is saying …

The colour … represents …

Participants who preferred not to write an explanation talked the researcher through their drawings while the researcher recorded and transcribed the explanations.

In their analysis of the drawings collectively generated by REds participants, researchers went back to some of the participants and engaged them in consensus discussions around themes emerging from the contents of their drawings and initial participant interpretations (see, for example, Theron, 2008; Theron et al., 2010).

5. A civic dissemination	A community-focused dissemination of drawings generated by REds participants is currently in process. Drawings like those in Figures 2.2 and 2.3 are being used to create themed posters to raise public and government awareness of the need to support teachers who are affected by HIV and AIDS. For example, Figures 2.2 and 2.3 form part of a poster that illustrates teachers' empathy for learners who are HIV+ or are affected by HIV and AIDS and how this empathy has the potential to jeopardise teacher resilience if teachers continue to be unsupported in their efforts to care for learners made vulnerable by the pandemic. Teachers who participated in REds and post-graduate students who acted as REds facilitators are collaborating with REds researchers to finalise the choice of themes, the selection of pictures to illustrate these themes, and the logistics of the public displays.

We have used here the example of one project that used drawings, but how to use drawings as a data-generation tool is not cast in stone. Nevertheless, because the value of drawings (both as knowledge production and as dissemination tool) is foregrounded in researcher-participant collaboration, any use of drawings that does not start with participatory process may invite criticism.

Part 2: Working with Drawings as Visual Images

As the preceding example of the REds project illustrates, there are many points of entry for working with the drawing process, ranging from (1) a consideration of what the individual participants themselves say about their drawings (either during interviews or in their captions), (2) an analysis of the shared discussions, (3) a thematic analysis of key issues (with supporting evidence of the drawings and commentary), (4) the responses of audiences at the time of civic dissemination (Who says what? Which images are particularly compelling to community audiences and to broader audiences? Are there thematic aspects that can be explored in audience response?), and of course, what is most desirable, and (5) the triangulation of these various data sources. But if there is no one right way to elicit drawings as research data, there is also no one way to work with the data. As pointed out in Chapter 7, the participants themselves can be involved in working with visual data with their own collections of drawings, but there is also the possibility of working across collections. Although in the preceding section we make it clear that drawing is a visual *participatory* methodology and relies on the engagement of participants, this does not mean that there is no place for analysis that runs across collections (not always possible for the participants) and analytic approaches that involve third-party audiences.

The illustrative case studies in the second part of *Picturing Research* draw attention to the various ways that different researchers generate and work with visual data. These case studies also highlight the multi-genred nature of producer generated data—from straightforward drawings to metaphorical productions (see Chapters 9 and 10) to such genres as cartooning (Chapter 15) and storyboarding (Chapter 16). Although the bulk of the images that are presented are done as individual drawings, work done in the area of storyboarding is often carried out in small groups, raising new questions about capturing the process as well as product and follow-up discussion.

In the REds project, civic dissemination is collaborative work between teachers and post-graduate students that leads to negotiated themes and poster development. Content analysis may be useful when a third-party audience, such as the research team, is looking for the emergence of themes or key issues across a large number of drawings or across collections of drawings created by different age groups and cultures or conducted at different times or in different geographical locations. These drawings might be from the same prompt, or they may be from collections from different categories of participants. For example, if researchers and peer educators look across teacher and learner drawings of HIV representations to see how HIV and AIDS is seen (Chapter 11), they might work towards solutions appropriate to what the drawings depict. According to Rose (2001), though, the method is challenging in that it requires the analyst to consider only what is actually in the drawings and to develop interesting and coherent coding categories that do not overlap. Even when conclusions are reached by a third-party audience through content analysis, it is still possible and often desirable to take the findings back to the participants for their comments and suggestions on ways forward or indeed to work with this method to develop the codes themselves. Although the approach is useful for looking systematically across a large number of drawings to see what *is* in them, it is often important to think also about what *is not* in them and to ask questions like 'How is gender represented and why?' or 'Who is not in the picture?' or 'Why does this group's drawings never depict living positively?' Something to bear in mind with content analysis is that it has its roots in quantitative analysis, and in its mechanical way may fail to provide a means of going beyond coding and counting, which is why approaches that are more interpretive (and ideally participatory) seek to study context.

A combination of interpretive methods for analysing drawings with participants or even third-party audiences (see Chapter 11) can also be considered. This is because beyond the drawing itself, its meanings and its value lie partly in the socio-cultural context from which the drawing arises, with the individual(s) who created the drawing, or in the social practices and discourses that may have shaped the drawing. The 'draw-and-write' technique and collaboration with participants ensures that the producer's intended meaning is central, but may not be able to take into consideration broader social constructions.

Discourse analysis pays attention to drawings as social constructions. According to Fairclough (1995), discourse practices are the mediators between texts (in our case, drawings) and social practices, and they can shape and be shaping. One of the most effective ways to activate discourse analysis would be through developing questions that facilitate thinking about the relationships between the drawings as sites of meaning on the one hand, and the social and cultural practices that relate to them, on the other. So, one might ask of a drawing, 'How does this drawing reproduce or change practices of stigma?' or 'What does this drawing say about social and/or sexual relationships?' Questions that call attention to the composition and interaction of elements in each drawing will contribute to taking a semiotic perspective on drawings themselves. Working with an audience of viewers and looking at a drawing that represents HIV through tombstones, rain, and sad faces, one may ask, 'What does this drawing mean to you?' or 'How do these three elements in this drawing combine to convey a strong message?'

Following from this, we also note the ways in which the research process might focus on the actual 'doing' of the drawing or, as Goodman called it in the 1980s, "kidwatching" (Goodman, 1985). As Wright (2007) observed in her work with young children's drawing-telling, there is a rich 'action' going on during the drawing process that can also be studied and analysed:

> In children's drawing, for example, the assembled signs can include graphically produced images (e.g. people, objects), which might also include written letters or words, numbers, symbols (e.g. flags) and graphic devices (e.g. 'whoosh' lines behind a car). In addition, this graphic content may be accompanied by children's sounds (e.g. expressive vocalisation) and imitative gestures to enhance the meaning. Hence, when children draw, they construct and interpret a range of verbal and non-verbal signs with reference to the conventions associated with this medium of communication. (p. 38)

Her work along with the work with children's drawing-telling-writing by Dyson (1990) adds an 'in process' dimension to the analysis, at least with the drawings of young children. Campbell's analysis "Two Boys Drawing" demonstrates kidwatching in action as he describes the art making of a 6-year-old and a 9-year-old. This type of observing, as Campbell explores, highlights the place of intertextuality and the performance element of drawings and the notion of 'you have to be there' as researcher in order to see (and hear) what is happening. Even the child's name may be woven into the drawing. This work also highlights the importance of video and audio recordings (something that is also emphasised in Chapter 13). Clearly, this is work that must be approached sensitively and with a concern for not being too intrusive.

"Two Boys Drawing"

Based on the sessions I spent drawing with the boys, a six-year old and a nine-year old, there are certain things I noticed, though I can't help feeling that there is a lot that is not represented by that experience. Certainly my role as both an adult and an 'art instructor' of sorts must have influenced the dynamic, as opposed to how the boys might draw and construct images on their own. It did, however, unlock memories from my own childhood, and remind me of how drawing techniques were often treated among my peers. Perhaps because of my background and formal training, I tend to see a bigger

---

schism between the way kids often draw at earlier ages, and the visualisation and observation process that defines drawing at more 'advanced' levels.

One of the things that struck me in particular was the relative *lack* of visualisation or reference based on sight. In one sense, it could be said that the act of drawing is, for them, not really drawing at all in the traditional sense, but something more akin to writing. Rather than describing an actual specific object, or referencing it from a sort of three-dimensional awareness in the mind's eye, it seems to be about a formula that, if followed properly, yields a specific result. The result is not necessarily an approximation of a particular person or familiar object, but an icon. It is a visual shorthand, a pictogram rather than a picture, constructed from abstract shapes, and congealed into a recognisable symbolic form.

Naturally, the act of drawing from observation can also be seen as a system of symbols, albeit on a more microcosmic level. Committing a three-dimensional object or space to a two-dimensional medium involves a certain degree of abstraction, and a system of visual codes understood between the artist and viewer. In observational drawing, one learns that specific types of mark-making can be used to describe those certain surfaces or edges that go together to create one's image, and on the receiving end, the viewer should understand these cues. Sometimes calculations are involved, to ensure that things such as proportion and perspective are maintained, in spite of the imperfect guidance of our eyes.

Images are also not necessarily meant to convey a whole idea. Often they are visual aides to facilitate talking points. The picture does not tell a story . . . it *comes with* a story. After the drawing is complete, the experience becomes a performance, in which the visual elements of a drawing become linked together by a verbal narration. A drawing can end up being the preparation for the main event, which is the performative explanation of the drawing.

When a child learns to draw a truck, or a dog, it is often according to a step-by-step recipe of shapes. This recipe may be passed on from schoolmates or an instructor as the 'right way' to draw these things, following a prescribed order. In this way, drawing becomes about building a vocabulary of these tricks and codes. "Do you know how to draw an airplane?" is a request for a simple formula to denote 'airplane' that may be added to one's repertoire, and repeated as needed. This pictorial language is highly imitative, but also very holistic. Television cartoons, comics, picture books, and other children's drawings all become sources for drawn/written symbols, such as text, onomatopoeic sound effects, movement lines, word bubbles, dust clouds to denote speed, or even diagonal rays to distinguish a sun from other circular objects. However, most of these methods are integrated from existing systems, rather than invented on the spot, and as such tend to be a few degrees removed from the act of looking at the object or person they seek to represent.

Six year old D talks about his friend at school who draws knights in armour, though in this case, the image is traced from a book photograph. D's own drawing of his friend's knight incorporates many of the details from the original tracing, but without any knowledge of what those details are meant to represent. The shapes are simply there because they were in the original tracing.

Nine year old J tells me about his friend from school who is very good at drawing army tanks, and offers to show me how this friend draws them. The result is a methodical exercise in formula, executed with the care and attention a student of calligraphy might use to trace out the form of a cursive capital "G". One always starts with the same oval, followed by the circles within the oval, the box on top, followed by the smaller oval, and topped with the rectangle of the cannon and the lines to denote treads.

If asked to draw a truck, J will draw the same two-dimensional profile of a truck he was shown how to draw, without significant variation, again and again. The type of truck, or the angle it is observed from doesn't change, though it may grow or shrink, or gain colours or insignia. The basic visual components, however, remain the same. When asked to explain why those components are present, or what they represent, the child may not have an answer. For him, some of these visual details don't have a practical correlation to the original object; they are merely one of the codified components of the icon. Some forms have an easily recognisable function and purpose, like the wheels on a car. Others might be more obscure, like the bands on a knight's suit of armour, and as such become parts of the symbol without requiring first-hand knowledge of how they relate to the original object. The object becomes abstracted even as it gains a certain symbolic universality.

Part 3: Drawing Ourselves into the Research: Self as Text

Finally, there is also the possibility of considering the positioning of the researcher. With an increased recognition of the importance of reflexivity in qualitative work, and the emergence of work in autoethnography (Ellis, 2004) and self-study (Pithouse, Mitchell, & Moletsane, 2009), we think it is critical to 'draw ourselves' into the research. In Chapter 1, we consider the backstory of how we ourselves came to be working in the area of drawing and how that influences what we focus on in this book. Readers might look, then, at these accounts in Chapter 1 as examples of our 'drawing ourselves' into the analysis. In Chapter 3, Kathleen Pithouse explores more broadly the issue of 'starting with ourselves' and the uses of self-study in participatory research, and we direct the reader to this chapter for further consideration of the researcher-self in participatory research.

CONCLUSION

In this chapter, we provide a foundation for considering the critical issues and illustrative case studies that follow. Drawing as a research methodology has often been overlooked by researchers in search of more high-tech (and sometimes more abstract) approaches. The simultaneous simplicity and complexity of drawing, however, are key for both beginning and experienced researchers. Drawing, as we show in the REds example, can be used as a single research tool, or, as can be seen in other chapters, may be one of several research tools used in tandem. In our concern for method, we are convinced that drawing as a participatory visual methodology offers researchers in sub-Saharan Africa and elsewhere a rich entry point for engaging participants in issues that are important to them, for studying the act of representation itself, for reaching multiple audiences, and ultimately, for social action.

REFERENCES

Backett-Milburn, K., & McKie, L. (1999). A critical appraisal of the draw and write technique. *Health Education Research, 14*(3), 387–398. doi:10.1093/her/14.3.387.

Banks, M. (2001). *Visual methods in social research*. London, England: Sage.

Boydell, K. (2009, October 26). *Transformative potential of the arts in research: Theoretical, methodological and practical considerations* [Workshop]. University of Toronto, Toronto, ON.

Buchli, V., & Lucas, G. (2000). Children, gender and the material culture of domestic abandonment in the late 20th century. In J. S. Derevenski (Ed.), *Children and material culture* (pp. 131–138). London, England: Routledge.

Burke, C., & Prosser, J. (2008). Image-based educational research: Childlike perspectives. In J. G. Knowles & A. L. Cole (Eds.), *Handbook of the arts in qualitative research: Perspectives, methodologies, examples, and issues* (pp. 407–420). London, England: Sage.

Carlson, E. A., Alan Sroufe, L., & Egeland, B. (2004). The construction of experience: A longitudinal study of representation and behavior. *Child Development, 75*(1), 66–83. doi:10.1111/j.1467-8624.2004.00654.x.

Cole, A. L., & McIntyre, M. (2008). Installation art-as-research. In J. G. Knowles & A. L. Cole (Eds.), *Handbook of the arts in qualitative research: Perspectives, methodologies, examples, and issues* (pp. 287–298). London, England: Sage.

Conrad, D. (2006). Entangled (in the) sticks: Ethical conundrums of popular theater as pedagogy and research. *Qualitative Inquiry, 12*(3), 437–458. doi:10.1177/1077800405284364.

De Lange, N., Mitchell, C., & Stuart, J. (2007). *Putting people in the picture: Visual methodologies for social change*. Rotterdam, The Netherlands: Sense.

Dyson, A. H. (1990). Symbol makers, symbol weavers: How children link play, pictures and print. *Young Children, 45*(2), 50–57.

Ellis, C. (2004). *The ethnographic I: A methodological novel about autoethnography*. Walnut Creek, CA: AltaMira Press.

Fairclough, N. (1995). *Media discourse*. London, England: E. Arnold.

Furth, G. M. (1988). *The secret world of drawings: Healing through art*. Boston, MA: Sigo Press.

Galvaan, R. (2007). Getting the picture: The process of participation. In N. de Lange, C. Mitchell, & J. Stuart (Eds.), *Putting people in the picture: Visual methodologies for social change* (pp. 153–161). Rotterdam, The Netherlands: Sense.

Goodenough, F. L. (1926). *Measurement of intelligence by drawings*. Yonkers-on-Hudson, NY: World Book.

Goodman, R. F. (2002). The day our world changed: Children's art of 9/11. In R. F. Goodman & A. H. Fahnestock (Eds.), *The day our world changed: Children's art of 9/11* (pp. 14–17). New York, NY: Harry N. Abrams.

Goodman, Y. (1985). Kidwatching: Observing children in the classroom. In A. Jaggar & M. T. Smith-Burke (Eds.), *Observing the language learner* (pp. 9–18). Urbana, IL: National Council of Teachers of English and Newark, DE: International Reading Association.

Gray, R. E., & Sindig, C. (2002). *Standing ovation: Performing social science research about cancer*. Walnut Creek, CA: Altamira Press.

Guillemin, M. (2004). Understanding illness: Using drawings as a research method. *Qualitative Health Research, 14*(2), 272–289. doi:10.1177/1049732303260445.

Knowles, J. G., & Cole, A. L. (Eds.), *Handbook of the arts in qualitative research: Perspectives, methodologies, examples, and issues*. London, England: Sage.

Kretzmann, J. P., & McKnight, J. L. (1993). *Building communities from the inside out: A path toward finding and mobilizing a community's assets*. Chicago, IL: ACTA.

MacGregor, A. S. T., Currie, C. E., & Wetton, N. (1998). Eliciting the views of children about health in schools through the use of the draw and write technique. *Health Promotion International, 13*(4), 307–318. doi:10.1093/heapro/13.4.307.

Mair, M., & Kierans, C. (2007). Descriptions as data: Developing techniques to elicit descriptive materials in social research. *Visual Studies, 22*(2), 120–136. doi:10.1080/14725860701507057.

McNiff, S. (2008). Art-based research. In J. G. Knowles & A. L. Cole (Eds.), *Handbook of the arts in qualitative research: Perspectives, methodologies, examples, and issues* (pp. 29–40). London, England: Sage.

Mertens, D. M. (2009). *Transformative research and evaluation.* New York, NY: The Guilford Press.

Miller, D. (2010). *Stuff.* Cambridge, England: Polity Press.

Mitchell, C. (2011). *Doing visual research.* London, England: Sage.

Pink, S. (2001). *Doing visual ethnography: Images, media and representation in research.* London, England: Sage.

Pithouse, K., Mitchell, C., & Moletsane, R. (2009). *Making connections: Self-study and social action.* New York, NY: Peter Lang.

Rose, G. (2001). *Visual methodologies: An introduction to the interpretation of visual materials.* London, England: Sage.

Springgay, S. (2008). *Body knowledge and curriculum: Pedagogies of touch in youth and visual culture.* New York, NY: Peter Lang.

Stuart, J. (2007). Drawings and transformation in the health arena. In N. de Lange, C. Mitchell, & J. Stuart (Eds.), *Putting people in the picture: Visual methodologies for social change* (pp. 229–240). Rotterdam, The Netherlands: Sense.

Theron, L. C. (2008). "I have undergone some metamorphosis!" The impact of REds on South African educators affected by the HIV/AIDS pandemic. A pilot study. *Journal of Psychology in Africa, 18*(1), 31–42.

Theron, L. C., Geyer, S., Strydom, H., & Delport, C. S. L. (2010). Progress towards resilience: Using visual methodology to illustrate how REds shaped teacher associations of the HIV&AIDS pandemic. *Education as Change, 14*(2), forthcoming.

Weber, S. (2008). Visual images in research. In J. G. Knowles & A. L. Cole (Eds.), *Handbook of the arts in qualitative research: Perspectives, methodologies, examples, and issues* (pp. 41–54). London, England: Sage.

Wright, S. (2007). Young children's meaning-making through drawing and "telling": Analogies to filmic textural features. *Australian Journal of Early Childhood, 32*(4), 37–49. Retrieved from http://www.earlychildhoodaustralia.org.au.

PICTURING THE SELF:
DRAWING AS A METHOD FOR SELF-STUDY

Kathleen Pithouse

INTRODUCTION

Self-study is an approach to the study of personal experience in a social context. What distinguishes self-study from many other methodologies for researching personal experience is that it focuses on the researcher's own self and experience. Self-study research has so far mostly been initiated and conducted by teacher educators and teachers who study their selves "in action ... within [their] educational contexts" (Hamilton, Smith, & Worthington, 2008, p. 17) with the aim of improving their own professional understanding and practice as well as contributing to public conversations about teaching and learning (see, for example, Kosnik, Beck, Freese, & Samaras, 2005; Loughran, Hamilton, LaBoskey, & Russell, 2004; Mitchell, Weber, & O'Reilly-Scanlon, 2005). However, self-study is now increasingly being undertaken by practitioners and scholars working across the human and social sciences (see Pithouse, Mitchell, & Moletsane, 2009b) who have a common commitment to exploring how study of the self "might illuminate significant social questions and make a qualitative difference to shared human experience" (Pithouse, Mitchell, & Moletsane, 2009a, p. 2).

Researchers who adopt a self-study methodology draw on a wide range of mainly qualitative research methods to produce, collect, and interpret data (Pithouse, Mitchell, & Weber, 2009). The use of a variety of methods enables self-study researchers to examine their selves and personal experience from a range of perspectives (LaBoskey, 2004). Methods for self-study can include commonly used qualitative research methods such as journal writing, interviews, and group discussions. They also often take on creative or arts-based forms, for instance, drama, poetry, narrative, collage, video, and drawing (see, for example, Mitchell et al., 2005; Pithouse et al., 2009; Tidwell, Heston, & Fitzgerald, 2009; Weber & Mitchell, 2004).

In this chapter, I consider three different published examples of drawing as a method for self-study (namely, Derry, 2005; Richards, 1998; and Tidwell & Manke, 2009) to identify some strategies for, and features of, this research method. My discussion explores the nature and value of self-study drawing as a social research method as well as some potential challenges of using such a method.

L. Theron et al. (eds.), Picturing Research: Drawing as Visual Methodology, 37–48.

STRATEGIES FOR DRAWING AS A SELF-STUDY METHOD

Sketches of Early Memories

Catherine Derry (2005) used drawings as a method for recollecting, representing, and examining her childhood memories of being a victim of bullying. Her aim was "to produce a study that would make teachers and teacher educators ... connect with [her] experience on an emotional level, to understand how it feels to be bullied" (p. 43). In her discussion of how she came to use drawings in her self-study research, Derry explains:

> I first used drawings when I was trying to write a description of being excluded by my best friend in third grade. I had trouble remembering exactly what happened. I sat down with a sheet of paper and some pencil crayons and I drew my memory of that incident. This drawing made all the feelings and details of the situation flood back and I was able to draw the picture [see Figure 3.1] and write my narrative .... The positive results of this drawing experience encouraged me to use drawings as a research tool for this study. (p. 37)

Figure 3.1. Being excluded by my best friend in the third grade.[i]

Derry combined her self-study drawings with written narrative descriptions to generate data about her childhood memories and also to present the findings of her research.

Self-Portraits of Practice

For Janet Richards (1998), drawings are a way to record and study her own decisions and actions as a teacher educator. Her self-study drawings take the form of self-portraits that "depict the ways we view our inner and outer selves" (p. 34). Creating self-portraits of her professional selves in action allows her to identify and examine both problematic and beneficial aspects of her current practice and to think of ways to enhance her future practice.

Richards uses a "four-step recursive cycle of thought and action" (p. 34) in developing her self-portraits of practice:

The first step involves a conscious effort on my part to monitor a particular aspect of my teaching that I wish to explore …. In step two, I carefully consider the teaching problem or event …. I reflect both in a systematic and a non-sequential, intuitive way until I develop some insights into my behavior. In the third step, I document my discoveries by creating a teaching self-portrait. [see Figure 3.2]

OK pre-service teachers. It's our first meeting of the semester. From now on we'll meet at Bayview School - not here on campus. I'll tell you how to get to Bayview later. Now remember everything that I'm going to tell you in the next two and ½ hours. Don't worry! Go with the flow! Delay gratification and you'll be just fine. In just two days you'll be teaching. Isn't that great? What's that? You say you don't know how to teach reading and language arts? Don't worry! You'll learn on the job! Just don't teach sight words in isolation or have kids do round-robin oral reading. What? You don't know what round-robin oral reading is? Well don't worry. Just trust me. You'll do fine. We'll go over that later. Now you'll need to make personal dictionaries, prediction logs, literature logs - oh-and you also need to create a hands-on interest inventory. What? Oh- we'll talk about that in a minute. Oh'- and don't forget - have lots of glue and childrens literature, and markers, crayons, and paper. And- devise a group management plan. Be at Bayview at 8:00 am. Don't chew gum. Park in the Playground. Don't worry. Everything will be fine. See you at Bayview. Don't worry…

Figure 3.2. A self-portrait depicting [Richards's] 'teacher talk' in the classroom: 'I talk too much'.[ii]

Finally, I reflect further about the portrait's content, searching for insights into my professional decisions and attempting to develop some deeper understanding about my actions ... [and to] come up with some alternative behaviors. (p. 35)

Metaphoric Representations of Professional Experience

Deborah Tidwell and Mary Manke (2009) developed metaphoric (or symbolic) drawings of significant experiences in their work as educational administrators to represent, examine, and better understand their professional lives and practice. Metaphoric drawings do not depict an event or experience factually or realistically. Instead, they use metaphors or symbols to show something important or meaningful about the event or experience. See, for instance, Manke's drawing of her professional self as a tightrope walker (Figure 3.3), which represents how she feels about her work as an administrator at a particular stage in her self-study research.

Figure 3.3. Mary's nodal moment #5.[iii]

Tidwell and Manke (2009) developed their method of metaphoric representation of professional experience through a year-long, collaborative process of self-study research:

We started each of us thinking about an experience that we found significant in our practice, and we created a simple drawing from that experience focusing on how that particular experience spoke to us. We allowed the drawing to represent both the event and how we felt about the event. The idea was not to ask, "What metaphor would help me to understand what is happening in my practice?" But instead, the self-study began when we thought about something that was happening in our professional work and represented those dynamics visually. This put less pressure on us to be clever and metaphoric. We could then focus on being in the meaning behind the moment. We think it is a good idea to create several metaphoric representations over a period of time. In the process of drawing metaphoric representations, a particular issue would arise that had been on our mind and a drawing related to that emerged. We found that once some salient issue has been represented, other issues are likely to arise as well. (p. 149)

In addition, Tidwell and Manke found it useful to write reflections to help to make sense of their metaphoric drawings. For example, Manke wrote the following reflection on her drawing of herself as a tightrope walker (see Figure 3.3):

Presto, I'm a tightrope walker carrying a long pole that should help me balance. I hope so, because there's a hole in the safety net below. My feelings here are related to the ones I drew in July. With a job so big I can't even remember all parts of it at one time, I sometimes feel unsure that I'll be able to do everything there is to do well enough to stay on the rope. So the fear of falling is always with me, someplace in my mind. (p. 144)

Tidwell and Manke also highlighted the value of working together to make meaning of their written reflections and drawings using email, telephone, and face-to-face meetings:

When we met, we recorded our discussions in summary notes. These notes were very helpful as a document of what we had said and as a source for thinking about these discussions after the meeting. The process of creating multiple layers of reflection on our metaphoric representations helped us generate deeper and deeper understandings of our practice. Because we were far apart, we relied on email and phone for much of our interactions. When we emailed each other our scanned drawings and our written reflections, we gave ourselves approximately 2 weeks to study our partner's drawing and to read through her reflections on that drawing. Having an electronic version of our drawings and reflections also helped make the data more accessible. We responded to each other with comments, questions, and queries about what we understood about each other's metaphors. These responses to our drawings helped us to see our metaphoric representations through a different perspective. We used our partner's comments and question prompts to push us further in thinking about our practice. Using these comments and questions, we would re-reflect upon our drawing and writing, then email our partner additional insights and comments about our metaphors. This recursive reflective process really helped us think about the meaning within our metaphoric representations. (p. 150)

FEATURES OF DRAWING AS A SELF-STUDY METHOD

Producing Detailed and Evocative Portrayals of Personal Experience

The work by Derry (2005), Richards (1998), and Tidwell and Manke (2009) shows how, by using diverse drawing strategies, self-study researchers can access and portray aspects of their personal experience that they might have forgotten, overlooked, not seen clearly, or even avoided thinking about. For example, Derry (2005) describes how the act of drawing helped her to remember details of, and feelings about, her early childhood memories of being bullied that she was not able to recover when she was trying to write descriptions of these memories:

> I encountered a problem as I started to write narrative descriptions of being bullied. I realized that something was missing in the reading and writing. My descriptions were dull, flat and the detail was sparse. What was missing was something that would help me to write fuller descriptions and would give the reader a multi-layered perspective of my experience. (p. 36)

Thus, for Derry, drawing allowed her to reconnect with and describe her early childhood experience in a more immediate and vivid way than writing had.

Richards (1998) acknowledged that portraying aspects of her professional practice through drawing encouraged her not only to look more carefully at her teacher educator self, but also "to publicly disclose parts of [herself] that [she] may prefer to remain hidden" (p. 35).

And Tidwell and Manke (2009) explained how creating metaphors to represent their professional experience allowed them to move beyond concrete or factual portrayals to produce images and written reflections that revealed the "more complex and possibly abstract meanings embedded within [their] own practice" (p. 137).

Deepening Researcher Self-Awareness and Self-Reflexivity

Because drawing as a method allows self-study researchers to look at their personal experience in detail and from different vantage points, it can prompt them to become more aware of, and reflexive (or thoughtful) about, their own viewpoints, feelings, and actions and of the possible impact of these viewpoints, feelings, and actions on themselves and others.

For Richards (1998), drawing as a self-study method can promote self-awareness and self-reflexivity by "[forcing] us to look carefully at who we are and [helping] us confront our strengths and shortcomings" (p. 34). To illustrate, Richards describes how by drawing her first meeting with a group of students (see Figure 3.2), she became aware that, despite her understanding of the importance of involving students in interactive learning, she was spending too much time telling students what she felt they needed to know.

Derry (2005) explained that drawing can function as "a mirror to view our perceptions of ourselves" (p. 39). She describes how drawing enabled her to give her and her research audience "a clear vision" of how her early experiences of bullying affected her view of herself at various points during her childhood "in a way that text alone could not" (p. 39).

Additionally, Tidwell and Manke (2009) highlighted the changes in practice that can result from the increased self-awareness and self-reflexivity that can come with using drawing as a self-study method. Tidwell explains:

> The most profound change that grew out of this process was my realization that administrative work, while important as a function of facilitating programs and supporting the needs of the larger institution, was not professionally fulfilling for me; and more importantly did not need to be a part of my professional life long term .... I made the conscious decision to step down from the role of coordinator for my program. (p. 148)

Engaging with the Emotions of Personal Experience

Drawing can be a way for self-study researchers to portray and engage with the emotions that give life to personal experience and yet are frequently overlooked or downplayed in public accounts of social research.

Derry (2005) drew attention to how drawing can bring forth the emotions of experiences that happened many years ago, and she emphasises the value of drawing for helping researchers to access and work with emotionally difficult information: "Many of the memories I recalled of being bullied were emotionally upsetting. I found it difficult to put the emotions that these memories contained into words ..... My drawing was an object used to remember an emotionally difficult situation" (p. 38).

Derry also explained how her drawings allow her to communicate the complexity and depth of the emotions of her personal experience with others and thus in turn "evoke [their] personal [memories] and emotion and make [them] think about how to deal with these issues, with their whole, embodied selves" (p. 41).

Tidwell and Manke (2009) described how developing and sharing metaphoric representations of their professional practice afforded them new insights into the relationships and emotions that are an integral and influential part of their professional lives and work. They discuss how, through their collaborative and recursive process of producing and examining drawings and associated written reflections, they were prompted to take action in response to the deeper emotional understanding they had gained. Manke elaborates:

> As I drew myself and represented what my practice looked like, I came to insights that were significant for me—and used them to make changes. When I saw myself cowed by Professor G-r-r-r, I was able to recognize what was happening in such interactions, and make a conscious effort to feel and act more courageously. When I drew the pleasure I felt in using my position to make connections, I became more attentive to opportunities to do so, and do so more often. (p. 148)

Stimulating a Dynamic Process of Working with Research Data

When drawing is used as a self-study method, research data are not collected, presented, and analysed in a linear sequence. Instead, data (drawings) are constructed and re-constructed through a creative, recursive, and sometimes collaborative process. Meaning is made and remade throughout this process.

Richards (1998) emphasised the cyclical and active nature of her method of developing self-portraits of practice. She explains that her approach to drawing as a self-study method is comprised of a cycle of reflection and action in which drawing is preceded, accompanied, and followed by deep thinking. And her self-study process does not end with definitive conclusions about the aspect of her professional practice that she is studying but rather with possibilities for enhancing her ongoing practice. These possibilities can in turn provide new avenues for ongoing self-study research.

For Tidwell and Manke (2009), a fundamental aspect of their year-long self-study process of creating and interpreting drawings was the collaborative nature of this process. They explain:

> Each of us had different issues concerning our practice, and each of us had different outcomes from this self-study experience. Yet we feel that we would not have reached the outcomes that changed our practice without our interactive process of discussing, reflecting, revisiting, and re-reflecting upon our data .... Neither of us believes that we could have experienced the knowledge building and practical change resulting from this process if we had worked alone. (p. 151)

Expanding Opportunities for Research Communication and Pedagogic Practice

Constructing and reconstructing self-study research data in creative ways and through dynamic processes such as drawing allows for vivid, evocative, and multidimensional forms of research communication "whose limits differ from those imposed by propositional discourse and number" (Eisner, 1997, p. 5) and that can stimulate lively research conversations. Drawing as a self-study method can also serve as an effective pedagogic strategy for learning through inquiry into personal experience.

Derry (2005) described how self-study drawings can function as a powerful stimulus to engage others in conversation about a research topic: "My drawings have provoked strong reactions from their audience .... [One] image can represent something that it could take many pages to describe" (p. 41). Furthermore, she explains how, in her capacity as a teacher educator, she used her drawing method as a pedagogic tool to engage a group of students in exploring their own experiences of, and thoughts about, bullying. Derry describes how the students, who initially had not seemed to be very interested in the subject of childhood bullying, became much more engrossed in the topic through drawing their own memories and sharing these drawings with others:

This drawing exercise got students in touch with their own feelings about and experiences with bullying. The dialogue that ensued was more personally and emotionally tinged …. These teachers learned that their own personal experiences could help them to better understand their own students' problems. (p. 43)

Richards (1998) also highlighted the value of self-study drawing as a pedagogic tool. She explains how she has used her own self-study drawings and reflections as a pedagogic resource to introduce her students (preservice teachers) to her method of creating self-portraits of practice. Richards has found that sharing her self-portraits and helping her students to create their own have enabled them to re-examine their own interaction with learners and to become more aware of possible inconsistencies between how they would like to teach and their actual teaching practices.

Richards draws attention to how this pedagogic interaction with her students has enhanced her own ongoing research into her professional practice. She highlights the benefits of collaborative inquiry through sharing the processes and products of self-study drawing: "Drawing and sharing self-portraits of teaching behaviors allow teacher educators and pre-service teachers to collaborate as partners and to engage in a synergistic process of mutual learning" (pp. 38–39).

CHALLENGES OF DRAWING AS A SELF-STUDY METHOD

Fear of Being 'Bad' at Drawing

A challenge highlighted by Derry (2005) and Tidwell and Manke (2009) is that adults who do not define themselves as artists are often afraid to draw or to share their drawings with others because they fear that they are not skilled or talented enough. As Derry acknowledges, "A few years ago, I was scared to draw. You could not have paid me to do it. My third grade teacher told me I was bad at drawing and I believed that" (p. 36). Derry describes how, despite her lack of confidence, she persisted with drawing because she began to experience the benefits of using it as a self-study research method. She also points out that she has gone on to use drawing as a method for many other projects.

Tidwell and Manke explain that because Manke was not comfortable with drawing at the start of their self-study process, she drew on work by Tidwell (2006) and Goldberg (1986, 1997) to develop strategies for, and confidence in, drawing as a research method. Tidwell and Manke also highlight how they both became less self-conscious about their drawing skills as they worked through the collaborative process of making meaning from their metaphoric representations. They caution that it is important for researchers who use drawing as a self-study method to remember that what is important is not how well one draws but, instead, what new insights one can gain through the drawing process.

Making One's Self Visible through Drawing

Drawing as a self-study method involves making one's self highly visible and thus vulnerable to one's own scrutiny and the scrutiny of one's research audience. Making public one's self-perceptions and self-questioning in a visual form is not something to be done lightly. As Richards (1998) pointed out, self-study drawing requires the researcher to face aspects of her self that she may not be entirely comfortable with. Tidwell and Manke (2009) emphasised that they "became less self-conscious about sharing [their] reflections and about responding to one another" (p. 151) when they were both engaged in the process of self-study through metaphoric representation. This suggests that a collaborative self-study process that involves sharing and mutual trust can help researchers to become more comfortable with revealing and examining their selves through drawing.

The research audience may also feel ill at ease with being presented with personal information about the researcher and with the emotions that may be aroused by that information. Derry (2005) described the initial, uneasy reaction of others to her memory drawings and reflections:

> Then I started reading them narrative excerpts from my self-study, which I presented along with my drawings. The room became quieter and the students seemed to be feeling emotion. They seemed, perhaps, to be a bit uncomfortable with feeling such emotion in the context of a university classroom and with knowing such vulnerable secrets about an instructor. (p. 42)

Derry goes on to explain how her research audience (in this case, her students) became more comfortable with the personal and emotional nature of her presentation when they engaged in the process of drawing and sharing their own memory sketches. However, as a researcher, one will not always have the opportunity to involve one's audience in producing their own self-study drawings and so it is important to be prepared to deal with any uneasiness one's drawings might trigger.

Dealing with the Emotional Weight of Self-Study Drawing

It is evident from the work of Derry (2005), Richards (1998), and Tidwell and Manke (2009) that self-study drawing as process and product both portrays and evokes emotion. As discussed earlier in this chapter, this can be a significant strength of this research method. However, it also means that researchers who use self-study drawing as a social research method take on considerable emotional responsibility towards themselves and others with whom they share their research processes and findings. Thus, before embarking on a process of self-study research through drawing, it would be advisable for researchers to be aware of the need to develop context-appropriate strategies for working with emotions in research (see also Pithouse et al., 2009).

TAKING SELF-STUDY DRAWING FORWARD

The work by Derry (2005), Richards (1998), and Tidwell and Manke (2009) highlights both the research and pedagogic potential of using self-study drawing as a method for inquiry into personal experience in a social context. Different forms of drawing such as memory sketches (Derry, 2005), self-portraits of practice (Richards, 1998), and metaphoric representations of professional experience (Tidwell & Manke, 2009) can assist self-study researchers to enrich and deepen their research processes and findings. It is, however, important to be mindful of the complexity and challenges of self-study drawing. Nonetheless, reference to the growing body of work in this area can provide valuable guidance and inspiration for researchers who wish to develop their own approaches to drawing as a method for self-study.

NOTES

i   I gratefully acknowledge kind permission from the copyright holder, Catherine Derry, to reproduce this image, originally published on p. 38 of Derry, C. (2005). Drawings as a research tool for self-study: An embodied method of exploring memories of childhood bullying. In C. Mitchell, S. Weber, & K. O'Reilly-Scanlon (Eds.), *Just who do we think we are?: Methodologies for autobiography and self-study in teaching* (pp. 34–46). New York, NY: RoutledgeFalmer. I also acknowledge kind permission from Catherine Derry to reproduce text from the aforementioned chapter.

ii I gratefully acknowledge kind permission from the copyright holder, Mary Lynn Hamilton, and from Janet Richards to reproduce this image, originally published on p. 36 of Richards, J. C. (1998). Turning to the artistic: Developing an enlightened eye by creating teaching self-portraits. In M. L. Hamilton (Ed.), *Reconceptualizing teaching practice: Self-study in teacher education* (pp. 34–44). London, England: Falmer Press.

iii I gratefully acknowledge kind permission from the copyright holder, Springer Science and Business Media, and from Deborah Tidwell and Mary Manke to reproduce this image, originally published as Figure 4 on p. 144 of Tidwell, D., & Manke, M. P. (2009). Making meaning of practice through metaphor. In D. Tidwell, M. Heston, & L. Fitzgerald (Eds.), *Research methods for the self-study of practice* (pp. 135–153). Dordrecht, The Netherlands: Springer. I also acknowledge kind permission from Springer Science+Business Media and from Deborah Tidwell and Mary Manke to reproduce text from the aforementioned chapter. Original copyright notice: No part of this work may be reproduced, stored in a retrieval system, or transmitted in any form or by any means, electronic, mechanical, photocopying, microfilming, recording or otherwise, without written permission from the Publisher.

REFERENCES

Derry, C. (2005). Drawings as a research tool for self-study: An embodied method of exploring memories of childhood bullying. In C. Mitchell, S. Weber, & K. O'Reilly-Scanlon (Eds.), *Just who do we think we are?: Methodologies for autobiography and self-study in teaching* (pp. 34–46). New York, NY: RoutledgeFalmer. doi:10.4324/9780203464977_chapter_4.

Eisner, E. W. (1997). The promise and perils of alternative forms of data representation. *Educational Researcher, 26*(6), 4–10. doi:10.3102/0013189X026006004.

Goldberg, N. (1986). *Writing down the bones: Freeing the writer within.* Boston, MA: Shambhala.

Goldberg, N. (1997). *Living color: A writer paints her world.* New York, NY: Bantam Books.

Hamilton, M. L., Smith, L., & Worthington, K. (2008). Fitting the methodology with the research: An exploration of narrative, self-study and auto-ethnography. *Studying Teacher Education, 4*(1), 17–28. doi:10.1080/17425960801976321.

Kosnik, C., Beck, C., Freese, A. R., & Samaras, A. P. (Eds.). (2005). *Making a difference in teacher education through self-study: Studies of personal, professional and program renewal.* Dordrecht, The Netherlands: Springer.

LaBoskey, V. K. (2004). The methodology of self-study and its theoretical underpinnings. In J. J. Loughran, M. L. Hamilton, V. K. LaBoskey, & T. Russell (Eds.), *International handbook of self-study of teaching and teacher education practices* (Vol. 2, pp. 817–869). Dordrecht, The Netherlands: Springer. doi:10.1007/978-1-4020-6545-3_21.

Loughran, J. J., Hamilton, M. L., LaBoskey, V. K., & Russell, T. L. (Eds.). (2004). *International handbook of self-study of teaching and teacher education practices* (Vol. 2). Dordrecht, The Netherlands: Springer.

Mitchell, C., Weber, S., & O'Reilly-Scanlon, K. (Eds.). (2005). *Just who do we think we are?: Methodologies for autobiography and self-study in teaching.* New York, NY: RoutledgeFalmer.

Pithouse, K., Mitchell, C., & Moletsane, R. (2009a). Introduction. In K. Pithouse, C. Mitchell, & R. Moletsane (Eds.), *Making connections: Self-study & social action* (pp. 1–9). New York, NY: Peter Lang.

Pithouse, K., Mitchell, C., & Moletsane, R. (2009b). *Making connections: Self-study & social action.* New York, NY: Peter Lang.

Pithouse, K., Mitchell, C., & Weber, S. (2009). Self-study in teaching and teacher development: A call to action. *Educational Action Research, 17*(1), 43–62. doi:10.1080/09650790802667444.

Richards, J. C. (1998). Turning to the artistic: Developing an enlightened eye by creating teaching self-portraits. In M. L. Hamilton (Ed.), *Reconceptualizing teaching practice: Self-study in teacher education* (pp. 34–44). London, England: Falmer Press.

Tidwell, D. (2006). Nodal moments as a context for meaning. In D. Tidwell & L. Fitzgerald (Eds.), *Self-study and diversity* (pp. 267–285). Rotterdam, The Netherlands: Sense.

Tidwell, D. L., Heston, M. L., & Fitzgerald, L. M. (Eds.). (2009). *Research methods for the self-study of practice.* Dordrecht, The Netherlands: Springer.

Tidwell, D., & Manke, M. P. (2009). Making meaning of practice through visual metaphor. In D. L. Tidwell, M. L. Heston, & L. M. Fitzgerald (Eds.), *Research methods for the self-study of practice* (pp. 135–153). Dordrecht, The Netherlands: Springer. doi:10.1007/978-1-4020-9514-6_9.

Weber, S., & Mitchell, C. (2004). Visual artistic modes of representation for self-study. In J. J. Loughran, M. L. Hamilton, V. K. LaBoskey, & T. Russell (Eds.), *International handbook of self-study of teaching and teacher education practices* (Vol. 2, pp. 979–1037). Dordrecht, The Netherlands: Springer.

CHAPTER 4

A POSITIVE, AFRICAN ETHICAL APPROACH TO COLLECTING AND INTERPRETING DRAWINGS: SOME CONSIDERATIONS

Linda Theron, Jean Stuart, and Claudia Mitchell

INTRODUCTION

All research is regulated by ethical principles that try to ensure that research participants are not harmed in any way by their participation in a research project. Universities and research bodies typically have robust ethical procedures and ethical codes that try to guarantee that researchers do ethical research. Ethical bodies at these institutions often have the power to enforce ethical requirements, and this results in researchers being coerced into ethical conduct that follows a trajectory of 'what I should do', rather than one of 'what, ideally, can I do?' Although we concur with the appropriate principles that ethical bodies legislate, this is not the focus of our chapter. We argue instead that ethical researchers need to be 'what-ideally-can-I-do'-minded. To this end, we focus on the notion of positive ethics (Bush, 2010; Handelsman, Knapp, & Gottlieb, 2005) or commitment to interpreting the ethical imperative of 'do least harm' as, instead, 'do most good' (Moletsane, Mitchell, Smith, & Chisholm, 2008, p. 114) and on the concept of African ethics (Murove, 2009b) or the normative, black African moral traditions and beliefs aimed at achieving fullness of humanity (Murove, 2009a; Prozesky, 2009; Shutte, 2009). Writing as we do from the perspective of three white women, we acknowledge, as Lather (2004) and Jansen (2009) did, that we could be on shaky ground in relation to taking up the idea of African ethics. However, in this chapter, we argue that researchers who use drawing as a methodology are ideally positioned to conduct research that both interrogates and celebrates the principles of positive, African ethics.

POSITIVE, AFRICAN ETHICS

We conflate notions of 'positive ethics' and 'African ethics' in this chapter. Although this has not been explicitly done in the literature, and even though our intention is not to simplify two profound philosophies, we fuse them because of the compatibility of their premises and visions. To illuminate this harmony, we briefly define each.

L. Theron et al. (eds.), Picturing Research: Drawing as Visual Methodology, 49–61.

CHAPTER 4

Positive Ethics

In essence, the concept of positive ethics speaks to an ethical fidelity that is integral to the researcher's *way of being* and not a way of doing as enforced by ethics committees (Handelsman et al., 2005). This way of being is rooted in personal values that are aligned with a deep commitment to the well-being of others and to transformational research (Mertens, 2009). What flows from this is an ethical integrity that is much more than an attempt to avoid lawsuits or censure.

An allegiance to ethical ideals is embedded in a deep awareness of personal and professional values and also the societal forces that shape these values. Positive ethics is not possible for anyone unless she or he confronts and articulates personal, professional, and socio-cultural values and considers what the possible social impact of a research agenda will be. In other words, positive ethics is intertwined with reflexivity (as is much visual research).

Implicit in positive ethics are the four core ethical principles of respect for autonomy, nonmaleficence, beneficence, and justice (Bush, 2010).

African Ethics

African ethics also speaks to a way of being that informs the ways of doing. This way of being embraces a number of core values, including that of Ubuntu or reciprocal, respectful relatedness, community, and generosity (Mokwena, 2007; Prozesky, 2009). These values ideally encourage Africans towards acts that promote community-building and human dignity, and towards a fundamental respect of, and for, persons. These values also teach human interdependence and an awareness that humans do not have the luxury of acting only in their own interest (Munyaka & Motlhabi, 2009). Although the idea of Ubuntu values has been tainted by forces of colonisation, Apartheid, urbanisation, and the HIV&AIDS pandemic (Mkhize, 2006; Munyaka & Motlhabi, 2009) and, as Lather (2004) and Jansen (2009) argued, sometimes misinterpreted and abused by academics and researchers, nonetheless the idea remains central to the African ethical vision (Shutte, 2009).

An Ethical Hybrid

The concord between the values that underscore positive ethics and African ethics is apparent. Both celebrate commitment to human dignity. Both observe respect. Both command doing most good. Both honour an anthropocentric community of being and an obligation to contribute to the good and growth of this community (Bujo, 2009). Because of this harmony and because of our situatedness as researchers in Africa, we advocate an approach to generating, interpreting, and displaying drawings that is rooted in a positive, African ethical hybrid.

A POSITIVE, AFRICAN ETHICAL APPROACH TO RESEARCH

Our approach to research is essentially transformative (Mertens, 2009). Because we seek to bring about social change, we advocate alternative data collection methods (like drawings) that give easier voice to marginalised groups or groups that might struggle in relation to language and literacy. Ethical rigour and allegiance to positive ethics (Bush, 2010) are central to this approach. From the perspective of African ethics, then, anything less than positive ethics, or, in other words, to an ethical commitment to the good of the communities and participants who participate in research projects, is unthinkable. This commitment is embedded in the processes of respect for autonomy, nonmaleficence, beneficence, and justice.

Respect for Autonomy

Respect for autonomy acknowledges the sovereignty of every human being. Implicit in this sovereignty is the right to choose. From an African ethics perspective, such an acknowledgement relates to perceiving fellow human beings as other selves (Shutte, 2009): The right to choose is something that most individuals would hold sacrosanct for themselves, so seeing a fellow human being as "another self" (Shutte, 2009, p. 94) encourages respect for autonomy. In being positive ethicists, researchers respect participants as other selves.

In research contexts, respect for autonomy is most often reflected in practices of informed consent, in terms of respect for the free choice to either participate or withdraw from the research process at any point. When a researcher strives towards observing positive ethics, informed consent processes purposefully and painstakingly address the participants' right to decide to participate by providing exhaustive detail on what participation in the research project will entail, especially in terms of time, activities that will generate data, and possible disadvantages that participation may hold for them as participants. The question the researcher asks is "What, *ideally*, can I do to ensure that my participant is fully informed and supported to make an informed decision about participation and termination of participation?" The answer to this question lies, in part, in detailed dialogue (preferably in the participants' mother tongues) complemented with comprehensive letters of information that participants can keep. It also lies in active communication (both verbal and non-verbal) of respect for the participant's choice, whatever this choice may be, with regard to participating in the research process.

When the research process involves drawing, respect for participant autonomy extends to respecting participant willingness to draw (or not). To this end, the informative dialogue preceding written consent (and the letter of information) must make it very clear that participants will be asked to make drawings as part of their contribution to the project. To complicate matters further, the ethical dilemma of ownership and public display of visual artefacts arises when drawings are involved (Karlsson, 2007; Moletsane et al., 2008). This is tricky and needs to be negotiated respectfully with participants: Researchers who align themselves with positive ethics need to explore the acceptability to participants of keeping their drawings, using them publicly, and even displaying them. Following this, the consent form must ask for *explicit* permission to keep these drawings and to use them publicly (e.g., in journals or in conference presentations):

> I am aware that I will be asked to make a drawing. I grant permission for the researcher to keep my drawing and to use my drawing publicly (i.e., my drawing can be shown anonymously in conference presentations, or reproduced in academic writings, or included in visual displays).
>
> **No**   **Yes**

Figure 4.1. Excerpt of a consent form.

Nonmaleficence

When researchers champion positive, African ethics, they reframe nonmaleficence positively as 'do most good' (Moletsane et al., 2008, p. 114). In so doing, researchers actively seek out ways in which to protect and enable participants and thus facilitate a positive experience of participating in a research project. Thus, positive ethicists enter more profoundly into a community with research participants and, in this manner, celebrate participants' dignity.

Expertise of the researcher.   One way of 'doing most good' is for researchers to ensure that they are competent in the methods they use (Mertens, 2005). As part of gaining and expanding expertise in the area of drawings, researchers should, of course, continue to read and participate in research forums focusing on the use of drawings and other visual methodologies. With regard to using drawings as a methodology, researchers themselves should draw (or should have drawn) what they are going to ask their participants to draw, both as a means of experiencing (to some extent) what the participants will experience and as a way of reflecting on the clarity of the prompt that will be used to guide the drawing. In rural African contexts, drawing might be an unfamiliar activity, so researchers will need to be sensitive about inviting drawing without distressing participants, in ways that are culturally compatible (such as drawing in the sand). Although drawing is a familiar activity in most communities, many adults last drew when they were children. In our experience, when adults are asked to make drawings, they often laugh nervously or protest that they cannot draw (see Weber & Mitchell, 1995). Some children, especially adolescents, do the same thing. Again, the onus is on the researcher to invite drawing in ways that celebrate the dignity of the participants.

It is vital to remind participants that they cannot be forced into making drawings, but that should they be willing to try, the focus is not on the quality of their drawings. As noted above, adults may be hesitant to engage in the process for fear of producing a child-like product. To further facilitate a positive experience of the methodology, researchers must allow participants sufficient time to reflect and to draw: Not hurrying participants will help to 'do good'.

Cultural sensitivity and awareness. Linked to the above notion of researchers being competent in the chosen methodology is prior affirmation (ideally at the design stage of the research project) that drawing will be culturally acceptable to the participants, especially if the drawings are to be made on paper. We recognise that this is not always easy to enact, and it is important to consider the ways in which cultural stereotypes may operate. We also acknowledge that the idea of 'culture' in and of itself is complex. By collaborating with community elders or community representatives (Mertens, 2009; Wassenaar, 2006), it may be possible to gauge how culturally appropriate the method of drawing will be. Such a collaborative partnership also encourages opportunities for adjustments to the methodology. For example, in some rural communities with low levels of literacy, it might be more appropriate to diagram in the sand, as done in the innovative study by van der Riet (2008). At the same time, we need to be aware of the various power dimensions operating in the community itself and the question of who can speak, and about what? As Moletsane (2011) argues, for example, in a context in which the adult voice dominates, particularly in relation to such issues as sexuality, we need to think about what that might mean in our fieldwork with children and young people. Similarly, in the study of an issue such as gender-based violence, we need to think about the consequences of girls and women speaking out through their drawings. As Leach (2006) asked, how can we ensure a safe space for this work? In a context of heteronormativity and homophobia, how can we prevent our fieldwork from further marginalizing participants or endangering their lives? And following from the work of Jansson and Benoit (2006), how do we take up work involving young people and the sex trade in ways that protect the participants? We are not, of course, arguing against studies on sexuality and violence; indeed, we are calling for the use of participatory methodologies as being particularly appropriate in addressing issues that are difficult to get at through more conventional interviews. However, we *are* drawing attention to the cultural (and sometimes political) context of studies of sexuality and violence, regardless of whether it is through drawings or other visual approaches or through direct interviews and focus groups.

Rights to privacy. Partly because some participants are self-conscious about their drawings and partly because as researchers we need to respect participants' rights to privacy, when drawings are made in a group context, it is important not to show any drawing to the rest of the group (even as part of a verbal exploration of the research focus). Rather, on completion of the activity, participants should be asked whether they would be willing to share their drawing with the others in the group, and their choice in this regard should be respected. Researchers need to give careful thought to how they will report and/or use participants' drawings when they are reporting the findings so that participants do not feel stereotyped or maligned in any way.

53

Artistic ownership. One of the challenges of working with visual productions such as drawings relates to the rights of the producer to be recognised for his or her artistic work. Ethics committees tend to insist on anonymity and confidentiality, but there may be cases where the very opposite may be necessary. As Mak (2006) highlighted, participants may be very keen to have their names appear on their art work (see Chapter 6 in this volume). In contexts where collective principles (like Ubuntu) are honoured, artistic ownership becomes an even more complex issue and one in which the values of positive, African ethics need to be foregrounded.

On the politics of group (or public) exhibition. Some researchers have noted the usefulness of encouraging the public display of drawings and other visual images as a way of inviting participants to engage in their own analysis of the issues being explored (De Lange, Mitchell, & Stuart, 2007). Again, rights to privacy should be respected. People should not be forced to display their images in a more public setting. At the same time, researchers should consider the value of this approach as a way to be more participatory and respectful of the voices of participants in the analytic process.

Debriefing. Because it is possible (depending on the focus of the study) that drawings might trigger uncomfortable or painful memories or thoughts, researchers aiming to 'do good' must consider how they will debrief participants (Babbie, 2007). Although there is no recipe for this, since the contexts will vary, we need to think about the ways in which the act of drawing can trigger painful memories, and we need, too, to be alert to this in the workshop or research setting.

Misuse (or abuse) of drawings. Following from the points noted above, we have the obligation, as researchers, to make sure that drawings are used ethically. Because of the power of visual images, especially children's drawings, which are often used in adult-related advertising (e.g., for purchasing life insurance or banking), social campaigns, and so on, there is the risk that they will be misused or overused in research reports and publications. Mitchell, Walsh, and Larkin (2004), for example, discussed the ways in which drawings produced by young people to accompany HIV&AIDS messages suggest, in their child-like quality, innocence and hence the need for protection from information rather than access to such information. Similarly, they highlight the way that children's drawings are sometimes inappropriately used to promote adult causes (see also Chapter 5 in this volume).

Beneficence

For researchers rooted in a positive, African ethical hybrid, the need for asset- or strengths-based approaches to research, and the need for research that transforms and encourages positive change (Mertens, 2009; Schratz & Walker, 1995), is pivotal, so the ethical principle of beneficence or taking action to advance the well-being of research participants and their communities is emphasised.

In many ways, drawings provide a unique opportunity for such agency. The process of drawing involves and invites reflection and makes visible a lived experience, perception, or thought, and this process is often therapeutic to the drawer (Rose, 2001; Stuart, 2007). In Africa, as in many other development contexts, opportunities for therapy and advocacy are limited, so when researchers use participatory techniques, like drawings, competently, they offer research participants opportunities to engage in therapeutic processes of agency, reflection, meaning-making, insight, and catharsis. For example, in the Resilient Educators (REds) study (see Chapter 2 in this volume), rural teachers in under-resourced communities who generated drawings associated experiences of beneficence with drawing. These included opportunities to express emotional pain, to make meaning of loss, and to summon attention to the challenges of teaching in the age of AIDS. One participant explained this as follows: "What I like about the drawing is that it explained the pain I felt about those people who are infected by this pandemic disease and the family of those who are infected." Another verbalised how drawing her real-life experience of HIV and AIDS defied denial and gave her an opportunity to broadcast her reality: "It reminds others about this pandemic. It will be an eye-opener to all." Another participant noted that drawing was beneficent for her because it facilitated advocacy: "I like to show the people what is happening in my world." When drawings are used as part of data generation in a pre-test, post-test intervention design, opportunities for reflection (and concomitant personal growth) can be maximised when researchers ask participants to contrast their pre- and post-test drawings and reflect on what they see (Stuart, 2007; see also Chapter 11 in this volume).

As we noted earlier in the section on nonmaleficence, the advocacy that participants verbalise in association with how their drawings communicate their message can be strengthened and extended more broadly when participants' drawings are used collectively, as in, for example, an exhibition. In exhibition format, drawings that are displayed publicly, as has been done with other visual media like photographs (Moletsane et al., 2008) and participatory video (Mitchell & De Lange, in press; Weber & Mitchell, 2007), constitute, potentially, a powerful collective message. Especially when drawings give voice to pressing social issues, such public displays disseminate rich messages and urge—or provoke, even—action (see also Mitchell, 2006). Rose (2001) also emphasises the power of the visual. Displaying provocative drawings can be a powerful means of stimulating social change and, in so doing, advancing the well-being of communities and groups.

One aspect of beneficence that is probably not afforded enough attention is the issue of how researchers are positioned. If as researchers we wish to advance the well-being of research participants, how do our positions as outsiders in terms of language, race, class, gender, sexuality, education, religion, ethnicity, and so on—and often powerful outsiders from moneyed or influential institutions—contribute to, or detract from, the well-being of the participants? Furthermore, because part of the fabric of traditional African ethics is generosity towards, and tolerance of, outsiders (Prozesky, 2009), what are the implicit pitfalls of this for the participants themselves? One caveat of this generosity is that researchers who are determined to encourage beneficence need to be sensitive to the ethical positions of African participants, especially when it comes to inviting drawing (which might not be common to their daily practice, but which participants could be loathe to refuse to do because this might imply lack of generosity to an outsider). Precisely because of the ethic of African generosity, we, as researchers, need to be cautious to position ourselves in such a manner that we do not behave rudely and thus exploit and abuse participant generosity.

Justice

The fourth core principle of positive ethics is ensuring the "fair, equitable and appropriate treatment" (Beauchamp & Childress, as cited in Bush, 2010, p. 25) of research participants. African ethics urge social justice, too (Mazrui, 2009). This is partly achieved by being sensitive to the needs and cultures of the participants and respecting them as co-knowledge producers and research partners. When drawings are used in the research style of 'draw and talk' (Backett-Milburn & McKie, 1999; Guillemin, 2004; Mair & Kierans, 2007), research participants are key to knowledge production. One of the criticisms levelled against visual methodologies is in relation to interpretation itself (i.e., how meaning is made of the visual) and the probability that different viewers will make different meanings out of what is visible (Guillemin, 2004; Rose, 2001). However, when participants themselves are asked to make meaning (provide a first-level analysis, if you like) of their drawn product, two things happen: On the one hand, the participant is then a co-researcher (justice) and, on the other, the research process becomes more trustworthy because the researcher is not superimposing her understanding of what was drawn onto the drawing. Where researchers go on to make so-called second levels of analysis, they should, of course, take into account the original meaning-making provided by participants and should consider, too, taking their new readings back to those participants to both verify them and to offer opportunities for truly collaborative meaning-making.

The process of 'draw and talk' allows research participants a safe opportunity to make pressing social issues visible and, in that way, give voice to their reality. Especially when communities partner researchers at the design stage and help shape the research focus, drawings provide real opportunity to concretise issues that shape (and even disrupt) daily life (Mertens, 2009). As noted previously, when these drawings are brought back to the community from which the participants come (in ways that will not threaten the participants), justice is experienced in the public airing of the messages embedded in the drawings (see Figures 4.2 and 4.3). Participants can actively help to shape this dissemination process by leading researchers to choose which drawings to foreground in such displays, where best to display them, and which forum to use. (For example, should displays be part of a public debate or education process, or should they be used for reflection? Are there any risks to the well-being of participants, either individually or collectively, if the drawings are displayed in a public venue?)

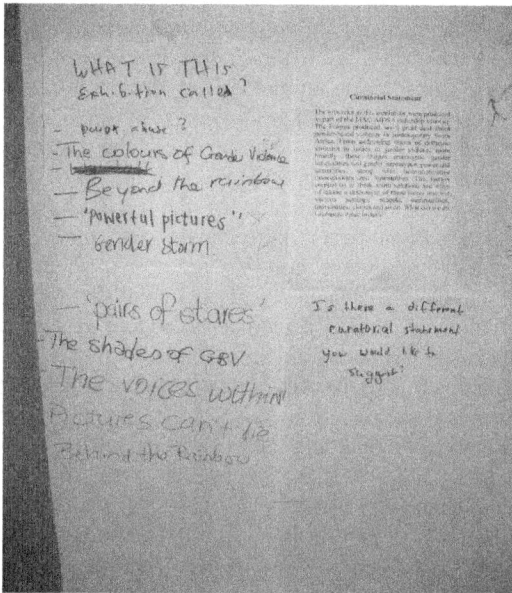

Figure 4.2. Public exhibition in action: A democratic process.

Figure 4.3. Public exhibition in action: A veridical process.

Interpretation and the democratic process of interpretation are integral to justice. Figure 4.2 depicts one aspect of an exhibition of drawings of gender violence and illustrates how participants' meaning-making can continue into a second level of interpretation in a situation in which drawings by individuals are displayed collectively. If researchers offer those who produced the drawings the opportunity to present and arrange their drawings as they see fit and to develop their own title and curatorial statement, the democracy of the research with, and into, the drawings is enhanced. Participants' perspectives are captured, participants are positioned as knowledge producers, and they are able to suggest ways forward in relation to images that may have been depicted originally as socially negative ones. There is no diminishing of the researcher's ethical responsibility when the exhibiting and meaning-making of drawings is democratised and due caution is needed to ensure that such a process does most good. But a possible advantage of opening the process to participants in this way is that open conversation about ethics can be broadened into including the participants.

In a very real sense, even though they are powerful and veridical, drawings provide 'nondogmatic answers' (Creswell, 2007, p. 206) to research questions because they literally reflect participants' views. This moves the researcher away from the traditional paternalistic position of being all-knowing, and it flattens the researcher-participant hierarchy that so often characterises research. And although the drawings may seem to 'speak for themselves', they often invite participants to say more about the issues than we as outsiders might see. Concrete 'non-dogmatism' encourages justice since it recognises the participants' truths.

CONCLUSION

In summary, researchers who employ 'draw and talk' (or 'draw and write') as a methodology (Backett-Milburn & McKie, 1999; Guillemin, 2004; Mair & Kierans, 2007) are well positioned to advocate the fundamentals of positive, African ethics. Respectfully inviting participants to draw, to interpret, and to participate in the dissemination of their drawn messages can facilitate powerful opportunities for participants and their communities to engage in research experiences that celebrate their autonomy, that focus on doing most good, and that promote justice. Throughout this chapter, we have suggested that this, of course, is far from simple and that the critical issues of addressing poverty, inequalities, sexuality, and the many pressing concerns of social research demand to be attended to in ways that respect and protect individuals and communities. When researchers operate from a positive, African ethics paradigm in ways that make the complexity of this work central to the research at hand, the potential for transformational, participatory research can be realised. We acknowledge that the full potential of this approach remains under-studied, and as a research community we do not know enough about the actual or perceived risks and harms of vulnerable populations participating in research that deals with sensitive issues. Furthermore, we often do not know enough about the full benefits—which may only be realised long after the fieldwork has been completed. These are areas to be studied, and as Leadbeater and

Glass (2006) noted, there is a need to "raise the profile of research on ethics" (p. 262). In proposing a positive, African ethics paradigm, it has been our aim to contribute to this project of raising the profile of research ethics. In this chapter, we have highlighted the idea of researchers and participants being able to say as one, "*Umuntu ngumuntu ngabantu.*"[i] and offer it as a (if not 'the') respectful way of doing visual research specifically and community-based research more broadly.

NOTE

[i] "A person is a person through other people."

REFERENCES

Babbie, E. (2007). *The practice of social research* (11th ed.). Belmont, CA: Wadsworth, Cengage Learning.
Backett-Milburn, K., & McKie, L. (1999). A critical appraisal of the draw and write technique. *Health Education Research, 14*(3), 387–398. doi:10.1093/her/14.3.387.
Bujo, B. (2009). Is there a specific African ethic? Towards a discussion with Western thought. In M. F. Murove (Ed.), *African ethics: An anthology of comparative and applied ethics* (pp. 113–128). Scottsville, South Africa: University of KwaZulu-Natal Press.
Bush, S. S. (2010). Legal and ethical considerations in rehabilitation and health assessment. In E. Mpofu & T. Oakland (Eds.), *Assessment in rehabilitation and health* (pp. 22–36). Upper Saddle River, NJ: Pearson.
Creswell, J. W. (2007). *Qualitative inquiry & research design: Choosing among five approaches* (2nd ed.). London, England: Sage.
De Lange, N., Mitchell, C., & Stuart, J. (Eds.). (2007). *Putting people in the picture: Visual methodologies for social change*. Rotterdam, The Netherlands: Sense.
Guillemin, M. (2004). Understanding illness: Using drawings as a research method. *Qualitative Health Research, 14*(2), 272–289. doi:10.1177/1049732303260445.
Handelsman, M. M., Knapp, S., & Gottlieb, M. C. (2005). Positive ethics. In C. R. Snyder & S. J. Lopez (Eds.), *Handbook of positive psychology* (pp. 434–445). New York, NY: Oxford University Press.
Jansen, J. D. (2009). *Knowledge in the blood: Confronting race and the apartheid past*. Cape Town, South Africa: UCT Press.
Jansson, M., & Benoit, C. (2006). Respect and protect? Conducting community-academic research with street-involved youth. In B. Leadbeater, E. Banister, C. Benoit, M. Jansson, A. Marshall, & T. Reicken (Eds.), *Ethical issues in communty-based research with children and youth* (pp. 175–189). Toronto, ON: University of Toronto Press.
Karlsson, J. (2007). The novice visual researcher. In N. de Lange, C. Mitchell, & J. Stuart (Eds.), *Putting people in the picture: Visual methodologies for social change* (pp. 185–201). Rotterdam, The Netherlands: Sense.
Lather, P. (2004, April). *Ethics now: White woman goes to Africa and loses her voice*. Paper presented to annual conference of American Educational Research Association, San Diego, CA. Retrieved from http://people.ehe.ohio-state.edu/plather/files/2008/09/ethics.pdf.
Leach, F. (2006). Researching gender violence in schools: Methodological and ethical considerations. *World Development. 34*(6), 1129–1147. doi:10.1016/j.worlddev.2005.11.008.
Leadbeater, B., & Glass, K. (2006). Including vulnerable populations in community-based research: New directions for ethics guidelines and ethics research. In B. Leadbeater, E. Banister, C. Benoit, M. Jansson, A. Marshall, & T. Riecken (Eds.), *Ethical issues in community-based research with children and youth* (pp. 248–266). Toronto, ON: University of Toronto Press.
Mair, M., & Kierans, C. (2007). Descriptions as data: Developing techniques to elicit descriptive materials in social research. *Visual Studies, 22*(2), 120–136. doi:10.1080/14725860701507057.

Mak, M. (2006). Unwanted images: Tackling gender based violence in South African schools through youth artwork. In. F. E. Leach & C. Mitchell (Eds.), *Combating gender violence in and around schools* (pp. 113–123). Stoke-on-Trent, England: Trentham Books.

Mazrui, A. A. (2009). Africa's wisdom has two parents and one guardian: Africanism, Islam and the West. In M. F. Murove (Ed.), *African ethics: An anthology of comparative and applied ethics* (pp. 33–59). Scottsville, South Africa: University of KwaZulu-Natal Press.

Mertens, D. M. (2005). *Research and evaluation in education and psychology: Integrating diversity with quantitative, qualitative, and mixed methods* (2nd ed.). Thousand Oaks, CA: Sage.

Mertens, D. M. (2009). *Transformative research and evaluation.* New York, NY: Guilford Press.

Mitchell, C. (2006). Visual arts-based methodologies in research as social change. In T. Marcus & A. Hofmaenner (Eds.), *Shifting the boundaries of knowledge: A view on social sciences, law and humanities in South Africa* (pp. 227–241). Scottsville, South Africa: University of KwaZulu-Natal Press.

Mitchell, C., & De Lange, N. (in press). Community based video and social action in rural South Africa. In E. Margolis & L. Pauwels (Eds.), *The SAGE handbook of visual research methods.* London, England: Sage.

Mitchell, C., Walsh, S., & Larkin, J. (2004). Visualizing the politics of innocence in the age of AIDS. *Sex Education, 4*(1), 35–47. doi:10.1080/1468181042000176524.

Mkhize, N. (2006). African traditions and the social, economic and moral dimensions of fatherhood. In L. M. Richter & R. Morrell (Eds.), *Baba: Men and fatherhood in South Africa* (pp. 183–198). Cape Town, South Africa: HSRC Press. Retrieved from http://www.hsrcpress.ac.za.

Mokwena, M. (2007). African cosmology and psychology. In M. Visser (Ed.), *Contextualising community psychology in South Africa* (pp. 66–78). Pretoria, South Africa: Van Schaik.

Moletsane, R. (2011). Culture, nostalgia, and sexuality education in South Africa in the age of AIDS. In C. Mitchell, T. Strong-Wilson, K. Pithouse, & S. Allnutt (Eds.), *Memory and Pedagogy* (pp. 193–208). New York, NY: Routledge.

Moletsane, R., Mitchell, C., Smith, A., & Chisholm, L. (2008). *Methodologies for mapping a southern African girlhood in the age of Aids.* Rotterdam, The Netherlands: Sense.

Munyaka, M., & Motlhabi, M. (2009). Ubuntu and its socio-moral significance. In M. F. Murove (Ed.), *African ethics: An anthology of comparative and applied ethics* (pp. 63–84). Scottsville, South Africa: University of KwaZulu-Natal Press.

Murove, M. F. (2009a). Beyond the savage evidence ethic: A vindication of African ethics. In M. F. Murove (Ed.), *African ethics: An anthology of comparative and applied ethics* (pp. 14–32). Scottsville, South Africa: University of KwaZulu-Natal Press.

Murove, M. F. (Ed.). (2009b). *African ethics: An anthology of comparative and applied ethics.* Scottsville, South Africa: University of KwaZulu-Natal Press.

Prozesky, M. H. (2009). Cinderella, survivor and saviour: African ethics and the quest for a global ethic. In M. F. Murove (Ed.), *African ethics: An anthology of comparative and applied ethics* (pp. 3–13). Scottsville, South Africa: University of KwaZulu-Natal Press.

Rose, G. (2001). *Visual methodologies: An introduction to the interpretation of visual materials.* Thousand Oaks, CA: Sage.

Schratz, M., & Walker, R. (1995). *Research as social change: New opportunities for qualitative research.* New York, NY: Routledge.

Shutte, A. (2009). Ubuntu as the African ethical vision. In M. F. Murove (Ed.), *African ethics: An anthology of comparative and applied ethics* (pp. 85–99). Scottsville, South Africa: University of KwaZulu-Natal Press.

Stuart, J. (2007). Drawings and transformation in the health arena. In N. de Lange, C. Mitchell, & J. Stuart (Eds.), *Putting people in the picture: Visual methodologies for social change* (pp. 229–240). Rotterdam, The Netherlands: Sense.

van der Riet, M. (2008). Diagramming as mediational means: Vygotskian theory and participatory research. *South African Journal of Psychology, 38*(3), 455–465.

Wassenaar, D. (2006). Ethical issues in social science research. In M. Terre Blanche, K. Durrheim, & D. Painter (Eds.), *Research in practice: Applied methods for the social sciences* (2nd rev. ed., pp. 60–79). Cape Town, South Africa: UCT Press.

Weber, S., & Mitchell, C. (1995). '*That's funny, you don't look like a teacher': Interrogating images and identity in popular culture.* London, England: Falmer Press. doi:10.4324/9780203453568.

Weber, S., & Mitchell, C. (2007). Imaging, keyboarding, and posting identities: Young people and new media technologies. In D. Buckingham (Ed.), *Youth, identity, and digital media* (pp. 25–47). Cambridge, MA: The MIT Press.

VISUALISING JUSTICE: THE POLITICS OF WORKING WITH CHILDREN'S DRAWINGS

Lara Bober

INTRODUCTION

To set aside the sympathy we extend to others beset by war and murderous politics for a reflection on how our privileges are located on the same map as their suffering, and may—in ways we prefer not to imagine—be linked to their suffering, as the wealth of some may imply the destitution of others, is a task for which the painful, stirring images supply only an initial spark. (Sontag, 2003, p. 76)

This chapter considers some of the ways in which children's rights are theorised, and implemented, through work with children's drawings as visual productions. As highlighted in Chapter 7, the use of children's drawings in human rights interventions and campaigns dates back to the Spanish Civil War and the Holocaust. Given the widespread use of children's drawings in human rights discourses, it is surprising that more attention has not been paid to their meanings, particularly in relation to broader structures and processes. It is important to recognise that children's rights discourses are most often grounded in the United Nations Convention on the Rights of the Child (UNCRC) adopted by the United Nations General Assembly in 1989. Like many international conventions, the UNCRC originated in the global North and is informed by Western norms (in this case, cultural and historical conceptions of childhood). It is also tied to the social and political agendas of capitalist countries mostly in Europe and North America (Boyden, 1997). The convention is an instrument that is legally binding to those states that ratify it and is seen, for this reason, as an important tool in advancing the rights of children. Conceptions of justice for children need to be understood in relation to children's everyday needs and experiences, rather than reduced to articulations of rights and freedoms (Aitken, 2001), something not obvious in the discourses of the UNCRC even though there is an apparent commitment to children's participation as actors. Children's rights discourses must also consider the ways in which children have been impacted by historical processes such as colonialism and by global inequalities created by neoliberal economic policies. In this chapter, I am interested in the ways in which children's drawings have been used as a research method and how this method fits into a framework of participatory research with children in relation to their everyday needs and experiences.

L. Theron et al. (eds.), Picturing Research: Drawing as Visual Methodology, 63–76.

There are many political contexts in which visual methods have been introduced. Here, I discuss case studies in which children use drawing to cope with violence and consequent displacement and discrimination as well as the use of these drawings by human rights organisations to help address these issues. Starting with drawings from Darfur (as part of the work of two different human rights organisations: Human Rights Watch and Waging Peace), I then look at drawings from Australia's National Inquiry into Children in Immigration Detention. Many of the children held in immigration detention in several countries, including Australia, have endured injustices and experienced similar atrocities as the children from Darfur. The concerns expressed visually on paper by children in immigration detention in Australia provide an example of children's drawings accepted as evidence of human rights abuses. The influence of visual productions on policy agendas will also be discussed in order to identify some of the ways in which visual productions can prompt concrete changes contributing to social justice. The chapter then goes on to consider the role of venues in displaying children's drawings of violence and atrocities, as well as other images representing displacement. Finally, I offer several critical questions for how (and why) policy makers should re-think their use of children's drawings.

VISUAL METHODS WITH CHILDREN

De Lange, Mitchell, and Stuart (2007) clearly articulated critical questions to consider in approaching visual methods: "How can visual interventions be used to educate community groups and point to ways to empower and reform institutional practices? What ethical issues come to the fore in these action-oriented studies?" (p. 3). There are many ethical issues arising in research processes with children. Social constructions of childhood must be examined in order to avoid essentialising children and replicating inequitable research relations. A greater understanding of the ways in which institutional practices have an impact on the lives of children can help to mobilise change. Using visual methods with children can be a valuable tool for research, enabling communities—that have historically experienced social, political, and economic exclusion—to identify realities that they would like to transform. Participatory research with children—much of it visual—has been informed by Participatory Action Research (PAR), which draws on the knowledge production and experiences of communities in struggle in order to effect change (Fals-Borda, 1979). By drawing on children's experiences and knowledge production, visual methods can contribute to producing policy recommendations across different sectors, including education and health.

Children are often (further) marginalised in that assumptions about their capabilities and intelligence do not necessarily reflect reality. Therefore, participatory research with children is even more critical in contexts of political instability and violence. Children's visual productions must be seen as *social* productions in order for children's perspectives to inform policies that have an impact on their lives. Rose (2001) discussed the importance of identifying the social relations of drawings and the settings of their production. For example, visual methods have been introduced with children who have experienced violence and atrocities leading to displacement. In reflecting on Glynis Clacherty's qualitative study of refugee and returnee children in UNHCR operations in Angola, South Africa, and Zambia (Clacherty, 2005), Stuart (2007) identified several benefits to arts-based research in this context. Through drawing, children were prompted to recount their experiences of violence and trauma. The drawings facilitated a "participatory and child-centred assessment of the effects of violence in these children's lives" (Stuart, 2007, p. 230). Researchers were able to hear children's perspectives and insights, which could then feed into policy and practice. Janzen and Janzen (2000), who conducted qualitative studies with children affected by the Rwandan genocide, also emphasised the benefits of using visual methods with refugee children, not only in providing historical documentation, but also for the therapeutic effect: "In the process of drawing, of telling a story visually, the child or adult explains and integrates traumatic experience and thus gives meaning to what otherwise would remain chaotic and therefore meaningless" (Janzen & Janzen, 2000, p. 121).

CASE STUDIES OF CHILDREN'S DRAWINGS

Case Study 1—Children's Drawings: Smallest Witnesses (Darfur)

> On a 2005 mission to refugee camps along Darfur's border with Chad, Human Rights Watch researchers gave children crayons and paper to draw while their families were being interviewed. Without any instruction or guidance, the children—some as young as eight—began to draw vivid and disturbing scenes of the violence and atrocities they had witnessed: the attacks by the Janjaweed, the aerial bombings by the Sudanese government, the rapes, the burning of entire villages and the flight to Chad. (Human Rights Watch [HRW], 2005, p. 1)

The HRW report *Smallest Witnesses* focuses on the role of external actors, including a paediatrician and a lawyer, visiting refugee camps along the Chad–Sudan border, with the intention of examining the consequences of "sexual violence on refugees as part of the conflict, and the services and protection provided" (p. 3). Annie Sparrow, the paediatrician who was involved with HRW offered the following reflections on her experiences of working with the children's drawings:

> Some drawings speak for themselves. Others require the child's translation, which suddenly transforms a non-specific squiggle into a family fleeing from attack and rape, an open mouth into a scream, a cell phone into a desperate appeal for help, a red scribble into a fatal gunshot wound. Others are so sophisticated that the material of war may be accurately identified by military analysts, giving the drawings the added gravity of bearing witness against the government as the true architects of this war. (2008, p. 132)

Although there is concern expressed for these children, the role of the children in analysing the conflict, in articulating their concerns and needs as well as in subsequent action to redress injustices and work towards political reconciliation, has not been made clear. Had the drawings been elicited in the context of a PAR study, perhaps the "unidirectional, top-down process of humanitarian assistance" (Cooper, 2005, p. 467) could have been challenged, thus providing opportunities to engage the children in more equitable research relations. There are centres specialising in conflict resolution at universities in each of the three states of Darfur (Mamdani, 2009), and researchers from these centres could be engaged in participatory processes with children. Mackenzie, McDowell, and Pittaway (2007) emphasised the importance of designing and conducting research projects "that aim to bring about reciprocal benefits for refugee participants and/or communities" (p. 301):

> The notion of reciprocity involves negotiating a research relationship with participants that not only respects, but also promotes their autonomous agency and helps re-build capacity. It is argued that the principle of respect for persons entails a responsibility on the part of researchers to try to understand and engage with the different perspectives and life experiences of research participants and to construct research relationships that are responsive to their needs and values. (p. 301)

In its report, HRW (2005) recounted its difficulty in obtaining documentation, through photographs or video footage, of Janjaweed militias or Sudanese soldiers attacking villagers. However, documentation came from an unexpected source:

> Thanks to the children of Darfur, we now have graphic representations of the atrocities. The drawings corroborate unerringly what we know of the crimes. From the point of view of humanitarian law, the drawings illustrate a compelling case against the government of Sudan as the architects of this man-made crisis in Darfur. (p. 5)

By describing the government of Sudan as the "architects of this man-made crisis in Darfur", the historical, political, and economic contexts of this conflict are not understood (i.e., the legacies of colonialism, geopolitics, and profound structural inequalities). Sparrow (2008) described the drawings as providing "a visual vocabulary requiring little or no translation that captures the hearts and minds, and may ultimately contribute to protection and peace in Darfur" (p. 137). Children's drawings do provide important historical documentation. However, it is critical that the meaning attributed to the drawings is clearly communicated by those who are producing the drawings, rather than defined by outside researchers. In the case of the children's drawings from Darfur, it is important to consider how the drawings were taken up by the international media in order to promote a political agenda that failed to address the complexity of this conflict. Mamdani (2009), drawing from extensive research and many years of work experience in Sudan, argued that what is required in Darfur is political reconciliation rather than punishment, which would necessitate "a regionally negotiated peace, reform of power in the nation-state of Sudan, and reform of land and governance systems within Darfur" (p. 16).

What is also missing from the HRW report are the perspectives of the children themselves in elaborating on how experiences of violence and atrocities have affected them and what significance they attribute to their drawings. Further consultations with children about the ways in which they are affected by humanitarian policies and human rights law are urgently needed. It is not clear from this report whether discussions took place with the children, or with their families if they were accompanied, around the politics of their refugee status and the terms of their care and protection. Visual methods could facilitate these discussions with children in similar situations.

Building on Rose's (2001) argument that the social relations of pictures and the settings of their production must be understood in an analysis of visual productions, it is useful to consider concerns articulated by Boyden (2001) regarding the structural exclusion of displaced populations. She identifies paternalistic attitudes, processes, and structures; relations of dependency; channels of political participation; values and attitudes of human rights and relief organisations; and lack of consultation as all contributing to structural exclusion. The lives of refugees have historically been governed from the perspectives of either charity and care or criminality and security (Lippert, 1999; Pratt, 2005, as cited in Moulin & Nyers, 2007; Soguk, 1999).

Malkki (1996) cautioned against homogenising representations of the refugee experience that do not allow for political and social engagement. Humanitarian discourse and practice of the 1990s have positioned migrants in certain ways, which Hyndman (2000) referred to as a "colonialism of compassion" (p. *xxi*). Boyden (2009) also problematised the concept of compassion from cultural and political economy perspectives, concluding that notions of power, equity, and rights must be critically analysed. There is an urgent need for further research on the political economy of forced migration, on gender dimensions of forced migration, and on an organisational sociology of humanitarian and refugee agencies (Castles, 2003). That the experiences of forced migrants are often represented by others, including the media, humanitarian agencies, and human rights organisations, is also a contentious issue:

> These representational forms come into play not only in media reporting on refugees but also in the policy discourse of humanitarian agencies, national governments, and nongovernmental organisations. Both discursively and transnationally mobile, these representations, by transmitting a certain idea of the refugee, have significant political and ethical repercussions. (Limbu, 2009, p. 268)

O'Neill and Harindranath (2006) provided a compelling analysis of the media politics of asylum by exploring the relations between journalistic discourse, social imagination, and immigration policies. They also address the absence of refugee perspectives and how this absence has an impact on policy and practice.

CHAPTER 5

Case Study 2—Children's Drawings: Waging Peace (Darfur)

Waging Peace is a UK-based human rights organisation working on campaigns and research reports, primarily in Africa. Its work in Darfur calls for "an immediate end to the atrocities and a stable and secure peace settlement that will bring about long-term safety and security for Sudan's citizens" (Waging Peace, 2009). In 2007, a Waging Peace researcher, Anna Schmitt, visited Eastern Chad to assess the current state of the conflict and to interview Darfuri refugees and displaced Chadians. Many of the adults she spoke with expressed concern about the violent events their children had witnessed when their villages were being attacked. Schmitt responded to their concerns by talking with the children, aged 6 to 18 years, giving them paper and pencils and asking them about their dreams for the future and their strongest memories. The majority of drawings describe the killing, bombing, and looting which took place during the attacks on their villages by Sudanese Government forces and allied Janjaweed militia. Approximately 500 drawings were collected by Waging Peace. The International Criminal Court accepted the drawings in November 2007 as contextual evidence of the crimes committed in Darfur, admissible in the trials of the accused as an illustration of the atrocities.

In accordance with my analysis in Case Study 1, my concern remains centred on how the drawings were collected, how they were used, and what the role of the producers was (or could have been) in the process.

Case Study 3—Children's Drawings: Immigration Detention (Australia)

Immigration detention for people seeking asylum and for those without documentation is a practice of deterrence in several countries. The policy of mandatory detention for asylum seekers was introduced by the Australian Labour Party in 1992 and came into force 2 years later (Gosden, 2006; Taylor, 2006). This deplorable practice, and concern for the health of those detained on tenuous grounds, has prompted outrage by several human rights organisations and migrant justice groups. The three main aspects of the mandatory detention regime that are of a concern in terms of human rights include the plight of especially vulnerable individuals, the problem of prolonged or indefinite detention, and the absence of independent review (Taylor, 2006).

It is important to consider the concept of the asylum–migration nexus introduced by Castles (2003), who argued that "many migrants and asylum seekers have multiple reasons for mobility and it is impossible to completely separate economic and human rights motivations—which is a challenge to the neat categories that bureaucracies seek to impose" (p. 17). Many individuals and organisations have worked hard to bring change to the policy of mandatory immigration detention and to ameliorate its effects through the provision of social, emotional, practical, lobbying, medical, and legal support (Gosden, 2006). A National Inquiry into Children in Immigration Detention began in 2001 and was undertaken by the Human Rights and Equal Opportunity Commission (HREOC).

Its aim has been to investigate the adequacy and appropriateness of Australia's treatment of children in detention. The inquiry has examined numerous issues including: health, education, culture, guardianship and security. Hundreds of submissions were received from community and government agencies and individuals. These submissions came from a diverse range of sources but share a common thread—a deep concern for the children held in detention and a desire to alleviate the injustices that they are currently facing. (Fauzee, 2003, p. 91)

The report of the National Inquiry into Children in Immigration Detention was tabled in parliament on May 13, 2004. The Inquiry found that children in Australian immigration detention centres

had suffered numerous and repeated breaches of their human rights. In particular, the Inquiry found that Australia's immigration detention policy failed to protect the mental health of children, failed to provide adequate health care and education and failed to protect unaccompanied children and those with disabilities. (HREOC, n.d.)

Drawings by children were included in the report and submitted to the inquiry. Some were drawn by children held in detention for 22 months, and other drawings were provided by former detainee children who participated in focus groups of the Inquiry. This is another example of children's drawings being considered as evidence of human rights abuses. On July 29, 2008, Senator Chris Evans, Minister for Immigration and Citizenship, made a speech titled "New Directions in Detention, Restoring Integrity to Australia's Immigration System". He stated that children would never be held in a detention centre again (Bowen, 2008). However, there are still many injustices and concerns articulated about the policy and practice of immigration detention, and many children continue to be detained in several countries as they wait for their immigration status to be determined.

REFLECTING ON THE CASE STUDIES:
POLICY AGENDAS AND THE ROLE OF VISUAL METHODS

The examples of children's visual productions noted in the preceding sections highlight the ways in which drawings serve as evidence of human rights abuses. An area for further exploration concerns the role of dissemination and the impact of research on children. Speaking more generally about ethical research practices with children, Christensen and Prout (2002) raised critical questions: "Will the children and adults involved be sent short reports of the main findings? Besides the effects of the research on the children involved, how might the conclusions affect larger groups of children?" (p. 491). How do children challenge and disrupt exclusionary practices? How can visual methods facilitate resolution or under-standing in these processes?

It is uncertain whether or not the children whose drawings were included in the HRW report were ever sent a copy of this document. Were they given an opportunity to reflect on the conclusions of the report and its intended purpose?

"While a picture may seem clear enough to the viewer, its communicative import exists in the drawer's intention" (Swart, 1990, as cited in Stuart, 2007, p. 238). In the case of Waging Peace, attempts were made to contextualise the children's drawings. What Rose (2001) referred to as the social relations of drawings and the settings of their production were identified.

There is a commitment expressed by human rights organisations to alleviate the suffering experienced in Darfur and elsewhere, and to prevent further violence. However, it is critical that the broader structures and processes shaping conflicts are understood and that humanitarian and human rights organisations engage in reflexive practices. What also needs to be questioned is the role that children have in assessing their own experiences and their commitment to social and political change. What are the social relations and practices that sustain them when they have experienced violence and displacement? "Incorporating children's views within legislation, policy and programmes definitely involves major institutional changes" (Boyden, 1997, p. 223).

Australia's National Inquiry into Children in Immigration Detention included focus groups with children in which their perspectives were sought and valued, a sharp contrast to their deplorable treatment in detention. In this case, their drawings appear to have an intended audience, urging people outside of the detention centre to consider the injustices experienced within. In what ways do the depictions of violence in children's drawings challenge representations of displacement in visual images provided by the media?

In reflecting on the representation of the Rwandan genocide through film (Razack, 2007), and the urgent need to elicit outrage and action regarding current conflicts, it is useful to consider questions raised by Apple (2009):

> How do the dynamics of class, gender and race determine 'cultural production'? How is the organization and distribution of culture 'mediated' by economic and social structures? What is the relationship between a cultural product—say a film or a book—and the social relations of its production, accessibility, and consumption? (p. 183)

These are all important questions to reflect on in considering the use of children's drawings in human rights interventions and campaigns. We must ask these questions in order to prevent the consumption of horrific images and stories; such consumption manifests as passive empathy, which is not followed by action or a critical examination of complicity (Razack, 2007; Sontag, 2003).

VENUES FOR DISPLAYING CHILDREN'S DRAWINGS

The venues where children's drawings are exhibited offer another 'entry point' to considering the political context of this work. Children's drawings from Darfur were exhibited in a variety of venues including art galleries, universities, and museums, primarily in North America. Given that the children who drew these pictures are living in precarious circumstances, what does it mean to place their drawings on display? There are many questions to consider regarding sites of representation and access to them, as well as the politics of display. Exhibits are not simply a collection of images but are images framed in particular ways with a sequence to follow, eliciting (and evoking) particular interpretations (Bal, 1996). What is the response of the children from Darfur to the inclusion of their drawings in these international venues? Who are the audiences for these drawings, and what will they do in response to these images? How can the exhibition of these drawings lead to action to mobilise change rather than perpetuating the consumption of horrific images and stories?

Such images representing experiences of refugees are not only exhibited in a variety of venues but have also been presented in different formats, including 'coffee-table books'. "The very existence of such books, in which the suffering of others is made into an aesthetic object, seems to invite questions about the politics and ethics of collecting and consuming images" (Szörényi, 2006, p. 24). Szörényi provides a compelling analysis of 'coffee-table books' comprised of photographs of refugees collected over many years by documentary photographers:

I find these books silent on the issue of the culture of imperialism, and its contemporary manifestation in a worldview in which the right of the 'developed' to assess and intervene in the destinies of the less privileged is taken for granted. (p. 39)

By reflecting on the politics of display, we can begin to add another level of context to children's drawings and, in so doing, focus on the position of children as active survivors rather than propagating only images of victims of war and violence. Not only must the significance that children attribute to these drawings be recognised, the political, economic, and historical contexts of their lived experiences must be understood in order to prevent passive empathy and the consumption of images. "Attending to the ways in which images are differently interpreted and to ways in which sites of viewing shape those interpretations can reveal hierarchies in relationships and in sites of translation, as well as differing interests and knowledge" (Mitchell, 2006, p. 63). Indeed, as Mitchell (2006) argued, it is important to reflect on the varied interpretations of children's drawings and what these interpretations may reveal about children's participation. She argued that the analysis of children's drawings needs to acknowledge relationships of power, authority, and difference.

Twum-Danso (2009) also pointed out that children's position in society is informed by cultural values and beliefs and that participatory research with children must integrate knowledge and practices of the communities in which studies are done. As 'outsiders' working with children from communities that have endured violence and injustices, adults need to be particularly sensitive about their roles as co-researchers so as to avoid reproducing inequitable research relations. Intergenerational relationships and social practices may facilitate in establishing trust and collaboration between members of a community and 'outsider' researchers. 'Outsider' researchers also encounter the painful reality that certain privileges are located on the same map as the suffering of others (Sontag, 2003), "and may—in ways we prefer not to imagine—be linked to their suffering, as the

71

wealth of some may imply the destitution of others" (Sontag, 2003, 76). As Szörényi (2006) suggested, the contemporary manifestation of the culture of imperialism needs to be acknowledged in order to engage in research that is genuinely collaborative and that can work towards equity and social justice. Fine (2006) emphasised the importance of "thinking critically about injustice in our everyday lives and analysing how unjust distributions of resources and opportunities affect our comfort and discomfort, our dependencies, privileges, joys, our moments of shared pain, and potential collective actions" (p. 102).

Since there may be multiple interpretations of drawings, it is critical that the producer's intent is made clear and that children are aware of, and consent to, the dissemination of their cultural productions. The consequences of misinterpreting drawings could be severe. Adults who might appropriate the voices of children in order to serve a political agenda could compound existing problems and further erode trust among communities and individuals who have already been treated deplorably. Such appropriations might also neglect to address the causes of political and socioeconomic exclusion or violence and instead further perpetuate relations of dependence.

Adults often underestimate children's capacity to understand the political aspects of war. Janzen and Janzen (2000), in reflecting on a study with refugee children from Rwanda, made the following observation:

That the children were aware of the explanations of the start of the war is evident in the many drawings that include the shooting down of President Habyarimana's plane: the depictions contradict those adults who think children are oblivious to the political aspects of the war and are shielded from the reality of the war. (p. 129)

Janzen and Janzen also referred to the "adult ideological supervision of the children" (p. 129) that comes from heterogeneous members of refugee communities with multiple perspectives, as well as humanitarian aid workers and other external actors.

SOME CRITICAL QUESTIONS AND ISSUES IN RELATION TO USING CHILDREN'S
DRAWINGS IN HUMAN RIGHTS STUDIES

In this chapter, I have drawn attention to some of the problematic issues of using children's drawings in human rights interventions. In so doing, my point has not been to criticise the method so much as to critique the ways in which the impact of studying children's voices might be further eroded if we do not pay attention to what could be described as 'the politics of children's drawings'. If we are to take children's voices seriously, we need to think critically and ethically about our responsibility to their engagement. Visual methods can facilitate in processes that enable children to articulate their concerns and needs. Children's rights discourses have been, and often continue to be, promoted by adults. "Children may be permitted to make history, but they are excluded from making policy. They can be very perceptive about the way adults colonise and reinterpret their activities"

(Ennew, 2000). The political and organisational skills among children could be strengthened by their inclusion in policy-making. In working towards significant institutional changes, we can incorporate children's views within legislation, policy, and programs (Boyden, 1997) so that the concept of children as social actors is not simply rhetoric.

The use of children's drawings in human rights interventions and campaigns has set important precedents. Children's visual productions have been accepted as evidence of human rights violations, which is a significant shift in how children are regarded in human rights law and discourses. There are still critical concerns to consider regarding the ways in which visual methods can empower and reform institutional practices as well as the ethical concerns relating to such interventions (De Lange et al., 2007). Perhaps, it makes sense to think of these concerns as a series of recommendations for practice that are informed by case studies and the research on children's participation.

Visual methods can engage children as active participants in the co-production of research, and these processes can be strengthened by careful consideration of concerns articulated in other studies. Engaging children as co-researchers through drawings and other participatory methods can facilitate opportunities to name and challenge the socioeconomic and political constraints children may live with as well as build on opportunities and resistances in which they are already engaged. However, I would argue that humanitarian and human rights organisations must engage in reflexive practices and consultations with children about their lives rather than just ascribing responsibility to social workers and teachers. Care must be taken to engage children as much as possible in follow-up to visual productions: Where will the drawings be exhibited? How will they be exhibited? Who will see them? Will there be any attempt to report back to the child participants?

Beyond these very concrete considerations, policy agendas and practices that are informed by children's rights discourses must be contextualised, taking into account the living conditions as well as the social, economic, and historical contexts in which children grow up (Reynaert, Bouverne-de-Brie, & Vandevelde, 2009). Contemporary debates around neoliberalism have prompted critical studies of the context of children's lives under economic and social transformation (Katz, 2004; Stephens, 1995). Researchers, policymakers, and practitioners working towards social inclusion and social justice must cultivate "a more nuanced, contextually grounded theorizing about children, childhood and children's participation" (Morrow, 2007, p. 7). There needs to be greater attention paid to the social, political, and historical construction of childhood. A paradigm shift in childhood studies—recognising children as social actors—has provided important, and often urgently needed, opportunities for consultations with children. In a welfarist/protectionist approach to work with children, teachers and social workers are ascribed responsibility for children's welfare without any requirement that they consult with children about their lives (Christensen & Prout, 2002). Conversely, the new sociology of childhood has prompted a significant shift in how children are regarded as participants in research processes. Situated in this paradigm, children are seen as active participants in the co-production of research. There has been, and continues to be, a welfarist/protectionist approach in work with children that has been challenged and contested by the new sociology of childhood (James, Jenks, & Prout, 1998), which positions children as social actors with agency and voice. "Recognition of children's agency does not necessarily lead to a rejection of an appreciation of the ways in which their lives are shaped by forces beyond the control of individual children" (Holloway & Valentine, 2000, p. 6), but it does make clear that researchers and policy makers need to start with children and the communities and social movements in which they are embedded. Drawings are one such way of doing this, but the project should not stop there.

REFERENCES

Aitken, S. C. (2001). Global crises of childhood: Rights, justice and the unchildlike child. *Area, 33*(2), 119–127. doi:10.1111/1475-4762.00015.

Apple, M. W. (2009). Controlling the work of teachers. In D. J. Flinders & S. J. Thornton (Eds.), *The curriculum studies reader* (3rd ed., pp. 199–213). New York, NY: Routledge.

Bal, M. (1996). *Double exposures: The subject of cultural analysis.* New York, NY: Routledge.

Bowen, C. (2008, July 29). *New directions in detention—Restoring integrity to Australia's immigration system.* Speech given at Australian National University, Canberra. Transcript retrieved from http://www.minister.immi.gov.au/media/speeches/2008/ce080729.htm.

Boyden, J. (1997). Childhood and the policy makers: A comparative perspective on the globalization of childhood. In. A. James & A. Prout (Eds.), *Constructing and reconstructing childhood: Contemporary issues in the sociological study of childhood* (pp. 190–229). London, England: Falmer Press.

Boyden, J. (2001). Children's participation in the context of forced migration. *PLA Notes, 42*, 52–56. Retrieved from http://www.planotes.org/documents/plan_04211.pdf.

Boyden, J. (2009). What place the politics of compassion in education surrounding non-citizen children? *Educational Review, 61*(3), 265–276. doi:10.1080/00131910903045914.

Castles, S. (2003). Towards a sociology of forced migration and social transformation. *Sociology, 37*(1), 13–34. doi:10.1177/0038038503037001384.

Christensen, P., & Prout, A. (2002). Working with ethical symmetry in social research with children. *Childhood, 9*(4), 477–497. doi:10.1177/0907568202009004007.

Clacherty, G. (2005). *Refugee and returnee children in southern Africa: Perceptions and experiences of violence. A qualitative study of refugee and returnee children in UNHCR operations in Angola, South Africa, and Zambia.* Pretoria, South Africa: UNHCR.

Cooper, E. (2005). What do we know about out-of-school youths? How participatory action research can work for young refugees in camps. *Compare, 35*(4), 463–477. doi:10.1080/03057920500331488

De Lange, N., Mitchell, C., & Stuart, J. (2007). An introduction to putting people in the picture: Visual methodologies for social change. In N. de Lange, C. Mitchell, & J. Stuart (Eds.), *Putting people in the picture: Visual methodologies for social change* (pp. 1–9). Rotterdam, The Netherlands: Sense.

Ennew, J. (2000). The history of children's rights: Whose story? *Cultural Survival, 24*(2). Retrieved from http://www.culturalsurvival.org.

Fals Borda, O. (1979). Investigating reality in order to transform it: The Colombian experience. *Dialectical Anthropology, 4*(1), 33–55. doi:10.1007/BF00417683.

Fauzee, Y. J. (2003). In the eyes of a child—behind the wire: Education for children in mandatory detention in Australia. *Contemporary Issues in Early Childhood, 4*(1), 90–95. doi:10.2304/ciec.2003.4.1.9.

Fine, M. (2006). Bearing witness: Methods for researching oppression and resistance—A textbook for critical research. *Social Justice Research, 19*(1), 83–108. doi:10.1007/s11211-006-0001-0

Gosden, D. (2006). "What if no one had spoken out against this policy?" The rise of asylum seeker and refugee advocacy in Australia. *Journal of Multidisciplinary International Studies, 3*(1), 1–21. Retrieved from http://epress.lib.uts.edu.au/ojs/index.php/portal/index.

Holloway, S. L., & Valentine, G. (2000). Children's geographies and the new social studies of childhood. In S. L. Holloway & G. Valentine (Eds.), *Children's geographies: Playing, living, learning* (pp. 1–23). New York, NY: Routledge.

Human Rights Watch (HRW). (2005). *The smallest witnesses: The conflict in Darfur through children's eyes.* Retrieved from http://www.thebigboxofcolors.org/images/HRW_SmallestWitnesses.pdf.

Human Rights and Equal Opportunities Commission (HREOC). (n.d.). *National inquiry into children in immigration detention.* Retrieved from http://www.hreoc.gov.au/Human_rights/children_detention/index.html.

Hyndman, J. (2000). *Managing displacement: Refugees and the politics of humanitarianism.* Minneapolis: The University of Minnesota Press.

Katz, C. (2004). *Growing up global: Economic restructuring and children's everyday lives.* Minneapolis: University of Minnesota Press.

James, A., Jenks, C., & Prout, A. (1998). *Theorizing childhood.* Cambridge, England: Polity Press.

Janzen, J. M., & Janzen, R. K. (2000). *Do I still have a life: Voices from the aftermath of war in Rwanda and Burundi* (Publications in Anthropology, Vol. 20). Lawrence: The University Press of Kansas.

Limbu, B. (2009). Illegible humanity: The refugee, human rights, and the question of representation. *Journal of Refugee Studies, 22*(3), 257–282. doi:10.1093/jrs/fep021.

Lippert, R. (1999). Governing refugees: The relevance of governmentality to understanding the international refugee regime. *Alternatives, 24*(3), 391–432.

Mackenzie, C., McDowell, C., & Pittaway, E. (2007). Beyond 'do no harm': The challenge of constructing ethical relationships in refugee research. *Journal of Refugee Studies, 20*(2), 299–319. doi:10.1093/jrs/fem008.

Malkki, L. H. (1996). Speechless emissaries: Refugees, humanitarianism, and dehistoricization. *Cultural Anthropology, 11*(3), 377–404. doi:10.1525/can.1996.11.3.02a00050.

Mamdani, M. (2009). *Saviors and survivors: Darfur, politics, and the war on terror.* New York, NY: Pantheon Books.

Mitchell, L. M. (2006). Child-centered? Thinking critically about children's drawings as a visual research method. *Visual Anthropology Review, 22*(1), 60–73. doi:10.1525/var.2006.22.1.60.

Morrow, V. (2007). Editorial: At the crossroads. *Childhood, 14*(1), 5–10. doi:10.1177/0907568207072539.

Moulin, C., & Nyers, P. (2007). "We live in a country of UNHCR"—Refugee protests and global political society. *International Political Sociology, 1*(4), 356–372. doi:10.1111/j.1749-5687.2007.00026.x

O'Neill, M., & Harindranath, R. (2006). Theorising narratives of exile and belonging: The importance of biography and ethno-mimesis in 'understanding' asylum. *Qualitative Sociology Review, 2*(1), 39–53. Retrieved from http://www.qualitativesociologyreview.org.

Razack, S. H. (2007). Stealing the pain of others: Reflections on Canadian humanitarian responses. *Review of Education, Pedagogy, and Cultural Studies, 29*(4), 375–394. doi:10.1080/10714410701454198.

Reynaert, D., Bouverne-de-Bie, M., & Vandevelde, S. (2009). A review of children's rights literature since the adoption of the United Nations Convention on the Rights of the Child. *Childhood, 16*(4), 518–534. doi:10.1177/0907568209344270.

Rose, G. (2001). *Visual methodologies: An introduction to the interpretation of visual materials.* London, England: Sage.

Soguk, N. (1999). *States and strangers: Refugees and displacements of statecraft.* Minneapolis: University of Minnesota Press.

Sontag, S. (2003). *Regarding the pain of others.* New York, NY: Farrar, Straus and Giroux.

Sparrow, A. (2008). Drawing attention to Darfur. In R. Solinger, M. Fox, & K. Irani (Eds.), *Telling stories to change the world: Global voices on the power of narrative to build community and make social justice claims* (pp. 127–137). New York , NY: Routledge.

Stephens, S. (1995). Children and the politics of culture in "late capitalism". In S. Stephens (Ed.), *Children and the politics of culture* (pp. 3–48). Princeton, NJ: Princeton University Press.

Stuart, J. (2007). Drawings and transformation in the health arena. In N. de Lange, C. Mitchell, & J. Stuart (Eds.), *Putting people in the picture: Visual methodologies for social change* (pp. 229–240). Rotterdam, The Netherlands: Sense.

Szörényi, A. (2006). The images speak for themselves? Reading refugee coffee-table books. *Visual Studies, 21*(1), 24–41. doi:10.1080/14725860600613188.

Taylor, S. (2006). Immigration detention reforms: A small gain in human rights. *Agenda, 13*(1), 49–62. Retrieved from http://epress.anu.edu.au.

Twum-Danso, A. (2009). Situating participatory methodologies in context: The impact of culture on adult-child interactions in research and other projects. *Children's Geographies, 7*(4), 379–389. doi:10.1080/14733280903234436.

Waging Peace. (2009). *Waging Peace homepage*. Retrieved from http://www.wagingpeace.info.

CHAPTER 6

THE VISUAL ETHICS OF USING CHILDREN'S DRAWINGS IN THE DOCUMENTARY *UNWANTED IMAGES*

Monica Mak

INTRODUCTION

From a black screen emerges the close-up shot of a coloured drawing. In it, a South African pupil stands by a doorway leading into a schoolyard. The camera pulls out to reveal the pupil watching an adult male zipping up his pants. Bearded and bespectacled, the grown-up casually walks away from a female adolescent lying on the ground; she is curled up in pain. A small pool of blood forms next to her body. The sounds of children gathered in a playground off-screen are faintly audible. The camera moves into an extreme close-up of the victim's distraught face. Her face dissolves into white text set against a black background. The text reads: "In South Africa it is estimated that a woman is raped every 35 seconds" (Mlamleli et al., 2001, p. 4). It is implied that the man is an authority figure, such as a teacher or principal, and that he has just sexually assaulted the young woman, a learner in his school. It is also suggested that another pupil, the figure by the doorway, has witnessed his criminal act.

This series of images make up the introduction to *Unwanted Images: Gender-Based Violence in the New South Africa* (Mitchell & Mak, 2001), an 8-minute educational documentary video produced by the Canada-South Africa Education Management Program (CSAEMP).[i] We created the video in response to the 1997 South African Gender Equity Task Team (GETT) Report imploring educators to provide young people with the knowledge and skills to repudiate gendered violence (Wolpe, Quinlan, & Martinez, 1997). Consequently, it has served as a discussion piece or conversation ice-breaker in facilitator-led workshops throughout South Africa that address various forms of sexual aggression.

Featured throughout the film are children's drawings done by 11- to 16-year-old participants at a violence awareness workshop organised by the Office on the Status of Women. These images were originally submitted to the Office to illustrate the trauma experienced by women and children, as seen through the eyes of learners.[ii] These images are juxtaposed with disturbing statistics presented as intertitles (simple texts on a plain matte inserted in between shots). Collectively, the images and intertitles demonstrate how gender-based violence, ranging from sexual harassment and rape to femicide (the killing of women) and homophobic attacks, affects South African youth in schools and at home. The narrative serves primarily to enlighten viewers about the different types of school-based and

L. Theron et al. (eds.), Picturing Research: Drawing as Visual Methodology, 77–88.

domestic violence. The concluding scene, however, urges educators to come up with strategies for eliminating this violence and for holding its perpetrators accountable.

The combination of hand-drawn imagery and written text is telling: The illustrations function as youth-generated visual data that corroborate rather than merely complement the given facts on violent and abusive behaviour.[iii] Many researchers have addressed the importance of drawings as a methodological tool in research on young people in the past. For instance, researchers have used sketches by children to study their views on educators (Weber & Mitchell, 1995) and their attitudes toward violence in refugee situations in southern Africa (Clacherty, 2005). Although there is a dearth of academic work on the ethics of utilising children's drawings as empirical data, much less work is being done on the ethics of incorporating such pictures into an art-based educational video.

This chapter therefore focuses on the ethical approach taken by the *Unwanted Image* production team to create a discursive space wherein young people, through their illustrations, could freely express their views on gender-based violence. This chapter presents six aspects of this approach. First, it studies anonymity in authorship. Second, it delves into the inclusion of actors for artistic enhancement. Third, it looks into magnification without distraction or exploitation, within the context of video. Fourth, it examines the use of drawing-inspired dramatisations. Fifth, it explores movement and music as solutions for integrating still pictures into a video setting. Sixth, it broaches the use of voiceover narration in moderation. I show how all six aspects adhere to an ethical code that is concerned with issues of safety. Safety, with regard to the first and second aspects, relates to authorial confidentiality. With regard to the third and fourth aspects, safety focuses on respect for a person's artwork by safeguarding its intended message(s).[iv] As far as the fifth and sixth aspects are concerned, safety pertains to sensitivity in the incorporation of still imagery into an audio-visual medium by acknowledging (and therefore preserving) cultural distinction. All in all, I demonstrate how these drawings serve as a secure and comfortable environment for young people's creative expression. I also reveal how process (i.e., their act of drawing) and product (i.e., the *Unwanted Images* video born of the drawings) are equally significant since each carries a specific reflexive benefit.

ANONYMOUS AUTHORSHIP

To protect the identities of the young artists, we (members of the *Unwanted Images* production team[v]) excluded their names from their illustrations and the end credits, thereby maintaining their anonymity throughout the whole video. Initially our South African collaborator (a Free State gender equity officer) and her test audience (primary and high school educators and parents living in a rural community) disapproved of our decision. For them, acknowledging authorship is essential for black South Africans since it symbolises a reclamation of their visibility and promotes their recognition as citizens in the post-Apartheid period (Mak, 2006). We, however, defended our decision since our primary responsibility was to protect the young artists. Revealing their names alongside their drawings or in the end credits could directly endanger their lives. Many of the featured images contain highly graphic depictions of domestic abuse targeting women and children and educator-to-peer and peer-to-peer acts of sexual violence. Therefore, if the real-life aggressors ever were to see this video and recognise themselves and the artists' names in it, they could retaliate. For instance, if the educator groping the female (see Figures 6.1 and 6.2) recognised himself in the film he could, by way of revenge, inflict physical harm on the artist, who might have been his victim or a witness to his crime. He could also sabotage her future by finding a way to have her fail her examinations or expel her from his school. As overseers of this project, it was our duty to maintain the illustrators' safety by keeping their names confidential.

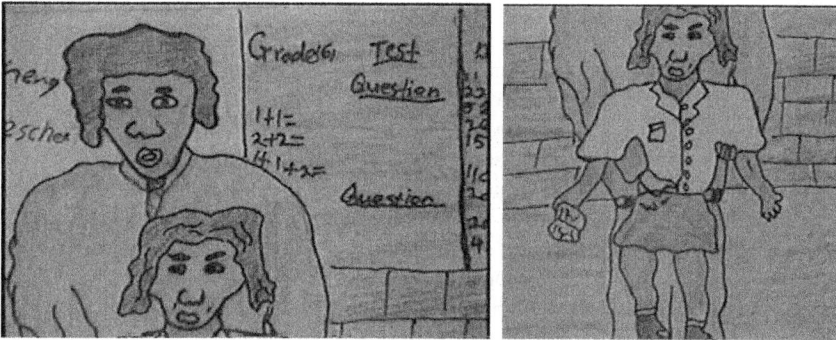

Figures 6.1 and 6.2. An educator sexually molests a learner in the classroom.

ACTORS FOR ARTISTIC ENHANCEMENT

Colourful illustrations of people trying to stop violent sexual acts dominate the second half of the video. In this part of the film, there are also shots of a rainbow over a sun interspersed with footage of three pre-teen boys sketching this image. During production on *Unwanted Images*, we included live action footage of these children drawing pictures of hope. This was to accentuate the sense of optimism present in the illustrations and to provide a glimpse of young artists at work. However, prior to production, we faced one obvious dilemma: How would we obtain footage of young people drawing without divulging the identities of those whose works are featured in the documentary? Just as we wished to protect these artists by excluding their names from their drawings and from the end credits, so too did we want to keep them safe by concealing their faces. This left us with two possible options. The first possibility was to hire a film crew who would film the artists participating at the anti-violence workshop from behind so that their faces would be hidden. But eventually we realised that this was not the appropriate course of action because the young artists might feel uneasy about being videotaped. Their reticence might arise from fear (of being associated with their drawings) or shyness (over drawing sexually explicit material in the presence of a film crew of strangers). In the end, we ascertained that, in front of a camera lens, they would not be so forthcoming in their portrayals of people in sexually violent scenarios. In retrospect, we might have lost the extent of the candour that their pictures currently bring to the narrative. For this reason, we went with our second option: the employment of amateur actors. Bently, Kristopher, and Rhyn, nephews of a member of the CSAEMP research team, graciously volunteered to be filmed drawing an image of their choice. The rainbow-over-a-sun imagery, for them, represents peace and happiness to all humankind—apt metaphors for a film section devoted to optimism. Their participation enabled us to continue upholding the workshop participants' anonymity.

MAGNIFICATION WITHOUT DISRUPTION OR EXPLOITATION

We wanted to integrate these drawings into the video so as to prevent the narrative from appearing stale and one-dimensional but this presented us with the challenge of how to combine the motion required by this medium with the stillness of the pictures. To resolve this, we often employed close-ups of the drawings to reinforce their core emotions and thematic sensibilities and to enliven them. Prompted by our need to respect the integrity of the illustrations, we used slow cross-dissolves[vi] to transition from medium and long shots to close-ups of drawings. We realised that cross-dissolves provided the most visually subtle—and therefore sensitive—way to usher in close-ups. Other transitional devices, such as wipes or jump cuts,[vii] would be disruptive since they would draw attention to the video's editing technology rather than to the drawing. By making viewers focus on showy effects, we would be distracting them from the serious message imbued in each picture. Employing such effects at a fast speed would also be disrespectful to the young artists. These effects, by virtue of their whimsical quality, would be making light of gendered violence and, in this way, subverting the artists' intended serious meaning.

In certain instances, we realised that close-ups of extremely violent drawings could be perceived as exploitative, and we omitted them for this reason. For example, in the illustration depicting 'jackrolling' (the gang rape of a young woman), two young men are pinning a girl to the table (see Figure 6.3). Her legs are spread apart, and the man with a scarred cheek wields a knife at her crotch. Our initial rough cut contained a close-up of the knife next to her legs. But our South African collaborator informed us that her test audience found this shot provocative and distasteful. As the director, I initially argued that the close-up's ability to draw attention to the picture's overall disturbing nature was the very reason we should keep it. But, in the end, we deferred to their suggestion to remove it. One reason was that our wide shot of this picture sufficiently demonstrated what was depicted in the drawing. We also theorised that our inclusion of this shot actually would be disrespectful to the artist since its shock value would overshadow the drawing's ability to raise audience awareness of gendered violence. In the end, showing courtesy to the artist's work meant removing this magnified shot from the film.

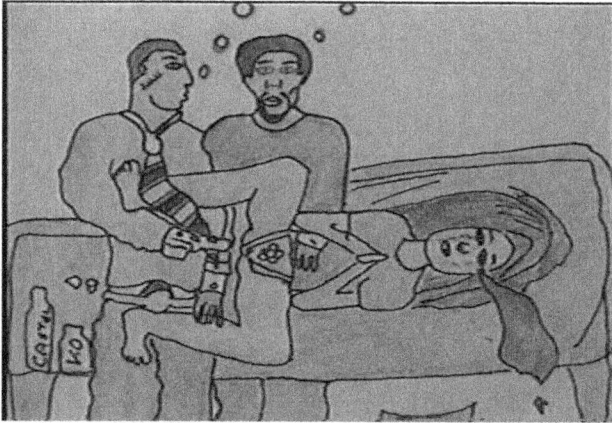

Figure 6.3. Two young men gang-rape (or 'jackroll') a young woman.

DRAWING-INSPIRED DRAMATISATIONS

To make the narrative more dynamic, we occasionally constructed dramatisations out of key symbols of gendered violence drawn from the children's illustrations. The two most overt examples involve a wine bottle and a caning stick. In 12-year-old L's[viii] drawing, a man is about to hit a woman, presumably his spouse or girlfriend, with a wine bottle. Frightened, she holds out her hand to shield her face from the blow. As the picture positions the wine bottle as the main instigator of aggression, we zeroed in on this negative connotation of alcohol-induced rage in the following shot. In this dramatisation, which we filmed in a dark room, the screen starts out empty. Eventually a wine bottle comes into view, slowly rolls across the floor, and then stops next to a wall. The camera next cuts to a close-up of the woman's terrified face, in the drawing. Then, it cuts back to the shot of the bottle on the floor and zooms in on it. By intercutting the dramatisation with the close-up of the female victim, we are suggesting that the man has already committed the brutal act and has just dropped his weapon on the floor.

Similarly, in a drawing by 14-year-old I, a male educator canes a boy on his bare buttocks in front of other learners (see Figure 6.4 on the next page). In this context, the raised rod epitomises the ruthlessness of corporal punishment, a practice declared unlawful by the Constitutional Court of South Africa in 1995. The educator stands beside the boy, where he has full view of his genitalia. The fact that the boy's arms are strapped down and that he is naked from the waist down underscores the sexually perverse nature of the situation. Moreover, the puddle of urine beneath his legs emphasises the cruelty of the punishment since it alludes to the boy's fear.

Figure 6.4. A male educator inflicts corporal punishment in full view of other learners.

Consequently, the dramatisation, in the following shot shows a stick striking in the direction of the camera. The camera then quivers to simulate the motion of being whipped and to suggest that the educator is in the midst of whipping the pupil. In both dramatisations, we adapted only elements integral to the drawings (i.e., the wine bottle and the rod) and refrained from introducing unrelated storylines. This was to preserve the original themes embodied in L's and I's drawings and, in this way, to honour their individual artistic intentions.

MOVEMENT AND MUSIC: STRATEGIES FOR ADAPTING STILL IMAGERY
INTO THE AUDIO-VISUAL REALM

Movement

Apart from using close-ups and slow cross-dissolves to invigorate the narrative of *Unwanted Images*, we relied on subtle camera movements to integrate the young artists' drawings into the medium of video. We often employed a gently roving shooting style to animate the still pictures but kept fancy filming techniques, such as rapid zoom-ins/-outs and pans, to a minimum.[ix] For example, the introductory scene, which depicts the schoolyard sexual assault, relies exclusively on a slow combination of zoom-outs, pans, and cross-dissolves. We wanted viewers to remain focused on the drawings' visual content instead of being distracted by the camera and any editing technology. From a theoretical standpoint, our effort to be sensitive to the artists' various messages involved rebelling against Canadian communications scholar Marshall McLuhan's (1967) famous 'the medium is the message' mantra.[x] We were drawing viewers' attention away from the way we made the video and turning it toward the content of the young artists' illustrations.

Music

Connotative soundscapes, just like camera movements, were pivotal for incorporating the children's drawings into the realm of video. We carefully chose two musical pieces that convey the two moods representative of the overall film. The sentiment of sorrow dominates the first half of the video in which different daily manifestations of sexual violence affecting South Africans at school and at home are portrayed. For this section, we employed "Blow the Wind—Pie Jesu" by British music composer/pianist Jocelyn Pook. This song features two female singers mournfully chanting the title words at different ranges. We found that the sadness in their voices aurally captured the agony shown on the faces of the drawings' victims of sexual violence.

The feeling of optimism—for an end to gendered violence through educational reform—informs the second half of the video. Here, the drawings contain slogans condemning gender-based violence and we see adults and children actively trying to stop it. One example is a 14-year-old girl's drawing in which a female teacher stops her colleague from beating a pupil. Another is a 13-year-old boy's illustration wherein a male teacher beats a female learner in a sexually charged manner. The picture includes a message box that reads: "Teachers don't beat girls on the buttocks." In this section of the film, we needed a musical track reflecting the hope in these drawings for a brighter future. We were also adamant about exercising cultural sensitivity. Therefore, the piece needed to honour the artists' South African heritage and, ideally, hint at life after 1994—the year that South Africa held its first democratic general election. As a result, we selected the instrumental version of *"Thula Sizwe Khay'Elisha"* ("Hush the nation, we will have a new home"), a well-known South African freedom song performed by the Soweto String Quartet.[xi] It was enthusiastically received by our South African collaborator and her test audience. In fact, our collaborator even admitted that every time she watches *Unwanted Images*, seeing the children's pictures set to that song always brings tears to her eyes.

NARRATION IN MODERATION

Rape, sexual harassment, assault, abuse, homophobia—the list of names is endless. But no matter what name we give to gendered violence, the children of South Africa are witnesses to its every incarnation of horror. Their drawings tell the story (Mitchell & Mak, 2001).

Delivered by the documentary's narrator during the opening credit sequence, this passage sums up the drawings' importance as the primary storytellers in the video. The pictures, rather than a faceless narrator, drive the film forward. We restricted the narrator's role to enable the young artists, through their illustrations, to recount their perceptions about gender-based violence with minimal interference from us. In other words, we did not want their drawings to serve as mere accoutrements to scripted dialogue created by academics and conveyed by an unseen grownup.

It was still important to have some narration to give context to the "5 W's" (who, what, where, when, and why)—essential to any documentary. A narrator was also necessary if we were to offer a conclusion to the film. Our solution was to have voiceover narration bookend the start and end of the film. However, we excluded narration from the bulk of the film's middle section in order to let the pictures speak for themselves. Julie Ally, a South African now residing in Canada, assumed the role of limited narrator. Her voice, like the Soweto String Quartet's musical piece, allowed us to pay homage to the artists' cultural background and, of course, to appeal to our South African audience.

DRAWINGS: PROVIDING A DISCURSIVE SPACE FOR SAFE, COMFORTABLE CREATIVE SELF-EXPRESSION

During the research and development phase of *Unwanted Images*, we recognised the need for a creative venue in which South African youth could express their views on gendered violence candidly, safely, and comfortably. In this instance, the traditional 'talking heads' approach of interview-driven social documentaries was inappropriate for our research purposes. Getting pre-teen and teen girls and boys to open up in recorded direct-camera testimonials or face-to-face interviews would have been challenging and possibly ineffective for three major reasons. First, we were studying the views of mainly black South African youth in the Free State and KwaZulu-Natal provinces. Getting them to express their thoughts accurately in English, which could be their third or fourth language or even their fifth after Sotho, Zulu, Afrikaans, and/or Xhosa, might have been impractical. They might have lacked the extensive vocabulary or fluency (attained through constant practice or advanced schooling) to express their thoughts. Second, because of their age group, they might have lacked the confidence or maturity to explain difficult and traumatic experiences or concepts—especially if they were themselves victims of sexual aggression. Third, even though we could blur out their faces in post-production, they might still have been scared to implicate themselves by being recorded. Even worse, they might have refused to cooperate with us.

Upon deliberation, we realised that their drawings on gender-based violence offered the solution around these obstacles. The drawings could help to resolve language barriers since the children could sketch out what they could not say or have trouble formulating in words. Chong, Hallman, and Brady (2006) stated that drawings can bestow upon children the opportunity to express themselves regardless of their linguistic aptitude. This is certainly the case of illustrations presented in *Unwanted Images*. For instance, in his sketch of a man about to strike his female partner with a wine bottle, 12-year-old L could elucidate, through coloured pencils and paper, the nefarious relationship between alcoholism and sexual abuse. Such a scenario might have been too difficult and painful for him to describe in words, particularly if the assault was by his father on his mother.

Drawings also provide young people with a secure environment in which they can freely confront the subject of gendered violence, while maintaining their anonymity. They can feel relatively more at ease disclosing their thoughts about their personal encounters with it. The ambiguous identities of the people depicted in their artwork may reassure them of their personal safety. Such personae, after all, could be fabricated characters, true depictions of themselves, or a mixture of fictional and real individuals. As artists with complete control over their creativity, they can provide a completely or partially autobiographical account or fictional representation of their impressions of this issue.

PROCESS, PRODUCT, AND REFLEXIVITY

A classic definition of participatory video-making posits that process (i.e., one's engagement in the act of filming and then the reviewing of raw footage) is more important than the final product (i.e., the narrative emerging from the filmed footage) (Caldwell, 2005). Within the context of *Unwanted Images*, process (defined by a young person's act of drawing) could theoretically be as important as the product (defined by our video showcasing such drawings). The integration of these young people's illustrations into the realm of documentary could generate therapeutic reflexivity from the artist's standpoint and could trigger reflexivity from the viewer's perspective.

As Malchiodi (1998) would argue, art therapy allows individuals to communicate what really happened to them before they can consciously accept the reality of their experiences (p. 12). Consequently, their involvement in artwork centred on abuse can serve as a mechanism for them to tap into their unconscious minds, reflect on such violence, and cope with the shock of enduring or seeing it.[xii] Within the context of *Unwanted Images*, an artist's therapeutic reflexivity referred to the way in which the drawing process could help young people gain catharsis following a traumatic experience, such as being victims or witnesses to gendered violence. Art therapy could enable them to concretise in images their recollections of heinous sexual acts committed to or before them. For example, during the drawing phase, some could explore the negative emotions that such brutal acts might have inflicted on them and could release such feelings into their artwork. The majority of the drawings featured in *Unwanted Images* meticulously detail the facial expressions—running the gamut from sadness to indignation—of victims and/or witnesses. This could possibly demonstrate the importance of drawings in helping young people to make sense of their feelings and, in this way, to gain some solace. Ultimately, we need to study in greater depth this form of reflexivity; researchers embarking on similar work need to explore it through in-depth conversations with youth artists regarding their feelings about their artwork.

Triggered reflexivity is a concept present in scholarly work on participatory video storytelling (for example, see Nair & White, 2003). In this context, video can function as an audio-visual product that triggers viewers to share their perspectives on an issue specific to the film in post-screening discussions. Extending their line of thought, I contend that participatory video, born out of a process-oriented endeavour (such as filming or, in the case of our documentary, drawing), can inspire spectators to ponder the topic's impact on their own lives. At the same time, it can encourage them to think of strategies to address the given problem.

Functioning as a participatory video product, *Unwanted Images* relies on pictures generated from the drawing process to motivate viewers to reflect on their own attitudes towards gender-based violence. In some cases, it may even inspire them to think of ways to confront or help eliminate this social abomination.

We have observed this type of reflexivity over the last 10 years. During this time span, many spectators have seen and analysed the documentary. Many of them have shared their own candid accounts of sexual violence (such as, for example, spousal abuse) and their solutions for ending it (such as, for example, fleeing the family home with their children). In December 2000, *Unwanted Images* was screened as part of the Men's Forum in the 16 Days Campaign of No Violence Against Women and Men in Pretoria, South Africa. Since then, it has been shown and discussed at educational conferences held in South Africa, Canada, the United States, and Great Britain. It has been deconstructed at the Lennoxville Women's Shelter, a Quebec community centre for battered women and their children. At this centre, art therapy is a common method for broaching the topic of domestic violence. Although it can exist as a stand-alone product, the video has also served as an audio-visual accompaniment to "Opening Our Eyes: Addressing Gender-Based Violence in South African Schools" (Mlamleli et al., 2001). This educational module was developed at CSAEMP to help South African educators conduct gendered violence awareness workshops in schools nationwide. All in all, to help spectators cope with the subject matter, we have encouraged them to communicate with us at post-screening Q & A discussions and to contact us directly through e-mail correspondence.

CONCLUSION

In this chapter, I have examined different notions of safety vis-à-vis the ethics of using drawings in documentary video. I have shown that safety refers to maintaining physical safety by excluding the artists' names from the narrative and substituting these individuals with amateur actors. I have pointed out that it means preserving the artist's original creative intent through slow close-ups and cross-dissolves, and limited use of voiceover narration and dramatised acts. I have demonstrated that it relates to safeguarding cultural distinctiveness through the inclusion of South African rhythms and a South African narrator. Ultimately, I have illustrated that guided by our set of ethical codes, we have tried to build a safe space wherein two kinds of reflexive discourse can flourish. First, during the process of artistic production, young people can 'look into' themselves or 'draw from within'. In other words, while they are drawing images, they can reflect on their direct/indirect encounters with gender-based violence. Through this reflection, they can then learn to cope with their memories and, in so doing, feel some sense of relief or comfort. Second, during screenings of *Unwanted Images*, their featured artwork can trigger viewers' engagement in an internalised dialogue with themselves or a conversation in discussion groups with fellow attendees. In this case, the film, as a finished media product, can compel viewers to ponder the issue and possibly come up with pragmatic measures for addressing it in South Africa and across the world.

Even though *Unwanted Images* was officially released in 2001, copies of the film continue to be requested by NGOs, women's rights organisations, and educational institutions to this day. In addition, it is still frequently screened at academic conferences worldwide. The video's longevity attests to the ability of its drawings to make it an effective educational tool for dealing with the issue of gender-based violence.

NOTES

i   The Canada–South Africa Education Management Program (CSAEMP) existed as a CIDA-funded partnership that involved McGill University, the South African National Department of Education, and the provinces of Gauteng, Free State, and Mpumalanga. It was in operation from 1996 to 2001.

ii Some of the illustrations were selected for a Women Against AIDS/Women Fight AIDS: No Condom No Sex! Calendar produced by the Office in 2000.

iii Although the statistical information was collected prior to the film's official release in 2001, such data is still relevant today.

iv Most participating artists provided a short written explanation about the meaning of their drawings. Located at the bottom of their illustrations, these artistic statements helped us to determine their intended messages. It was important to include these statements with the drawings. It would have been too difficult to verify artistic intentions once these artists left the workshop.

v   During the making of *Unwanted Images*, I served as principal videographer; Dr. Claudia Mitchell was the producer; and my fellow CSAEMP researchers and the Gender Focal representatives of the Free State, Gauteng, and Mpumalanga contributed to all stages of production. Therefore, the pronoun 'we', which is employed throughout the essay, refers to all of us since the video grew out of our collaborative efforts.

vi A cross-dissolve is a transitional effect whereby one screen image appears to 'melt' into the second image. It is used to gently switch from one shot to another. For more details, see Compesi and Gomez (2006).

vii A wipe is a transitional effect whereby one screen image replaces another in a 'wiping' horizontal or vertical motion. In contrast, the jump cut is a discontinuous transition from one shot to another caused by a difference in the size and position of the subject in the two shots. The wipe and the jump cut are very noticeable effects and for this reason are used mainly to achieve a highly stylised look. For more details, see Compesi and Gomez (2006).

viii To continue preserving the young artists' anonymity, I identify them by the first letter of their first names.

ix A zoom-in refers to the camera focusing closer on an object, whereas in a zoom-out the camera moves out of the object, thereby showing the space around it. A pan is the camera moving left to right or vice-versa.

x   Although there are numerous interpretations of the phrase 'the medium is the message', the most common is the notion that any given medium (e.g., a film) determines how the message (e.g., a drawing) will be interpreted. By this logic, the medium affects the way in which the message will be perceived. So we kept fancy camerawork and editing effects to a minimum in an effort to present the drawings as they were originally drawn.

xi The Soweto String Quartet consists of four black classically-trained musicians originating from the Soweto township. The ensemble achieves its unique fusion sound by drawing out native African rhythms and intonations from traditional European string instruments.

xii Since sexual violence can cause severe psychological wounds, I am not suggesting that drawing is the sole solution for children who have been affected by it. Certainly, other healing practices, such as extensive psychological counselling, medical testing for sexually transmitted diseases, and complete physical examinations (to look for fractures or severe bruises), should be sought. However, art-based therapy can be one major strategy to help with emotional recovery.

REFERENCES

Caldwell, G. (2005). Using video for advocacy. In S. Gregory, G. Caldwell, R. Avni, & T. Harding (Eds.), *Video for change: A guide for advocacy and activism* (pp. 1–19). London, England: Pluto Press.

Chong, E., Hallman, K., & Brady, M. (2006). *Investing when it counts: Generating the evidence base for policies and programmes for very young adolescents.* New York, NY: UNFPA. Retrieved from http://www.unfpa.org.

Clacherty, G. (2005). *Refugee and returnee children in Southern Africa: Perceptions and experiences of violence.* Pretoria, South Africa: UNHCR.

Compesi, R. J., & Gomez, J. S. (2006). *Introduction to video production: Studio, field, and beyond.* Boston, MA: Allyn & Bacon.

Mak, M. (2006). Unwanted Images: Tackling gender-based violence in South African schools through youth artwork. In F. E. Leach & C. Mitchell (Eds.), *Combating gender violence in and around schools* (pp. 217–225). Stoke-on-Trent, England: Trentham Books.

Malchiodi, C. A. (1998). *The art therapy sourcebook.* New York, NY: McGraw-Hill.

McLuhan, M., & Fiore, Q. (1967). *The medium is the message: An inventory of effects.* New York, NY: Random House.

Mitchell, C. (Producer), & Mak, M. (Director). (2001). *Unwanted images: Gender-based violence in the new South Africa* [Documentary video short]. Canada: Canada-South Africa Education Management Program.

Mlamleli, O. et al. (2001). *Opening our eyes: Addressing gender-based violence in South African schools* [Module for educators]. Pretoria: South African National Department of Education.

Nair, K. S., & White, S. A. (2003). Trapped: Women take control of video storytelling. In S. A. White (Ed.), *Participatory video: Images that transform and empower* (pp. 195–214). Thousand Oaks, CA: Sage.

Weber, S., & Mitchell, C. (1995). *'That's funny, you don't look like a teacher': Interrogating images and identity in popular culture.* London, England: Falmer Press. doi:10.4324/9780203453568.

Wolpe, A., Quinlan, O., & Martinez, L. (1997). *Gender equity in education: A report by the Gender Equity Task Team.* Pretoria: South African National Department of Education.

LOST AND FOUND IN TRANSLATION: PARTICIPATORY ANALYSIS AND WORKING WITH COLLECTIONS OF DRAWINGS

Katie MacEntee and Claudia Mitchell

> The task of interpretation is virtually one of translation.
> Susan Sontag, 1966

INTRODUCTION

As researchers in the social sciences, we glibly use the term 'data collection' in our research studies, but how do we really think of 'collections' in the data collection process? We ask this question because work with drawings (and indeed other forms of visual representation such as photos or collage) typically yields what might be regarded as an art collection. How does the term 'collection' itself imply something of an archive? How might the idea of working with an art collection or a collection of visual arts-based artefacts such as drawings contribute to the interpretation/translation process? And finally, what are some of the opportunities (and challenges) we face when we re-frame our thinking about collections of drawings, particularly in relation to the voice of the producers and audiences? This chapter focuses on the notion of participatory analysis and the ways in which the producers themselves might be engaged in analysis, but the ways in which third-party analysis can deepen an understanding of the issues are also covered.

Our interest in thinking about collections and archives stems from the association between data collecting involving drawings and the various collections of children's drawings in the public domain. If you google "children's drawings", you will find references to a fascinating array of different collections and information on institutions dedicated to displaying them—from the Jewish Museum of Prague's collection of drawings produced by children in the Terezin Concentration camp to the World Awareness Children's Museum's mission to "foster awareness, understanding, and appreciation worldwide of cultural diversity for children and adults" (World Awareness Children's Museum, 2009). As Sarah Henry (2002) pointed out, these collections highlight the ways in which children move from being the observed to the observers:

> Children are among history's most elusive witnesses. Museum and libraries are full of objects and documents that appear to tell the stories of childhood but are actually the creations of adults. The books, toys, clothes, and child-rearing manuals that inform what we think we know about childhood tell us

L. Theron et al. (eds.), Picturing Research: Drawing as Visual Methodology, 89–102.

much more about what society wanted children to be than children actually saw, heard, believed, or felt. Thus children are more often than not the observed, rather than the observers of history. This gap in the historical record troubles historians of childhood and leaves the rest of us with a seriously impoverished understanding of our own history. For when we do have the opportunity to listen to children, their testimony is powerful. And art is one of the most compelling ways children have of expressing what they have experienced. (p. 18)

One can access virtual collections, such as the drawings produced by children during the Spanish Civil War (Avery Architectural & Fine Arts Library, 2004). The references generally include the size of the collections: 2000 pieces of art created from over 100 countries at Paintbrush Diplomacy, 1300 words in the Stone Soup Museum of Children's Art, 4500 children's drawings from Terezin, and so on. And if you visit the virtual collections, you will discover some of the coding and categorising; it is often possible to know the age, sex, and location of the child producer, along with, in some cases, even the name. The circumstances in which the drawings were collected are also part of the information provided. In the case of the Terezin drawings, it is noted that Mrs. Friedl Dicker Brandeis taught art classes to children at the camp before she was sent to Auschwitz and that she was able to hide two suitcases full of the children's drawings. Some of this coding and categorising complements what has been done in published book collections such as Volovková's (1993) *I Never Saw Another Butterfly: Children's Drawings and Poems From Terezin Concentration Camp, 1942–1944* or Geist and Carroll's (2002) *They Still Draw Pictures: Children's Art in Wartime. From the Spanish Civil War to Kosovo.*

This work on collections of children's drawings is interesting for a number of reasons. First, it highlights the ways that children's drawings serve as evidence of some of the most horrific moments in history. As Colin Rhodes (2000) pointed out, the whole movement of children's drawings dates back to Jean-Jacques Rousseau in the 18th century, after which, in the late 19th century, the notion of a raw primitivism speaks to natural expression that is "outside the complex social structures that govern the lives of most adults" (pp. 26–27). A second reason for highlighting these collections of children's drawings is a methodological one. These collections can be read as a validation of children's drawings as method, in and of itself. Notwithstanding the many debates and discussions about the truth value of images, and of course the challenges of interpretation, the sheer volume of drawings produced by children and, furthermore, the fact that they are produced in relation to so many different social justice issues, suggests that we need to take seriously—though not uncritically—the genre itself. If so many images exist, so do these questions: How, under what circumstances, and in whose interests were they collected? We need to ask questions that point back to the responsibility of adults to resist trivialising the time, the hopes, the dreams, and the safety of children. The focus of this last question is particularly critical because so many children's drawings have been collected during times of war. What is the impact of these drawings, if any, on the adults who collected them in the first place? What about the impact on child audiences? The existence of so many public collections also raises the question of why we do not make better use of these collections. If, for example, we are interested in studying the effects of conflict on children, do we not have a responsibility to seek out other collections that are in the public domain (on websites, in museums, in published collections) so that we are building on and adding to what is already there rather than simply collecting more data? Finally, as noted above, we are interested in the idea of fully mining collections of drawings, particularly those that we elicit in our fieldwork with participants. For us, there is a crucial question: How can the voices of the producers themselves become central to research being carried out on their images?

THE BACKSTORY OF THREE ARCHIVES

In this section, we offer three brief cases of working with collections of drawings. Although we refer to these as three 'archives', their genesis is far from sophisticated: Not unlike the two suitcases that originally contained the Terezin drawings, these archives started out as cardboard boxes, folders, and a drawer in a file cabinet.

Draw a Teacher (Canada)

One of the 'archives' of children's drawings is a collection made up of more than 500 drawings produced by Quebec primary school children in response to the prompt: *"Draw your teacher."* As described in Chapter 1, Sandra Weber and Claudia Mitchell came upon the drawings somewhat by accident when they saw a reference to the collection in the local newspaper. The artist who had organised the project turned over the collection to the research team (Weber & Mitchell, 1995, 1996) when they contacted her. The sheer size of the initial collection moved the team into an interpretive paradigm related to the question of what to do with 500 drawings. Their first response was not to start coding and categorising (something they eventually did) but rather to lay out the drawings on the floor, on desks and tables, and simply engage in a 'walk about' around the images. The visual lay-out, they realised, served as an invitation to others to engage in the interpretive process. A group of beginning teachers, for example, looked at this visual lay-out and began to talk about particular images in relation to their own teachers ("This one looks like ..."). In their comments, they often spoke about their own hopes and dreams: "This is the kind of teacher I want to be" and "Here is an example of what I DON'T want to be". They engaged in something that Weber and Mitchell eventually termed 'future oriented remembering' (hooks, 1994). Thus, although these two researchers ultimately came to code drawings according to age, sex, and subject area depicted on the blackboard, and according to such emerging categories as romance, the individual responses of beginning teachers highlighted the significance of memory and the past in such coding. Interestingly, beginning teachers ended up doing their own drawings in due course (Weber & Mitchell, 1996) and, therefore, expanding the collection.

Let Every Child Learn (South Africa)

On a larger scale, we encountered examples of this kind of 'future-oriented remembering' (hooks, 1994) in the dialogue of a group of beginning teachers in South Africa as they looked through drawings of teachers and schools produced by South African school children. The drawings were produced by over 12,000 school children in response to two art competitions, one sponsored by the South African Post Office ("Let Every Child Learn") and the other by the Checkers supermarket chain ("Back to school: Draw your teacher"). Both collections were created in 1994–1995. As a visiting professor at the University of the Witwatersrand (Wits) in Johannesburg (and as a relative outsider to South African education), Claudia Mitchell worked with a group of beginning teachers at Wits to study the drawings. What started as a project of analysing these drawings, however, ended up, for these teachers, becoming a memory project in which the drawings served as visual memory prompts. The tape recordings of their group discussions were filled with questions and comments like "Do you remember ...?", "Oh no—this is just like what our classroom was like", or "I remember this ..." as they proceeded to talk about struggling with the legacy of schools as sites of oppression—places in which teachers are often seen to be overly punitive, unprofessional, lazy, and authoritarian. Many of the teachers in this group focused on a particular image to recall school, and the memories offered were often very poignant. The teachers also made many references to issues of power and the disciplinary role of teachers—again prefacing many of their comments by "I remember ...". The archive, then, is a memory one, and the types of comments made by the teachers highlighted the possibility of reflection and looking back but also the need for comparative data. What would the images look like 10 years later? Would the teachers have a more future-oriented analysis?

Draw Gender-Based Violence (Rwanda)

The two preceding cases highlight the significance of personal memory in the interpretive process. We were aware of other dimensions of translation in such a process when we were working with a collection of drawings on gender-based violence produced by children and young people in Rwanda. As part of a project in Rwanda related to children's participation in addressing gender violence in and around schools, Claudia Mitchell worked with children and young people in every region of the country to get their perspectives on the issues. One of the data collecting tools was the production of drawings on gender-based violence (see Table 7.1).

Table 7.1.

In one primary school in Rwanda, children were asked to visually express 'feeling unsafe', which included drawing places where they might feel frightened. Comments by the children are listed beneath each caption.
Drawing 1 Caption: "Fear behind the Toilets" – *I fear behind the toilet because I can easily be raped from there or else they kill me.* – *Inside the toilettes I fear there because a boy can rape me from there.* – *Behind the school I fear there because every one can easily harm you from there.* – *I fear in the corridor because some one can rape you from there when it is dark.*
Drawing 2 Caption: "Because the Headmistress Punishes Us" – *On the administration block I fear there because the headmistress punishes us seriously.* – *Near the toilets are bushes so we fear there because like a girl can easily be raped from there.* – *On the road we fear there because car can knock you to death.*
Drawing 3 Caption: "Boys or Men Can Easily Catch Me" – *Behind the classes we fear there because of the bush and someone can rape you.* – *We fear the barracks because they can beat us from there and we meet bombs.* – *On the toilet I fear there and boys or men can easily catch me and rape me.* – *On the road I fear there because the car can knock me down.*
Drawing 4 Caption: "The Soldiers Can Beat You" – *Behind the classes I fear there because there are snakes that can bite me.* – *On the road I fear there because some one can rape me from there.* – *On the barracks I fear there because the soldiers can beat you or you are bombed.*

Many of the images produced included captions written in Kinyarwanda, so translation relied on the help of a young Rwandese medical student named Jean-Paul. In total, he worked with approximately 1000 drawings. He would work with them for a few days and then return them to the research team with translations of the captions but also a page or two of general comments. In fact, he was not just involved in translating the captions from Kinyarwanda to English but also in translating the images themselves: "This is what I think the drawing means." Unlike the responses of the beginning teachers to the children's drawings in the South African case mentioned previously, Jean-Paul's responses were less explicitly about his own memories and more about his perspective on the social reality of contemporary Rwanda. The backstories that he provided were critical to how we worked with the drawings.

We gained an even greater appreciation for an insider perspective when we had occasion to explore the images in an outsider context. A research assistant at McGill University became interested in working with the same collection of drawings that Jean-Paul had worked with. We were uncertain about what she might do with the drawings: Would she simply organise them according to sex, location, and age? Or would she try to look at the actual themes? The task proved to be a difficult and frustrating one because she felt so far outside the context of the actual collecting of the drawings, or the context of contemporary Rwanda:

> My ability to read scenes of men and girls with cars and cells phones as prostitution was inhibited by lack of familiarity with this type of exchange in my urban North American childhood where cell phones and cars are a "natural" part of middle-class life. So too was my ability to interpret scenes of children in forests as a commonplace threat to a Rwandan child's safety impeded by my cultural estrangement from having to cross wide-open, un-policed spaces daily without the provision of a trusted adult. (field notes, 2009)

What the three cases in this section highlight are some of the opportunities for using archival data to evoke new stories. Working with beginning teachers' interpretations of children's drawings of teachers led to some critical findings on the role of memory in becoming a teacher (Mitchell, 2004; Mitchell & Weber, 1999). At the same time, these examples, especially those dealing with issues of social justice, draw attention to the following questions: How might the producers (in this case, the children who produced the drawings), or at least members of their community, interpret the collection of images? And how might the processes of using-reusing, coding-recoding, and playing-replaying contribute to deepening an understanding of the phenomenon under study?

PARTICIPATORY ANALYSIS PART 1:
THE PRODUCERS AND THE IDEA OF THE DIGITAL ARCHIVE

In this section, we consider the idea of engaging the children themselves in the process of working with the images. As explored elsewhere (see Mitchell, 2009; Mitchell, Walsh, & Moletsane, 2006; Moletsane, Mitchell, Smith, & Chisholm, 2008), the significance of the visual (drawings, video making, and photography) in breaking the silence related to such issues as gender-based violence in and around schools is critical. In the case of the drawings of gender-based violence from Rwanda, where policy-making was key, how might the voices of the producers— the girls who drew images of such violence—be further invoked within grassroots policy-making? Such a question is located within what Patricia Maguire (1987, 2001) and others refer to as feminist participatory research, an approach to research that acknowledges participants as more than 'subjects' and in so doing recognises the critical perspectives of girls and women in identifying both gender issues as well as possible solutions at the community level.

Participatory Archiving

The participatory archive, as Huvilo (2008) and Shilton and Srinivasan (2008) noted, is a relatively new concept that refers to the ways in which users (including producers) can also be engaged in designing the archive as well as in coding and re-coding the data. A digital archive (regardless of whether it is a public site or a restricted research site created by a research team) is simply a collection of records in a digital form that makes it possible to both store data and to retrieve it via software applications (Pearce-Moses, 2005). Digital images are described using a metadata protocol and saved in a database for retrieval, access, and preservation. As outlined elsewhere (Park, Mitchell, & De Lange, 2007) in the actual digitisation, the activity of connecting original materials and their apparent objective and subjective descriptions with newly created digital surrogates form the database (Hughes, 2004). As Shilton and Srinivasan (2008) observed, the reason for creating a new participatory method in working with archives is to prevent, as much as possible, the distortion of cultural histories of marginalised populations. Implementing a system that allows marginalised groups to become engaged in the entire archiving process allows a community to ensure the authenticity of the individual pieces, with the archive depicting a more accurate history of the community. In his essay "Reading the Archive", Allan Sekula (2003) observed that archives are far from neutral. He cites numerous examples of the ways in which both the content and management of archives shape what knowledge (and ultimately whose knowledge) is stored in the first place and how it is coded and categorised, how it can be retrieved, and who has access to the archive. The examples in the previous section of this chapter of how beginning teachers interpreted the drawings of children according to their own histories and memories, or the example of the research assistant who found it difficult to associate forests with danger, speak to the presence of multiple meanings but perhaps also to the absence of the meanings intended by the producers. Although much of the work related to participatory archives links to the use of public archives in such settings as libraries and universities, the nature of interactivity offers promising developments that could be incorporated into the participatory work of community-based archives or restricted sites. Work on digital archives of local photo data on a restricted site in a rural South African context highlights the possibility for community members to be more directly engaged in contributing to analysis, management, and dissemination of the data/knowledge production (see also De Lange, Mitchell, & Park, 2008; De Lange, Mnisi, Mitchell, & Park, 2010; Dyson & Leggett, 2006; Mnisi, DeLange, & Mitchell, in press; Park, Mitchell, & De Lange, 2007, 2008).

An archive, then, can become a democratic space, one that invites the producers themselves (for example, adolescent girls in Rwanda) to participate along with 'users' in the case of stakeholders and researchers. We draw on the successes of work with photo archives to consider how these successes can transfer to work with drawings. Our interest is in the development and application of interactive digital formats (within an archive) so that producers can play with, remix, and rework the visual data (their own and others) and in so doing, fully exploit the dynamic nature of the archive and the data. Producers (and users) can add their voices to the data in a variety of ways, ranging from the use of social tagging to creating stories (as a type of analysis) using the images and digital technology.

PARTICIPATORY ANALYSIS PART 2:
INSIDER AND OUTSIDER PERSPECTIVES ON ART-MAKING

Participatory analysis can go beyond work with the participants, even if such work is clearly the starting point. Much has been written on using arts-based techniques, reflexivity, and the potential for arts-based methods to open the door to alternative forms of data representation and knowledge production (Eisner, 1997; Knowles & Cole, 2008; Knowles, Luciani, Cole, & Neilson, 2007; Leavy, 2009; Mitchell & Weber, 2004; Moletsane et al., 2007). However, there is a paucity of research concerning the role of participant-produced art in participatory arts-based research and little consideration of the role of audiences (those not directly involved with the initial research process) who view the art. In this section, we explore the potential of integrating third-party perspective analysis into arts-based research. We do this by focusing on participant-produced images created during arts-based research committed to a change-centred approach (Schratz & Walker, 1995). Responding to critiques of participatory research, raising questions about participant-produced art and the participatory nature of the research, and interrogating the role of aesthetics in facilitating change, we argue the potential of participatory analysis that contains an explicit critique of artistic forms and what it means to do research for social change. We conclude by discussing the value of incorporating the audience voice into participatory arts-based research analysis.

As discussed above in 'Participatory Analysis Part I', the inclusion of the participants' voice and understanding, through coding and analysis of the drawings, can contribute to a more democratic approach to the research process. It helps ensure that the art is accurately represented and explained. But the inclusion of participants in research analysis also carries challenges. It requires training, it can be difficult for participants to review data that presents them (or their situation) in a negative light or that is painful for them, and the process can be tedious (Cahill, 2007). Of particular note is the risk of romanticising the participant's voice. Kincheloe (2009) wrote of Participatory Action Research (PAR) techniques:

> Too many contemporary advocates of PAR have failed to ask hard questions about the nature of participation. Without such complex and intense questions, PAR too often migrates to one of two positions: a research method/design that (1) romanticizes and essentializes the perspectives of the oppressed and fails to question the diversity of viewpoints among subjugated groups; (2) embraces facile notions of participation that serve as new and more hegemonically sophisticated modes of exclusion. (pp. 119–120)

Although the inclusion of participant interpretation and analysis is important, without a critical exploration of the limitations of any particular participant or group of participants' perspectives, we risk constructing a positivist universalism. We argue that participatory arts-based research can also be trapped into glorifying the perspective of the participant and therefore risks essentialising participant voices, glossing over difference, and/or creating further marginalisation within an already struggling group. Without taking away from the importance of participant analysis, Kincheloe's critique leads us to consider how participant-centred research may benefit by finding ways to incorporate a wider range of perspectives or voices into its analysis process.

A participatory arts-based approach—with participants creating art for the sake of research and typically without any formal training in the arts—has been important in marginalised communities (Lykes, 2001a, 2001b; Mitchell & Kanyangara, 2006; Umurungi, Mitchell, Gervais, Ubalijoro, & Kabarenzi, 2008; Wang, 1999) because it helps 'give a voice' to otherwise overlooked groups and experiences. Although not always participatory, arts-based research is politically motivated, with a significant proportion of participatory research dedicated to ensuring that participant needs and goals are realised, at least in part, through the research process and findings. This type of collaborative and interdisciplinary work has ties to PAR and its "key question of how we go about generating knowledge that is both valid and vital to the well being of individuals, communities, and for the promotion of larger-scale democrative social change" (Brydon-Miller, Greenwood, & Maguire, 2003, p. 11). An emancipatory approach commits this work to challenging an oppressive status quo (for example, gender-based violence in Rwanda) and including a critical analysis of the everyday lives and insights of traditionally oppressed individuals and communities. As we see with the drawing work by girls in Rwanda, the participants become the centre of the research and are inextricably involved in the act of knowledge production. It is their knowledge of risk and unsafe spaces (represented in part by their drawings of toilets and forests) that inform policy change. Therefore, displaying the girls' drawings for community members and for ministry officials was integral to the research process. The power of exhibiting the participant-produced art is one of the valuable aspects of this type of research and can play a key role in ensuring that participant objectives are met.

Exhibiting participant work helps ensure that participants receive recognition for both their work and their role in the research. Other 'showings' of the art may be through the inclusion of individual images in academic books and journal articles or as projected conference slides (100 times magnified) in PowerPoint presentations. Still other work might be 'adopted' by the community: hung in offices, archived in museums, incorporated into a coffee table book, or re-presented digitally online. This art can be presented in a variety of forms, sometimes without the accompanying information recorded from the participant. In the case of photographs on the topic of HIV and AIDS taken by teachers and community health workers in a rural area of KwaZulu-Natal, South Africa, the collection still hangs in the community health clinic 7 years after the completion of the research project. Hundreds of people pass by these photos every week. What do these images mean to the people who work at this clinic? How are the images understood by the clients who visit the clinic?

When we are showing art to a wider audience, there is potential for a third-party perspective that might shed new light on the research process and lead to new understandings of the actions required to bring about social change. In this sense, it can seem as though the knowledge production process of participatory research is never ending. What might be gained by incorporating these perspectives into the analysis? Guided feedback, question and answer periods, comments in a visitors' book, and focus groups are all examples of how a third-party perspective analysis of the issues under research might be captured. The audience can describe its relationship to the issues, its understandings, its ability to effect change, and its potential to take action. Given Kincheloe and Cahill's critiques, how might the formal incorporation of this type of analysis into the research process contribute to avoiding the essentialisation of the participant voice? Indeed, what responsibility do we have as researchers to capture alternative understandings of participant-produced art? How might an outsider lend a constructive analysis to the art?

Third-party analysis, of course, also has its challenges, especially in relation to aesthetics. On the role of aesthetics in arts-based research, Leavy (2009) wrote:

> The issue of aesthetics is central to the production of arts-based texts as well as our evaluation of them. Although in the best cases art provokes, inspires, captivates, and reveals, certainly not all art can meet these standards. Throw novices into the mix who create art for their scholarly research and even less of what is produced is likely to meet the aesthetic ideals developed in the fine arts. (pp. 16–17)

On the one hand, participants may feel uncomfortable being judged on their work, and it can seem unfair for outsiders to judge pieces created by amateur research participants. In turn, outsiders may not be experienced at responding to art. As Eisner (1985) explained, "the reward and insights provided by aesthetically shaped forms are available only to those who can read them" (p. 25). Those unaccustomed to viewing art may lack the language to review it or may have no interest in doing so. The aesthetics of a drawing produced by a participant can fall anywhere along a subjective scale from aesthetically 'good' to 'bad'. And these judgments can be made by the participant, the researcher, the research group, the community, or a larger population—some or all of whom may differ in opinion. On the other hand, aesthetics is more than simply evaluating 'prettiness'. As Springgay, Irwin, and Kind (2008) discussed, Bourriaud's (2002) concept of relational aesthetics has to do with the viewer and the art both being active, meaning-making subjects within an exhibition space. In this sense, once the artist-participant completes the piece, the art takes on a life of its own and is separate and independent from the artist-participant. Following relational aesthetics, the display of participant-produced art (with or without the presence of the artist or the re-representation of the artist's voice) takes on a central role in the construction of meaning by allowing for multiple interpretations to be evoked and understood from any one piece of art.

However, regardless of these challenges, the aesthetic—the ability of the art to 'do something'—can have lasting consequences and can have an impact on the research. Under most circumstances, a researcher is likely to include an aesthetically pleasing or dramatic image to exemplify various research findings and observations in publications and conference presentations. In Chapter 1, for example, Claudia Mitchell discusses the haunting drawing from Rwanda of the perfectly formed baby in the toilet, an image that she has used in a variety of presentations. Although researchers ask permission to show images again in their publications, how is this understood by participants? Does the girl living in rural

Rwanda who drew the image of the baby at the bottom of the toilet have any real understanding of what it means to have this image projected onto a screen as part of a PowerPoint presentation? What is the researcher's responsibility regarding the incorporation of a discussion of aesthetic consequences into participatory work? On the one hand, participants who produce a drawing that is aesthetically pleasing to members of their community may enjoy praise and admiration from within their community context. This may motivate a participant, who knows that her or his end product will be exhibited to a larger audience, to make compromises in terms of content for the sake of aesthetics. Does this take away the validity of the research? On the other hand, both the participant and the researcher may benefit from an aesthetically pleasing drawing if it is more likely to sway policy makers towards political action that will benefit those involved in the research. Given that aesthetics can have an impact on the research process and outcomes, it cannot be ignored and needs to be more deeply explored. At the least, there should be explicit discussions within research groups of the potential consequences of aesthetics in arts-based research.

Finally, we consider the significance of an emerging conceptual framework to examine the various audiences in participatory analysis approaches, especially in the context of collections (or data sets). By this, we mean the responses of all those who view the art produced during the research process, including community members, policy makers, and, of course, the participants themselves who, in a participatory group, are also audience to co-participants' work as well as to their own work. Here, we consider a number of key questions: How does a consideration of aesthetics inform the 'reach' of the work? Should we be considering what would be entailed in the development of a 'participant aesthetic'? What is the potential of the audience to give a (guided) analysis of art produced during arts-based research? How might documenting the analysis of the audience help inform our understanding of the role of participatory methods on making positive change in participants' lives or in taking action? Will including audience perspectives encourage viewers to engage more in the work and provoke action on their part? These questions, we suggest, might form a foundation for interpreting and translating participant art in ways that more fully mine collections, and as noted at the beginning of this chapter, 'honour' the art work of children, many of whom face difficult circumstances.

CONCLUSION

We began this chapter with Susan Sontag's words on the interpretation process as a process of "translation". Critical to this process is ensuring that participants and politically invested third-party individuals and groups are given space to participate in the translation process. A consideration of the various perspectives in this process suggests the beginnings of a framework within which one might incorporate the idea of participatory analysis into participatory arts-based research. We have highlighted terms such as 'audience' and 'aesthetics' and have considered the possibilities for deeper engagement with the drawings by those who produce the art in the first place, as well as the various audiences. Indeed, there remains the potential to incorporate a more dynamic and nuanced understanding of how aesthetics and drawings can inform the knowledge production process. Collections should not be static, and perhaps the most critical aspect of this work is to consider how adult researchers can keep the types of archives described here (and the collections and issues they house) alive.

REFERENCES

Avery Architectural & Fine Arts Library. (2004). *Children's drawings of the Spanish Civil War* [Online exhibition]. Retrieved from http://www.columbia.edu/cu/lweb/eresources/exhibitions/children

Brydon-Miller, M., Greenwood, D., & Maguire, P. (2003). Why action research? *Action Research, 1*(1), 9–28. doi:10.1177/14767503030011002.

Cahill, C. (2007). Participatory data analysis. In S. Kindon, R. Pain, & M. Kesby, (Eds.), *Participatory action research approaches and methods: Connecting people, participation and place* (pp. 181–187). London, England: Routledge.

De Lange, N., Mitchell, C., & Park, E. (2008, April). *Working with digital archives: Giving life (to data) to save lives in the age of AIDS*. Oral presentation at the American Education Research Association, New York, NY.

De Lange, N., Mnisi, T., Mitchell, C., & Park, E. G. (2010). Giving life to data: University–community partnerships in addressing HIV and AIDS through building digital archives. *E-Learning and Digital Media, 7*(2), 160–171. doi:10.2304/elea.2010.7.2.160.

Dyson, L. E., & Legget, M. (2006, December). *Towards a metadesign approach for building indigenous multimedia cultural archives*. Proceedings of the 12th ANZSYS conference: Sustaining Our Social and Natural Capital, Katoomba, New South Wales, Australia. Retrieved from http://www-staff.it.uts.edu.au/~laurel/Publications/TowardsAMetadesignApproach.pdf.

Eisner, E. (1985). Aesthetic modes of knowing. In E. Eisner (Ed.), *Learning and teaching: The ways of knowing* (pp. 23–26). Chicago, IL: National Society for the Study of Education.

Eisner, E. (1997). The promise and perils of alternative forms of data representation. *Educational Researcher, 26*(6), 4–10. doi:10.3102/0013189X026006004.

Geist, A. L., & Carroll, P. N. (2002). *They still draw pictures: Children's art in wartime from the Spanish Civil War to Kosovo*. Champaign: University of Illinois Press.

Henry, S. (2002). Children as witnesses to history. In R. F. Goodman & A. H. Fahnestock (Eds.), *The day our world changed: Children's art of 9/11* (pp. 18–22). New York, NY: New York University Child Study Centre & Museum of the City of New York.

hooks, b. (1994). In our glory: Photography and black life. In D. Willis (Ed.), *Picturing us: African American identity in photography* (pp. 43–53). New York, NY: The New Press.

Hughes, L. M. (2004). *Digitizing collections: Strategic issues for the information manager*. London, England: Facet.

Huvilo, I. (2008). Participatory archive: Towards decentralised curation, radical user orientation, and broader contextualisation of records management. *Archival Science, 8*(1), 15–36. doi:10.1007/s10502-008-9071-0.

Kincheloe, J. (2009). Critical complexity and Participatory Action Research: Decolonizing "democratic" knowledge production. In D. Kapoor & S. Jordan (Eds.), *Education, Participatory Action Research, and social change: International perspectives* (pp. 107–121). New York, NY: Palgrave MacMillan.

Knowles, J. G., & Cole, A. L. (Eds.). (2008). *Handbook of the arts in qualitative research: Perspectives, methodologies, examples, and issues*. Thousand Oaks, CA: Sage.

Knowles, J. G., Luciani, T. C., Cole, A. L., & Neilson, L. (Eds.). (2007). *The art of visual inquiry*. Halifax, NS: Backalong Books.

Leavy, P. (2009). *Method meets art: Arts-based research practice*. New York, NY: The Guilford Press.

Lykes, M. B. (2001a). Activist participatory research and the arts with rural Maya women. Interculturality and situated meaning making. In D. L. Tolman & M. Brydon-Miller (Eds.), *From subject to subjectivities: A handbook of interpretive and participatory methods* (pp. 183–199). New York: New York University Press.

Lykes, M. B. (2001b). Creative arts and photography in participatory action research in Guatemala. In P. Reason & H. Bradbury (Eds.), *Handbook of action research: Participative inquiry and practice* (pp. 363–371). Thousand Oaks, CA: Sage.

Maguire, P. (1987). *Doing participatory research: A feminist perspective.* Amherst: Center for International Education, School of Education, University of Massachusetts.

Maguire, P. (2001). Uneven ground: Feminisms and action research. In P. Reason & H. Bradbury (Eds.), *Handbook for action research: Participative inquiry and practice* (pp. 59–69). Thousand Oaks, CA: Sage.

Mitchell, C. (2004). Just who do we think we are? Memory work and self-study with beginning teachers. In R. Balfour, T. Buthelezi, & C. Mitchell (Eds.), *Teacher development at the centre of change* (pp. 45–54). Durban, South Africa: University of KwaZulu-Natal Press.

Mitchell, C. (2009). Geographies of danger: School toilets in sub-Saharan Africa. In O. Gershenson & B. Penner (Eds.), *Ladies and gents: Public toilets and gender* (pp. 62–74). Philadelphia, PA: Temple University Press.

Mitchell, C., & Kanyangara, P. (2006). *Violence against children and young people in and around schools in Rwanda: Through the eyes of children and young people.* Kigali, Rwanda: National Youth Council and UNICEF.

Mitchell, C., Walsh, S., & Moletsane, R. (2006). Speaking for ourselves: A case for visual arts-based and other participatory methodologies in working with young people to address sexual violence. In F. E. Leach & C. Mitchell (Eds.), *Combating gender violence in and around schools* (pp. 103–112). London, England: Trentham Books.

Mitchell, C., & Weber, S. (1999). *Reinventing ourselves as teachers: Beyond nostalgia.* London, England: Falmer Press. doi:10.4324/9780203454497.

Mitchell, C., & Weber, S. (2004). Visual arts-based approaches to self-study. In J. Loughran, M. L. Hamilton, V. K. LaBoskey, & T. L. Russell (Eds.), *International handbook of self-study of teaching and teacher education practices, Volume 1* (pp. 979–1038). Toronto, ON: Kluwer.

Mnisi, T., De Lange, N., & Mitchell, C. (in press). Learning to use visual data to 'save lives' in the age of AIDS. *Communitas.*

Moletsane, R., De Lange, N., Mitchell, C., Stuart, J., Buthelezi, T., & Taylor, M. (2007). Photo-voice as a tool for analysis and activism in response to HIV and AIDS stigmatisation in a rural KwaZulu-Natal school. *Journal of Child & Adolescent Mental Health, 19*(1): 19–28. doi:10.2989/17280580709486632.

Moletsane, R., Mitchell, C., Smith, A., & Chisholm, L. (2008). *Methodologies for mapping a southern African girlhood in the age of Aids.* Rotterdam, The Netherlands: Sense.

Park, E. G., Mitchell, C., & De Lange, N. (2007). Working with digital archives: Photovoice and meta-analysis in the context of HIV & AIDS. In N. de Lange, C. Mitchell, & J. Stuart (Eds.), *Putting people in the picture: Visual methodologies for social change* (pp. 163–172). Rotterdam, The Netherlands: Sense.

Park, E. G., Mitchell, C., & De Lange, N. (2008). Social uses of digitization within the context of HIV/AIDS: Metadata as engagement. *Online Information Review, 32*(6), 716–725. doi:10.1108/14684520810923890.

Pearce-Moses, R. (2005). *A glossary of archival and records terminology.* Chicago, IL: Society of American Archivists.

Rhodes, C. (2000). *Outsider art: Spontaneous alternatives.* London, England: Thames & Hudson.

Schratz, M., & Walker, R. (1995). *Research as social change: New opportunities for qualitative research.* New York, NY: Routledge.

Sekula, A. (2003). Reading an archive: Photography between labour and capital. In L. Wells (Ed.), *The photography reader* (pp. 443–452). New York, NY: Routledge.

Shilton K., & Srinivasan, R. (2008). Participatory appraisal and arrangement for multicultural archival collections. *Archivaria, 63,* 87–101. Retrieved from http://journals.sfu.ca/archivar/index.php/archivaria.

Sontag, S. (1966). *Against interpretation and other essays.* New York, NY: Farrar, Straus and Giroux.

Springgay, S., Irwin, R. L., & Kind, S. (2008) A/r/tographers and living inquiry. In J. G. Knowles & A. L. Cole (Eds.), *Handbook of the arts in qualitative research: Perspectives, methodologies, examples, and issues.* Thousand Oaks, CA: Sage.

Umurungi, J.P., Mitchell, C., Gervais, M., Ubalijoro, E., & Kabarenzi, V. (2008). Photo voice as a methodological tool to address HIV and AIDS and gender violence amongst girls on the street in Rwanda. *Journal of Psychology in Africa, 18*(3), 413–420.

Volovková, H. (1993). *I never saw another butterfly: Children's drawings and poems from Terezin Concentration Camp, 1942–1944* (2nd exp. ed.). New York, NY: Schocken Books.

Wang, C. C. (1999). Photovoice: A participatory action research strategy applied to women's health. *Journal of Women's Health, 8*(2), 185–192. doi:10.1089/jwh.1999.8.185.

Weber, S., & Mitchell, C. (1995). *'That's funny, you don't look like a teacher': Interrogating images and identity in popular culture.* London, England: Falmer Press. doi:10.4324/9780203453568.

Weber, S., & Mitchell, C. (1996). Drawing ourselves into teaching: Studying the images that shape and distort teacher education. *Teaching and Teacher Education, 12*(3), 303–313. doi:10.1016/0742-051X(95)00040-Q.

World Awareness Children's Museum. (2009). *About the World Awareness Children's Museum.* Retrieved from http://www.worldchildrensmuseum.org/Pages/about.html.

SECTION TWO

ILLUSTRATIONS FROM PRACTICE:
DRAWING FROM RESEARCH

DRAWING ON STRENGTHS:
IMAGES OF ECOLOGICAL CONTRIBUTIONS TO
MALE STREET YOUTH RESILIENCE

Macalane Malindi and Linda Theron

INTRODUCTION

Multitudes of youth worldwide leave their homes, permanently or temporarily, and take up street life because of harsh personal and contextual factors that are out of their control (Donald, Lazarus, & Lolwana, 2010). Youth who adopt street life lose opportunities to play, to be educated, and to experience the rest needed for their physical and mental development (Bartlett et al., as cited in Ataöv & Haider, 2006). These young people are labelled 'street youth'—an umbrella term that includes youth *of* the street (i.e., young people who have no family ties and whose primary home is the street), youth *on* the street (i.e., young people who spend time on the streets to make a living to supplement family income while maintaining family ties), and former youth of the street who have moved to welfare-run homes for street youth (Panter-Brick, 2002). Blanket use of the term 'street youth' is problematic because it suggests erroneously that these young people are a homogeneous group, it characterises street youth according to the public spaces that they use or occupy, it is riddled with derogation, and it bears negative emotional overtones (Evans, 2002). We use the term to refer to a heterogeneous group of young people who are traditionally classified as 'at-risk' and 'vulnerable' in popular literature.

Street youth are mostly categorised as at-risk and vulnerable since they are affected by manifold risks, including violence, abuse, and/or adverse socio-economic circumstances (Kelly, as cited in Eloff, Ebersöhn, & Viljoen, 2007) and deprivation of family-based upbringing (UNICEF, 2009). However, in spite of the aforementioned risks, some street youth have displayed remarkable resilience, which is frequently ignored by researchers and the larger community.

Their resilience, or ability to cope well with the compound challenges they face (Masten, 2001), often lies in their effective survival and coping strategies, which are habitually underplayed by researchers. Some of these strategies (like begging) are unconventional because young people should ideally receive parental care and support. In the light of this, begging, which could be seen as a sign of helplessness, typically hides resilience if taken at face value (Ungar, 2004). In spite of what begging might appear to suggest, these strategies assist street youth to cope adaptively. In essence, this suggests that street youth present a unique paradox of vulnerability, on the one hand, and resilience, on the other (Donald & Swart-

L. Theron et al. (eds.), Picturing Research: Drawing as Visual Methodology, 105–117.

Kruger, 1994; Panter-Brick, 2002). Although most researchers assume that street youth are vulnerable, others like ourselves (see, too, Donald & Swart-Kruger, 1994; Evans, 2002; Kombarakaran, 2004) have become intrigued with what feeds this resilience. Masten (2001) asserted that resilience is not such an uncommon phenomenon among individuals leading difficult lives and that resilience results from the effective functioning of basic human adaptational systems. What is lacking in the studies of street youth resilience to date is rich evidence that access of street youth to ordinary supportive resources encourages their resilience. Furthermore, few studies with street youth engage them as authoritative voices on their lived experiences or heed their interpretations of collected data (Ennew, 2003). Instead, most studies with street youth script the adult researcher as the authority and thus generate 'adultist assumptions' (Ennew, 2003).

In the light of this, then, the purpose of our study was to explore the resilience of street youth in the Eastern Free State in South Africa by means of a phenomenological study using symbolic drawings (see Guillemin, 2004) to generate such rich and youth-centred evidence. We believed that our findings would be significant to teachers, mental health practitioners, and service providers working with street youth, especially if our study afforded these adults opportunities to *see* and better understand that street youth need not be viewed only in terms of negative stereotypes and to *see* exactly what nurtured their resilience. We hoped this would spur adults on to enable street youth towards resilience.

WHY USE DRAWINGS AS METHODOLOGY?

There is renewed interest in the use of drawings in research since traditional methods often fail to elicit the socially silenced voices of vulnerable and marginalised youth (Driessnack, 2005). Because street youth are often illiterate or have low levels of literacy, quantitative pen-and-paper instruments present limited opportunities to generate such evidence. Our personal experience in working with street youth in the Eastern Free State and Gauteng suggested that one-on-one interviews were a limited possibility because the participants were often reluctant to open up and became easily saddened when they were talking about their lives. Furthermore, Ennew (2003) and Aptekar and Heinonen (2003) recommended the generation of projective or concrete data that present street youths' voices in undistorted ways.

For these reasons, we chose to use a visual methodology (drawings) to explore the resilience of street youth. Some previous experience of exploring drawings in other studies (Theron, 2008) led us to anticipate that drawings would enable participants to express the roots of their resilience in a non-threatening, creative way. We anticipated that the drawings would 'speak' for the participants and provide a prompt for a brief written explanation of what encouraged their 'doing well' despite the many challenges of street life.

In order for us to appreciate what the participants would reveal via their drawings, we needed to engage them as co-interpreters of their drawings, but we also needed to ground ourselves in what was already known about street youth resilience.

WHAT CONTRIBUTES TO STREET YOUTH RESILIENCE?

Before discussing what encourages resilience among street youth, it is worthwhile to briefly review what is understood by resilience. Although the exact meaning of the concept 'resilience' is much debated (Luthar, Cicchetti, & Becker, 2000), it is generally accepted that resilience connotes both a process and an outcome that is synonymous with a 'doing well' when life circumstances predict the opposite. This 'doing well' is often linked to socially and developmentally appropriate indicators, such as academic progress, peer acceptance, normative mental health, normative behaviour, and participation in age appropriate activities (Masten & Reed, 2005). Such 'doing well' is encouraged by young people navigating towards, and negotiating for, health-affirming resources (like education, material resources, and adult mentorship) in culturally appropriate ways. In addition to these efforts, the ecologies of these young people need to collaboratively reciprocate and make health-affirming resources accessible in culturally appropriate ways (Ungar, 2008). In other words, resilience is a bi-directional, ecosystemically embedded transaction (Lerner, 2006).

As already noted, not much research evidence is available on the process of street youths' navigation towards resilience. The handful of studies on resilient street youth suggest that resilient youth who frequent the streets rely on ordinary human adaptational systems to deal competently with adversity, albeit through precocious means (Ataöv & Haider, 2006). Street youth adapt and survive by stealing, begging, engaging in transactional sex, shining shoes, and selling goods (Beazley, 2002; Kruger & Richter, 2003). As mentioned previously, these behaviours may encapsulate a hidden resilience (Ungar, 2004).

Street youth resilience is also to be found in such commonplace resources as social networks (like group protection, peer support, and peer bonding), access to food and schooling (along with other health-promoting resources), higher levels of intelligence (often manifested as the ability to problem solve), and personal strengths (like agency and self-efficacy) (Donald & Swart-Kruger, 1994; Evans, 2002; Kombarakaran, 2004). Orme and Seipel's (2007) study on resilient street youth in Ghana reported that spirituality and hope also encourage resilience.

Once young people move onto the streets, they lose the much-needed social support that typifies microsystems such as the family and school. Nevertheless, street youths' survival is encouraged by street-based social networks. Some street youth rely on social services (Malindi, 2009), but more often, a young person who joins street life is absorbed into an existing group of street youth led by a streetwise leader. The newcomer is enveloped in street culture and socialised within this group towards survival (Vogel, 2001).

A recent South African study (Malindi, 2009) reinforces the finding that street youth resilience is rooted in intrapersonal and ecological resources. The individual resources include (among others) being able to identify with positive role models, a propensity towards optimism, flexibility, assertiveness, the capacity for self-regulation, and an internal locus of control. The ecological resources include (among others) varying experiences of social support and a sense of belonging; access to education, health care, and police services; cultural groundedness and religious belief.

Central to the studies reported above is a defiance of the traditionally deficit-based conception of street youth. Our present study sought to extend this in a way that would generate artefacts (i.e., drawings) that would shed light on the roots of street youth resilience.

METHOD

Our previous work with street youth enabled us to develop rapport with various non-governmental organisations (NGOs) that work with street youth in the Eastern Free State. Therefore, when we needed to recruit participants for our current study, we identified the shelter that was nearest to us and asked the resident welfare workers to collaborate in the recruitment of resilient street youth. From previous research collaborations with us, these welfare workers were familiar with the concept of resilience and so acted as gatekeepers who sampled purposefully and competently on our behalf (Terre Blanche, Durrheim, & Painter, 2006). Twenty resilient street youth were identified (see Table 8.1).

Table 8.1. Summary of participant demographics.

Participant	Age (at time of study)	Highest school grade completed	Sex	Duration on streets
1	14	4	M	7 months
2	17	5	M	14 months
3	10	4	M	6 months
4	11	4	M	5–8 months
5	18	5	M	19 months
6	13	5	M	13 months
7	16	5	M	7 months
8	14	6	M	9 months
9	13	3	M	8 months
10	16	6	M	17 months
11	10	2	M	4 months

12	16	5	M	10 months
13	16	6	M	14 months
14	15	6	M	11 months
15	18	6	M	18 months
16	12	5	M	15 months
17	16	9	M	3 months
18	15	6	M	13 months
19	16	6	M	13 months
20	9	2	M	3 months

The welfare workers introduced us to these participants, and this helped us to develop rapport with them. We regarded rapport and a trusting relationship as paramount since street youth are wary of adults if they doubt their intentions. All the participants were male, aged 10 to 18 years, and resident at a local shelter at the time of our study. Our sample reflected that in South Africa, as in other countries, the majority of street youth are boys since girls typically tolerate abuse at home longer than boys do, or become part of the sex industry, thereby being less visible on the streets (Kombarakaran, 2004).

All the participants attended school during the day, so we engaged them after school at the shelter. We explained the purpose of our study in careful detail and requested voluntary participation. We explained that there were no potential risks to them—their participation would be anonymous to protect their privacy—and that we were going to share our findings with other interested parties. We expressly requested permission to keep and reproduce their drawings. All the participants were keen to take part and all signed consent forms.

We prepared a drawing brief that we presented to the participants. The verbal and written brief was: "*Think about what helps you to cope well with your life. Draw something in the space below that will show or illustrate what helps you to cope well with your life. Remember, how well you draw is not important.*" According to Ennew (2003), earlier studies that used drawings to access young people's worlds failed to ask those youth to articulate what their artefacts represented, and this led to gross misinterpretations of the drawings. Therefore, we invited participants to do so: "*Explain what your symbol is saying about what helps you to cope well with your life. Write 3–4 sentences, or ask the researcher to write them for you.*" Because the participants spoke Sesotho and isiZulu, we code-switched in order to ensure that they fully understood the written brief. Those who were not proficient in English wrote their explanation in Sesotho. Some of the participants described their drawings verbally, and Macalane Malindi (co-author of this chapter) recorded this verbatim, before translating it.

The participants were excited to participate, and they bragged about how well they were going to draw. They took approximately 35 minutes to finish their drawings and descriptions. As a token of appreciation, we gave the participants a hamburger each when they had completed their drawings.

In order to make further meaning of the contents (drawn symbols and explanations), we engaged in individual inductive analysis and then held a rigorous consensus discussion (Creswell, 2009).

FINDINGS

An inductive analysis of the contents of the drawings and explanations yielded six themes that shed light on what contributed to our participants' resilience. In order of frequency, these themes were self-reliance, reliance on others, respect for school and education, safe spaces, adherence to religion, and recreation. We discuss the themes in this ascending order of frequency.

Self-Reliance

Three drawings depict the participants' reliance on themselves in order to cope with street life. All three drawings are of individuals, two of which show only a head (see Figure 8.1 for an example).

Figure 8.1. Produced by Participant 16.

The explanation for Figure 8.1 is as follows: "If someone beat me or hurt me … I think to beat him, but I use my mind: I didn't beat him …. And my mind help me to ask if I need something, and my mind help me to think good things." This illustrates Participant 16's ability to regulate his thoughts and make pro-social behavioural choices.

Likewise, the explanations of the other two drawings reflect this self-reliance. Participant 18 explained that his drawing related to his capacity to care for himself, and this encouraged him: "I can take care of myself; it makes me happy when I'm upset. It makes me to be proud of who I am; it helps me not to hide how I feel."

Participant 9 drew himself working on a car, which demonstrated (he said) his ingenuity in taking care of himself. He indicated that if he lacked clothes and food, he could find gainful work. That way, he could meet his needs in a pro-social way.

Reliance on Others

Three drawings depict reliance on others as a resource that encourages resilience. Significantly though, only one of these drawings includes a picture of another person providing support (in this instance, the support is advice from a male peer). The other two pictures depict resources that can be gained from unselfish others (such as transport, food, and clothing) and so imply reliance on others. In both these drawings, the participants emphasise that other people are resilience-promoting resources but suggest that such others could be anyone. For example, Participant 20 explained, "Someone could buy me shoes", and Participant 4 said, "If I am injured somebody can take me to hospital. Knowing that someone can help me makes me happy!"

Respect for School and Education

Three drawings fall into this category. Two depict well-dressed young men holding/reading books (see Figure 8.2).

Figure 8.2. Produced by Participant 11.

The participants' explanations of these drawings indicate an appreciation of access to school since this facilitates education and a future with concomitant social and financial standing. The third drawing shows a well-maintained school building and gardens. The explanation that Participant 12 provided was about how school encourages enabling life skills: "School helps me to gain knowledge. I learn about life. School opens my mind and I avoid crime. School teaches me how to live like other people who support themselves."

Safe Spaces

Three drawings suggest that resilience is nurtured when youth have access to safe spaces. All the drawings include houses and two also include soccer fields. One (see Figure 8.3) includes resources such as a garden, running water, and a toilet, along with nearby recreation facilities.

In all three explanations, the youth refer to the security of having access to a safe space (like a shelter). One participant (Participant 8) wrote, "I have a place to sleep and I feel safe", and another (Participant 5) wrote, "Having a place to sleep makes me feel safe. I have food and receive care." Participant 5 also suggested that attending school was part of this safe space and that caregivers had negotiated this for him.

Figure 8.3. Produced by Participant 6.

Adherence to Religion

Four drawings depict religion as a resource that encourages resilience. The contents of the drawings are quite diverse, including a church building, a bible, God, and the hand of God. In their explanations, two participants indicate that when they face hardships they pray. For example, Participant 1 explained that his drawing meant "the hand of God, He blesses me when I am in hardships and I pray". There was a sense that God was a benevolent father who would provide for their needs.

The remaining two participants emphasised that church provided opportunities to learn pro-social values and behaviours. For example, Participant 7 wrote, "I also learn that I should not hit other youth." The other (Participant 17) explained:

> The church makes me happy to be a South African, to live in this free country. And this church I love it because it helps me a lot to focus to [on] good life things like school. I cope well after Sundays … proudly to be a Christian of Methodist, proudly to be South African.

Recreation

Six of the drawings focus on soccer or include soccer as part of what helps these youth to 'do well' despite the multiple difficulties of their lives. All six drawings include soccer paraphernalia, such as soccer balls or fields, or well-kitted soccer players (see Figure 8.4).

Figure 8.4. Produced by Participant 10.

The explanations are illuminating: "Football brings back my happiness" (Participant 8); "If anyone upsets me I go out to play football, because while I am playing no one can upset me. I can continue being happy." (Participant 15); and "When I am facing difficult times, I like playing football to make myself forget" (Participant 19). In short, with the exception of two participants who linked soccer to future goals and opportunities to dream (wanting to learn soccer skill or wanting to become a famous player), the participants viewed soccer as an opportunity to do what young people do: play.

DISCUSSION

Our findings provide a rich answer to what enables male street youth to do well despite the many challenges of street life. In summary, the drawings by our participants show that the resilience of these street youth is anchored in the ordinary structures of regular everyday life, as posited by Masten (2001) 10 years ago. On one level, our participants' ability to bounce back is apparently rooted in self-reliance, other-reliance, access to safe spaces and to schools, religion, and opportunities to play (typically soccer). Implicit in these resources are additional resilience-promoting resources, such as the capacity for hope ("If I am injured somebody can take me to hospital."), belief in benevolent strangers ("Knowing that someone can help me makes me happy!"), and positive collective identity ("proudly to be South African") (Malindi, 2009; see also Ungar et al., 2007) All of these are 'ordinary magic' (Masten, 2001, p. 227).

Most of these resources have been noted in previous studies with different cohorts of resilient youth. For example, self-reliance and the capacity to demonstrate self-help skills are reported to have promoted resilience in populations of high-risk children from marginalised families (Werner, 1995). Access to education, reliance on others, and adherence to religious beliefs were shown to promote resilience among at-risk children and youth as far back as the early 1990s (Masten, Best, & Garmezy, 1990). Opportunities for recreation have also been associated with resilience (Masten & Powell, 2003). All these, except for opportunities for recreation, have been reported in association with resilient street youth (Donald & Swart-Kruger, 1994; Kombarakaran, 2004; Malindi, 2009; Orme & Seipel, 2007).

A review of our emerging findings in terms of themes that were not touched on by the participants is hugely significant. Resilience literature and studies on resilient youth emphasise the enabling role of peers and supportive adults, such as social workers (Kombarakaran, 2004; Masten, 2001). Many resilience studies suggest that teachers are key players in the process of youth resilience (Dass-Brailsford, 2005). Yet, these themes were not evident in the drawings that our participants generated. It is possible that further studies with larger numbers of resilient street youth might introduce these traditionally reported resources. It is, however, also possible that when youth are engaged directly in reporting the sources of their resilience, they focus on what is most meaningful to them. In the instance of our study, a grouping of the six emergent themes suggests street youths' resilience lies in three key resources: opportunities to play like a young person, and dream; opportunities to learn (be it increased knowledge, spiritual or citizenship values); and opportunities to have basic needs (a safe place to sleep, somebody who cares enough to provide material resources like shoes, access to medical care) met safely.

The studies detailing what contributes to the resilience of street youth to date have not reported the above resources so unequivocally. We believe this relates to our visual method of data collection: By inviting youth to draw and explain their artefacts (Guillemin, 2004), we engaged them on a level that allowed them to show us unmistakably what nurtures their resilience. Although most of the themes that emerged matched previous findings from earlier street youth resilience studies, the details do not. The evidence relating to opportunities to play soccer, to make up their own minds, or to have a safe place to sleep is unambiguous.

In this regard, the drawings point to the existence of the participants' individual and ecological strengths and ways of coping that are mostly underestimated in the literature on street youth and not as clearly defined in the literature on resilience. The drawings also indicate that the roots of street youth resilience are in the restoration of ordinary developmental processes such as ordinary opportunities to be young people again who can associate with others, play as the young should, dream, recreate, learn spiritual values, gain valuable knowledge through attending school, and meet their basic needs for food, shelter, and health-care. These findings open our eyes to the fact that interventions should attempt to afford street youth opportunities to reclaim their childhoods (Le Roux, 2001).

We acknowledge the main limitation of our study: It involved only boys. This suggests that our emerging findings are gendered and raises questions about what findings would have emerged had girls been represented in the sample. Our study also included boys of various ages: A re-analysis of the data from a developmental perspective might engender further insight into what promotes the resilience of male street youth.

Another limitation related to language. The boys spoke IsiZulu and Sesotho, the major language groups in the Eastern Free State, so it is possible that their responses were nuanced by their Sotho and Zulu cultures (Ungar, 2008).

Furthermore, all our participants were residents in a local shelter. Future studies need to include street youth from other ethnic groups who are not accessing social services in order to explore how street youth resilience might be informed by services and culture.

CONCLUSION

Despite the limitations of our cohort as noted above, our study illustrates the value of engaging vulnerable young people (like street youth) in participatory studies that motivate active data generation and reflection on generated artefacts (Guillemin, 2004). In this study, our participatory approach encouraged non-'adultist' (Ennew, 2003) data that provided unequivocal, detailed evidence of what it is that encouraged the resilience of our male street youth participants. Their drawings introduced understandings (albeit gendered) of resilience (like the opportunity to play soccer) that are new to the body of knowledge on street youth resilience. We doubt that traditional quantitative or interview-based qualitative methods would have generated this deep insight.

Perhaps, the greatest value of our study lies in the explicit findings that reinforced the belief that street youth, like other youth living at home with their parents, need opportunities to be young people, to play, to be protected, and to learn. In fact, the resilience of our participants could be aligned with the fundamental rights of young people. This study's methodology gave voice to participants who are typically a marginalised, disenfranchised, and socially silent group of youth (Driessnack, 2005).

That drawings bridged traditional barriers to communication with street youth and offered youth opportunities to project *their* understanding of what contributed to their resilience is patent. These artefacts introduce convincing evidence that street youth resilience is not only possible but probably facilitated by everyday resources or 'ordinary magic' (Masten, 2001, p. 227). These youth-generated messages leave us as adults (teachers, service providers, policy makers, and others) with an irrefutable exhortation to champion street youth resilience by making everyday resources available and accessible.

REFERENCES

Aptekar, L., & Heinonen, P. (2003). Methodological implications of contextual diversity in research on street children. *Children, Youth and Environments, 13*(1). Retrieved from http://www.colorado.edu/journals/cye.

Ataöv, A., & Haider, J. (2006). From participation to empowerment: Critical reflections on a participatory action research project with street children in Turkey. *Children, Youth and Environments, 16*(2), 127–152. Retrieved from http://www.colorado.edu/journals/cye.

Beazley, H. (2002). 'Vagrants wearing make-up': Negotiating spaces on the streets of Yogyakarta, Indonesia. *Urban Studies, 39*(9), 1665–1683. doi:10.1080/00420980220151718.

Creswell, J. W. (2009). *Research design: Qualitative, quantitative, and mixed methods approaches* (3rd ed.). Thousand Oaks, CA: Sage.

Dass-Brailsford, P. (2005). Exploring resiliency: Academic achievement among disadvantaged black youth in South Africa. *South African Journal of Psychology, 35*(3), 574–591.

Donald, D. R., Lazarus, S., & Lolwana, P. (2010). *Educational psychology in social context: Ecosystemic application in Southern Africa* (4th ed.). Cape Town: Oxford University Press Southern Africa.

Donald, D., & Swart-Kruger, J. (1994). The South African street child: Developmental implications. *South African Journal of Psychology, 24*(4), 169–174.

Driessnack, M. (2005). Children's drawings as facilitators of communication: A meta-analysis. *Journal of Pediatric Nursing, 20*(6), 415–423. doi:10.1016/j.pedn.2005.03.011.

Eloff, I., Ebersöhn, L., & Viljoen, J. (2007). Reconceptualising vulnerable children by acknowledging their assets. *African Journal of AIDS Research, 6*(1), 79–86. doi:10.2989/16085900709490401.

Ennew, J. (2003). Difficult circumstances: Some reflections on "street children" in Africa. *Children, Youth and Environments, 13*(1). Retrieved from http://www.colorado.edu/journals/cye.

Evans, R. (2002). Poverty, HIV, and barriers to education: Street children's experiences in Tanzania. *Gender & Development, 10*(3), 51–62. doi:10.1080/13552070215916.

Guillemin, M. (2004). Understanding illness: Using drawings as research method. *Qualitative Health Research, 14*(2), 272–289. doi:10.1177/1049732303260445.

Kombarakaran, F. A. (2004). Street children of Bombay: Their stresses and strategies of coping. *Children and Youth Services Review, 26*(9), 853–871. doi:10.1016/j.childyouth.2004.02.025.

Kruger, J. M., & Richter, L. M. (2003). South African street children at risk for AIDS? *Children, Youth and Environments, 13*(1). Retrieved from http://www.colorado.edu/journals/cye.

Lerner, R. M. (2006). Resilience as an attribute of the developmental system: Comments on the papers of Professors Masten and Wachs. *Annals of the New York Academy of Sciences, 1094*, 40–51. doi:10.1196/annals.1376.005.

Le Roux, C. (2001). A historical-educational perspective of urbanisation and its contribution to the street child phenomenon in South Africa. *Educare, 30*(1&2), 94–114. Retrieved from http://www.unisa.ac.za/contents/publications/educ3012.pdf.

Luthar, S. S., Cicchetti, D., & Becker, B. (2000). The construct of resilience: A critical evaluation and guidelines for future work. *Child Development, 71*(3), 543–562. doi:10.1111/1467-8624.00164.

Malindi, M. J. (2009). *The antecedents of resilience among street children* (Unpublished doctoral thesis). North-West University, Vaal Triangle Campus, Vanderbijlpark, South Africa.

Masten, A. (2001). Ordinary magic: Resilience processes in development. *American Psychologist, 56*(3), 227–238. doi:10.1037/0003-066X.56.3.227.

Masten, A. S., Best, K. M., & Garmezy, N. (1990). Resilience and development: Contributions from the study of children who overcome adversity. *Development and Psychopathology, 2*(4), 425–444. doi:10.1017/S0954579400005812.

Masten, A. S., & Powell, J. L. (2003). A resilience framework for research, policy, and practice. In S. S. Luthar (Ed.), *Resilience and vulnerability: Adaptation in the context of childhood adversities* (pp. 1–25). New York, NY: Cambridge University Press.

Masten, A. S., & Reed, M. J. (2005). Resilience in development. In C. R. Snyder & S. J. Lopez (Eds.), *Handbook of positive psychology* (pp. 74–88). New York, NY: Oxford University Press.

Orme, J., & Seipel, M. M. O. (2007). Survival strategies of street children in Ghana: A qualitative study. *International Social Work, 50*(4), 489–499. doi:10.1177/0020872807077909.

Panter-Brick, C. (2002). Street children, human rights, and public health: A critique and future directions. *Annual Review of Anthropology, 31*, 147–171. doi:10.1146/annurev.anthro.31.040402.085359.

Terre Blanche, M., Durrheim, K., & Painter, D. (Eds.). (2006). *Research in practice: Applied methods for the social sciences* (2nd rev. ed.). Cape Town, South Africa: University of Cape Town Press.

Theron, L. C. (2009). "I have undergone some metamorphosis!" The impact of REDs on South African educators affected by HIV/AIDS pandemic. *Journal of Psychology in Africa, 18*(1), 31–42.

Ungar, M. (2004). *Nurturing hidden resilience in troubled youth.* Toronto, ON: University of Toronto Press.

Ungar, M. (2008). Resilience across cultures. *British Journal of Social Work, 38*(2), 218–235. doi:10.1093/bjsw/bcl343.

Ungar, M., Brown, M., Liebenberg, L., Othman, R., Kwong, W. M., Armstrong, M., & Gilgun, J. (2007). Unique pathways to resilience across cultures. *Adolescence, 42*(166), 287–310.

UNICEF. (2009). *Child poverty and disparities in Ghana.* Retrieved from http://www.unicef.org/socialpolicy/index_43137.html.

Vogel, H. M. (2001). *Coping skills for street children.* Pretoria: University of South Africa Press.

Werner, E. E. (1995). Resilience in development. *Current Directions in Psychological Science, 4*(3), 81–84. doi:10.1111/1467-8721.ep10772327.

TEACHER SEXUALITY DEPICTED: EXPLORING WOMEN TEACHERS' POSITIONING WITHIN SEXUALITY EDUCATION CLASSROOMS THROUGH DRAWINGS

Mathabo Khau

INTRODUCTION

Lesotho has the third highest HIV prevalence in the world with 260,000 out of 2,000,000 people, most of them still in school, living with HIV and AIDS. Of these people, 56% are women (UNAIDS, 2008). Education has been described as a 'vaccine' against HIV and AIDS (Coombe, 2003) because of relatively lower rates of HIV infection among people with higher levels of educational participation. This places teachers at the forefront of the pandemic as prevention agents expected to teach about sexualities and safer sex practices and therefore equip learners with the necessary knowledge to make informed decisions regarding their sexual lives. But teachers are also gendered and sexual beings. So how does this enable or interfere with teachers' effectiveness in handling sexuality and HIV and AIDS in education?

This chapter draws attention to how teachers' personal identities play a key role in how they tackle sexuality and HIV and AIDS in the classroom and highlights the impossibilities and contradictions embedded in female teacherhood. It presents data on how Basotho women teachers see themselves as women and the implications of such positioning on their experiences of teaching sexuality education in rural schools. Teachers' drawings and stories are used as case material for thinking about the role of teachers' gendered and sexual identities within the sexuality education classroom.

WHO AM I?

Doing research on issues of sexuality in the rural villages of Lesotho forced me to acknowledge the baggage that I brought into the field in terms of my biases. I am a divorced woman and a science teacher interested in sexuality education in rural schools in the age of HIV and AIDS—an abominable combination for rural villagers. I was aware that my education and marital status positioned me as deviant in relation to the constructions of proper womanhood within the villages, where it is still believed that a woman does not need an education but a good husband. The villagers believed that in talking about sex I would be corrupting the participants into loose morals. The husbands thought I would incite their women to

L. Theron et al. (eds.), Picturing Research: Drawing as Visual Methodology, 119–131.
© 2011 *Sense Publishers. All rights reserved.*

divorce, and the women thought I was going to take off with their husbands. Thus, my choice of methodology and approach had to take into account all these factors so that I could gain the trust of the participants and all stakeholders.

METHODOLOGY

Guided by a feminist approach to research, the data production involved three phases: the preparation phase, the data production phase, and the debriefing phase. The preparation phase was intended to create better rapport between myself and the participants. The data production phase revolved around a 'starting with ourselves' framing. I placed myself at the centre of the inquiry as a participant-researcher, and I contributed my experiences as I employed the various methods. The debriefing phase served to address any issues that arose from partaking in the study.

Data was produced with eight purposively selected Basotho women science teachers from two rural secondary schools. The women had to be science teachers who had been involved in the teaching of sexuality education through the Population and Family Life Education (POP/FLE) framework and who are currently involved with teaching sexuality education in the life skills education curriculum. Drawings were used to explore how the women teachers see themselves as women and how their positioning is implicated in their teaching of sexuality education. The following prompt was used:

In the space provided, draw a picture that represents your woman self. There are no good or bad drawings just draw. Below each drawing explain why you have chosen this representation and what it means to you.

Figure 9.1. Drawing prompt.

Drawing is a powerful technique for eliciting attitudes and beliefs and generating discussion around an issue of interest (Stuart, 2006). Martin (1998) also argued that drawings can offer an entry point and provide insight into the experiences and perceptions of the people producing the drawings. Additionally, Schratz and Walker (1995) observed:

> Where photographs can take us behind the scenes and allow us to share witness with the researcher, drawings can take us inside the mind of the subject ... the ways in which people draw things, their relative size and placement of objects for example can at least give us a starting point from which to ask questions. (p. 77)

My choice to use drawing as the tool for data production was based on the sensitivity of the topic of sexuality, especially within a context in which talk about sex is highly taboo. Basotho communities still regard women as children under customary law (Guma, 2001). Thus, as children, women are expected to be sexually innocent. This implies that sex talk by women is against social norms. I was aware that the women teachers would not talk freely to me about issues related to their sexuality and their teaching because they would be policing themselves to abide by socially constructed norms of good womanhood. Therefore, I used the drawings to allow me to get "inside the minds" (Schratz & Walker, 1995, p. 77) of the women teachers in order to explore how they see themselves as women. The women used their drawings as reflection tools in constructing narratives of their woman selves. All narratives were written in English by the women teachers and have been used verbatim as data for this chapter. Even though the drawing prompt did not specify sexual identity, the woman self has been depicted in sexual terms. This implies that for these teachers, their womanhood revolves around their sexuality.

The drawing sessions were followed by focus group discussions in which the women explained their choices of drawings and the meanings they made of them. Before the discussions, each group was informed of issues of confidentiality and requested to keep the contents of our discussions within the group. Group members were also informed that only those drawings and discussion issues they felt free to share would be used in the study. I started the discussion by sharing my own drawings and explanations in order to ease the participants' uncertainties.

The narratives presented in this chapter represent women teachers' analysis of drawings of their women selves. My discussion of these narratives presents a second level of analysis. Thematic analysis was used to identify and categorise common threads of meaning in the stories. According to Munro (1998), "to be a woman is to lack authority, knowledge and power. To be a teacher is to have authority, knowledge and power" (p. 1). In line with Munro's argument, I discuss how the women teachers make meaning of their gendered and sexual identities and how this creates (im)possibilities for effective facilitation of sexuality education.

FINDINGS

The drawings are dominated by animal metaphors, with inanimate objects often pictured, as well. The women teachers had no particular reason for why they portrayed themselves as animals. They chose the particular animals because of certain traits of these animals that reflected their own lives. They did not consider the chosen animals in totality in relation to their characteristics. Thus, the reading of the animal metaphors should be at the level at which the participants have placed them. Any deeper relationship of the animals to the selves they chose to depict—for example, why is it that the women have not specified the sex of the animals they have chosen except for the hen—would warrant another study.

As for the inanimate objects, the women teachers argued that they had not seriously thought of the lifeless, unresponsive, or inert nature of the objects they had chosen. However, these characteristics were clearly reflected in the women's narratives of why they chose the particular depictions. The women chose the inanimate objects only for their usefulness and importance in everyday life. This means that these portraits and their explanations are open to several readings depending on which lens one uses: My reading of them is not the only possible one.

Portraits of the Woman Self

In this section, I present some of the ways in which the women teachers see themselves as women.[1] For purposes of this chapter and in the interest of brevity, I discuss only five randomly selected drawings out of the eight produced. The drawings and narratives bring to light the dominant discourses in relation to womanhood and femininity and the regulation of female sexuality.

The chamber pot.

> My woman self is a chamber pot (*thuana*).[ii] A chamber pot is a container that people have in the bedroom and is used for urinating in at night. In the village, a chamber pot is kept under the bed, out of sight of visitors. In the morning, people try as hard as they can to make sure that they empty the chamber pot without being seen. Even when carrying it outside one has to hide it. It is a shameful thing to be seen, despite its important use.

Figure 9.2. Woman self-portrait.

> I see myself as a chamber pot because I think that my husband only thinks of me when he wants sex. I have no say even in the sex itself. He jumps on and then he jumps off and he is through, while I am left wondering what happened. I am just like the chamber pot where he just deposits his sperms and goes off. During the day I have no use to him. *Ke mosali, ke sala hae* (I am a woman, I should stay at home). I am only good for the bedroom. I am expected to be there for him if and when he wants me and I should never query his decisions in anything in the household.

The hen.

My woman self is a hen. I have chosen a hen because I have been watching my chickens daily and seeing the life of a hen. The duty of the hen is to produce eggs and chicks. The cock just comes by, jumps on the hen and rushes off after the next hen and can even have sex with the other hen in the presence of the previous one. I think I always hear my hens complaining that they did not have enough, I think they do try to complain by the noise they make when the cock jumps off, but the cock never listens. It is too busy chasing after the next conquest.

Figure 9.3. Woman self-portrait.

I am also expected to understand that my husband has needs which have to be satisfied, so I am not expected to complain about my husband's infidelity. When I am heavy with child or breast-feeding, my mother-in-law and my own mother just tell me that I should know that my husband is at another woman's house because he has needs. How about mine? Would they be happy to see another man in my house? Just like the cock, he can chase other hens but does not want to see other cocks after his hen. Just as I said about my own chickens, the hens do complain but they are never heard. It is amazing that when a cock has sex with several hens per day people say it is a good cock; it is doing its job well. The same thing applies with Basotho men. If they have sex with many women then they are real men. A hen is never commented on having lots of sex with many cocks.

The blanket.

As a woman I see myself as a blanket. A blanket is a possession that one can do whatever they please with. Because you pay for it, you can do anything you want with it. You can sleep on it, walk on it, sleep under it, wipe your feet on it, or even use it as a bed for your dogs. The duty of the blanket is to keep the owner warm and happy, protecting him from the coldness of the world outside. I am a blanket for my husband. He beats me when he wants, he cares for me when he wants and sometimes he wants to be seen with me in public when he is happy. Just like with the blanket, my husband has several women in this village that I know of but I cannot complain to anyone. Who would listen to a jealous wife?

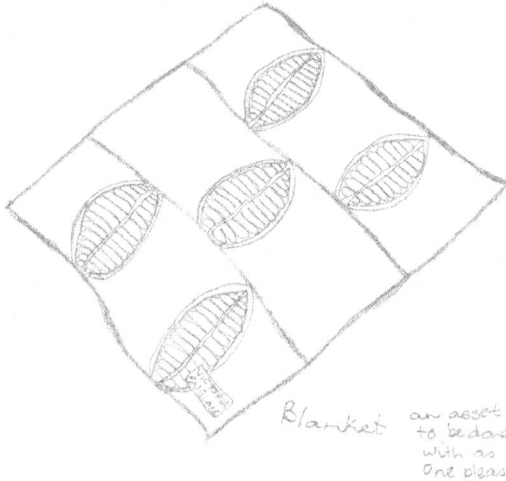

Figure 9.4. Woman self-portrait.

When he is not with one of his other women then he comes to me for sex. We do it if and when he wants and he never uses any protection because he has "bought" me by paying *lobola*,[iii] just like a blanket is bought. I am lucky that I have two sons; otherwise I am not sure what would have happened to me. Because of my sons, my in-laws value me as their mother but not as another human being. My mother told me that "*Mosali o ngalla mots'eo*" ("a woman does not run away from her marital problems"). Just like the blanket I think I will be in this marriage until I am worn out and of no use to anybody, then they will throw me out.

The fruit tree.

As a woman I see myself as a fruit tree. A fruit tree is expected to produce fruits for the family to enjoy at the right season. In the village we do not care much for the fruit trees until it is time for us to get some fruits from them. This is how I see myself as a woman. In my family I am expected to produce as many children as "God has given me" to repay the *lobola* that was paid when I got married. Without my children I am nothing. I cannot be called a woman, a real woman. I am lucky that my first child was a boy otherwise I would have been sent back home. Despite the fact that I have two children already, my in-laws keep telling me that I need to have more children. They argue that at least four children will have repaid their cows. They say that culturally a woman should have as many children as possible to show that she is a real woman. They put a lot of pressure on my husband for more children. I may have more children but there are other needs in life that one has to consider before filling a house with children.

Figure 9.5. Woman self-portrait.

The donkey.

A donkey is one of the most overworked animals in the world. In the rural areas it does all sorts of work without even being taken care of. You find that the farmer takes good care of his horse and brushes it and feeds it properly and builds a stable for it. Even if he has a donkey too, you will find the donkey sleeping out in the cold but in the morning the donkey will be out going to collect food for the horse and doing all the hard work. I see my woman self as a donkey because as a woman I am expected to do all the hard work in the family. I am overworked and under-appreciated. I am taken for granted by my husband, my in-laws, and even my own children. I do everything for them even when I am sick. When they are sick I take care of them but no one takes care of me even if I am sick. Even when I am lying in bed ill, they still ask me "What are we eating today?" I am everything for them, but unfortunately *there is no one for me.* You should see a donkey from the mill. It will be having big bags of maize and sorghum flour and the shepherds would also be riding on it. The poor thing just goes on with its heavy load while no one cares. The passers-by cannot even ask why the donkey is over-loaded. They take it for granted that a donkey can do it all.

Figure 9.6. Woman self-portrait.

What Do the Portraits Mean?

These drawings present powerful metaphors of women teachers' positioning as women within rural communities. The narratives for the drawings provide the meanings that the women make of their positioning and hence are useful texts for understanding the women's lives. They highlight the patriarchal gender-order characteristic of Basotho communities. These Basotho women teachers are expected to perform certain scripts of proper womanhood in order for them to be accepted as respectable citizens within the rural community. Although the stories explaining the drawings show that the women are aware of the oppressive conditions of their womanhood, they seem to have taken these circumstances as their lot in life (see hooks, 1981). This is reflected in their complicity in their subordination (see Arndt, 2002). To highlight this, I will discuss the portraits within the following themes: 'Women as Mothers' and 'Passive Female Sexuality'.

Women as mothers. The portrayals of the woman self show that good womanhood centres on being a mother and nurturing family members. The explanations of the drawings highlight how Basotho womanhood is constructed in relation to bearing children, especially boys. Basotho people place great value on women's fertility and ability to bear male children (see Ashton, 1967; Setiloane, 1976). The woman's body is thus objectified as a conduit for the passage of the child into the clan. Krais (1993) added to this argument: "Women are seen simply as receptacles for the male seed, passive vessels, a kind of safe place where the product of male potency may rest for a while and unfold its human potential" (p. 163).

Arndt (2002) has also observed that "women's identity and the justification of their existence is [sic] rooted in their motherhood" (p. 126). These women teachers consequently see their worth as women as being based on their ability to provide heirs for their husbands and keep the family name going.

The women teachers argue that they are also subject to the double burden of family and profession. Arndt (2002) argued that irrespective of educational and professional accomplishments, women get "reduced to their role as wives and mothers and [are] positioned as subordinate to men" (p. 29). Thus, despite professional employment, women are still expected to be nurturers within the family. Because the nurturing role is performed within the private sphere of the home, it is not seen as work (Nussbaum, 2002). Nussbaum has argued that women's work as nurturers and caregivers has been taken for granted worldwide. She argued that women often have taxing professional employment alongside full responsibility for housework and childcare, leaving them limited time for play and personal development.

Bourdieu (1991), however, posited that people always act out of self-interest under all circumstances. He suggested that disinterested actions do not exist. All activities are informed by the notion of self-interest to some extent, and are embedded in, and governed by, the rules of the specific field in which the activity takes place, as well as the agent's place within that field. Any action, Bourdieu suggested, is conceivable only in self-denial. These Basotho women teachers, by implication, conform to societal norms of motherhood and nurturing through self-denial and in accordance with their self-interest. Conformity provides them with safety as accepted players in the field of motherhood and womanhood. Although this situation may seem to position women as powerless, Foucault (1978) argued that there is nothing wrong in exercising power over others "in a sort of strategic game, where things can be reversed" (p. 129). He observed that power cannot be "acquired, seized or shared, something that one holds on to or allows to slip away; power is exercised from innumerable points" (p. 94). Individuals are positioned as powerful or powerless by different discourses. Thus, through discourse, individuals can be subjected to power or can exercise power over others. Although these women teachers occupy disadvantaged positions in relation to men, they are never completely powerless.

The fluidity of power and gender relations is evidence that the borders between femininity and masculinity are permeable and fragile, allowing for slip-ups and the performance of alternative scripts. This implies that even though the women teachers in this study are subjected to particular constructions of femininity, there are possibilities for shattering the fragile border between femininity and masculinity. Hence, there are possibilities for resistance and the performance of alternative scripts. If exercising power over others is a strategic game and things can be reversed, and if there are possibilities for these women teachers to perform their womanhood differently, then why do these Basotho women teachers choose to perform the normative scripts of womanhood and femininity?

Passive female sexuality. The women teachers' metaphors present female sexuality as good only in relation to heterosexual relationships and procreation. Otherwise, female sexuality is something that should be policed and kept under control because it disrupts the moral and social order of society (Kimmel, 2004). However, there are subtle hints of the women's desire for sexual fulfilment and their need to make sexual advances. The narrative of the hen provides this example: "When I am heavy with child or breast-feeding, my mother-in-law and my own mother just tell me that I should know that my husband is at another woman's house because he has needs. How about mine?" And the narrative of the chamber pot provides the following statement: "I have no say even in the sex itself. He jumps on and then he jumps off and he is through, while I am left wondering what happened."

These questions show that these women also need sexual fulfilment and hence question the kind of sexual lives they lead with their husbands. In accordance, I argue that Basotho female sexuality is not completely passive but has some agency, which the women as actors in the field of sexual relationships strategically use or ignore in accordance with their interests. Basotho girls and women are raised to believe that to be sexually active is to transgress the rules of femininity. Kimmel (2004) observed that "men will always try to escalate sexual encounters to prove their manhood, and that women—or rather, "ladies"—either do not have strong sexual feelings, or that those they do must be constantly controlled lest they fall into disrepute" (p. 240). These women actively choose to suppress their sexual needs in favour of being labelled as good women. Despite being teachers and having all the power that goes with the field of teacherhood, the women teachers are regarded only as 'women' in their interactions with their families and the community. Their womanhood is used to reduce the power they are afforded by being teachers (see Arndt, 2002). This is exemplified in the narratives of the hen and the blanket in which the women are expected to accept without question that their husbands have sexual needs that must be fulfilled by other women. This expectation is contradictory to teacherhood, which centres on questioning and critiquing life events.

One insightful comment by the women teachers was that "we are women before we are teachers". The implication of this comment is that despite the prestige afforded them by their qualifications and teaching positions, the most valued self for them is the woman self. The value placed on womanhood and motherhood in their communities is reflected in the value the women teachers themselves place on these identities. They are women and they are also mothers. As discussed earlier, motherhood is associated with purity and virtue (Acholonu, 1995; Arndt, 2002; Emecheta, 1979). Mothers are expected to protect children from harm. Thus, these women teachers are expected to protect their students from the supposed corruption of sexual knowledge. One can therefore assume that the way these Basotho women teachers approach the teaching of sexuality education in their rural classrooms is largely dictated by the womanhood scripts that they are performing. The implication is that their effectiveness in facilitating sexuality education is compromised because good women are supposedly sexually innocent and pure and always protect their children from any form of corruption, including sexual knowledge. Although Paechter (1998) argued that knowledge is power, the discourse of childhood sexual innocence that is applied to these women teachers as well as their students creates challenges for effective sexuality education.

As discussed earlier in this chapter, whatever people choose to do they do because they have some interest in the decision or something to gain from the action. These women teachers choose to privilege their performance of proper womanhood because it serves their self-interest. I argue that submitting to the normative scripts in the manner that these women teachers do is a survival strategy of avoiding conflict and ensuring their acceptance within the community. As educated women, they are expected to perform differently than other rural women and to challenge the status quo, but this is not in their interest, and they actively choose instead to conform to the societal norms of womanhood and motherhood. Conforming to the dictates of society does not reflect weakness but can be read as strength. By submitting to the scripts of proper womanhood, these women teachers avoid the discrimination and violence that they could otherwise be subjected to within the rural patriarchal villages. They are not hopeless victims of circumstance and actively choose what to do in relation to what can best suit their interests. In this manner, they secure their share in the patriarchal dividend.

SO WHAT?

The contestation between good womanhood and teacherhood still remains a challenge for the effective facilitation of sexuality education by women teachers in rural villages. There is a need to find common ground between womanhood and teacherhood such that women teachers do not have to choose between the two identities in performing their professional duties. A teacher is expected to mould students in such a way that they can fit into their positions in the adult world, and thus, by implication, a sexuality education teacher is also expected to prepare students to fit into socially acceptable sexuality scripts. However, the era of HIV and AIDS requires a sexuality education that embraces all sexual identities, irrespective of their acceptability in society, in order to understand how they are linked to HIV infection. There is a need for sexually inclusive sexuality education classrooms that are norm-critical and sex-positive. In this way, children will be taught about HIV prevention through addressing sexualities positively and highlighting the pleasures inherent in healthy sexuality.

WHAT DIFFERENCE DO DRAWINGS MAKE?

In simple drawings, the women were able to bring up their perceptions, emotions, and understandings of their lived realities as women teachers in rural schools, thus providing very rich information of their positioning as women. The intensity of the discussions in relation to the drawings was evidence of the women's emotional engagement in the study. I became aware that, through the drawings, I had created a platform for the women teachers to come face-to-face with their being in a manner they had never before been able to do. They were able to interrogate and challenge their positioning and experiences as women teachers even though they still had to conform to societal norms in order to avoid violence. The drawings assisted the women teachers to think about their womanhood and develop narratives of their lived experiences. I believe that drawings used in this way to address sensitive and emotional issues can provide a tool for exploring people's lived realities in a non-intrusive manner.

NOTES

[i] These are verbatim accounts.

[ii] *Thuana* is a derogatory word used for chamber pot. A more welcome word for chamber pot is *pitsana* (a small pot).

[iii] This refers to the bride price paid to the woman's family as a token of appreciation by the man's family.

REFERENCES

Acholonu, C. O. (1995). *Motherism: The Afro-centric alternative to feminism. Women in Environmental Development Series, Volume 3.* Owerri, Nigeria: Afa.

Arndt, S. (2002). *The dynamics of African feminism: Defining and classifying African-feminist literatures.* Trenton, NJ: Africa World Press.

Ashton, H. (1967). *The Basuto: A social study of traditional and modern Lesotho* (2nd ed.). London, England: Oxford University Press.

Bourdieu, P. (1991). *Language and symbolic power* (G. Raymond & M. Adamson, Trans.). Cambridge, MA: Harvard University Press. (Original work published 1982).

Coombe, C. (2003). HIV/AIDS and education: Managing for disaster in the SADC region. In K. Lewin, M. Samuel, & Y. Sayed (Eds.), *Changing patterns of teacher education in South Africa: Policy, practice and prospects* (pp. 84–90). Cape Town, South Africa: Heinemann.

Emecheta, B. (1979). *The joys of motherhood.* London, England: Alison and Busby.

Foucault, M. (1978). *The history of sexuality, Volume 1: An introduction.* (R. Hurley, Trans.). New York, NY: Random House. (Original work published 1976).

Guma, M. (2001). The cultural meaning of names among the Basotho of Southern Africa: A historical and linguistic analysis. *Nordic Journal of African Studies, 10*(3), 265–279. Retrieved from http://www.njas.helsinki.fi.

hooks, b. (1981). *Ain't I a woman? Black women and feminism.* Boston, MA: South End Press.

Kimmel, M. S. (2004). *The gendered society* (2nd ed.). New York, NY: Oxford University Press.

Krais, B. (1993). Gender and symbolic violence: Female oppression in the light of Pierre Bourdieu's theory of social practice. In C. Calhoun, E. LiPuma, & M. Postone (Eds.), *Bourdieu: Critical perspectives* (pp. 156–177). Cambridge, England: Polity Press.

Martin, E. (1998). Immunology on the street: How non-scientists see the immune system. In S. Nettleton & J. Watson (Eds.), *The body in everyday life* (pp. 45–63). New York, NY: Routledge.

Munro, P. (1998). *Subject to fiction: Women teachers' life history narratives and the cultural politics of resistance.* Buckingham, England: Open University Press.

Nussbaum, M. (2002). Women's capabilities and social justice. In M. Molyneux & S. Razavi (Eds.), *Gender justice, development, and rights* (pp. 45–77). New York, NY: Oxford University Press. doi:10.1093/0199256454.003.0002

Paechter, C. F. (1998). *Educating the other: Gender, power and schooling.* Abingdon, England: RoutledgeFalmer.

Schratz, M., & Walker, R. (Eds.). (1995). *Research as social change: New opportunities for qualitative research*. New York, NY: Routledge.

Setiloane, G. M. (1976). *The image of God among the Sotho-Tswana*. Rotterdam, The Netherlands: Balkema.

Stuart, J. (2006). *From our frames: Exploring visual arts-based approaches for addressing HIV and AIDS with pre-service teachers* (Doctoral dissertation, University of KwaZulu-Natal, Durban, South Africa). Retrieved from http://hdl.handle.net/10413/858.

UNAIDS. (2008). *Report on the global AIDS epidemic*. Retrieved from http://www.unaids.org/en/KnowledgeCentre/HIVData/GlobalREport/2008.

DRAWING IN AND ON MATHEMATICS TO PROMOTE HIV&AIDS PRESERVICE TEACHER EDUCATION

Linda van Laren

INTRODUCTION

The various South African HIV&AIDS education policy documents (South African National Department of Education, 1999, 2001, 2002, 2003) set out what is expected of school teachers and higher education lecturers in integrating HIV&AIDS education into disciplines. These expectations are, however, not offered in conjunction with strategies or guidelines to achieve integration. The changes required of educators to explore innovative ways of including HIV&AIDS education in disciplines necessitate the development of new approaches, so before educators can begin to think about the implementation of such integration, they must explore issues related to their beliefs and mindsets. The use of hand-drawn metaphors (Van Laren, 2007) to address this integration in the discipline of mathematics is offered as one of the first steps in an implementation project. This chapter answers the question: How can the goal of integration of HIV&AIDS education in a discipline be initiated while working with a large number of preservice teachers who are registered for a compulsory module?

South African policy documents dictate that a variety of models may be used for HIV&AIDS education. The models suggested for delivering HIV&AIDS education in the institutional curriculum range from what is loosely termed the Integrated Model (HIV&AIDS education integrated across the curriculum) to what is called, also loosely, the Discipline/Subject Area Model (HIV&AIDS education integrated into one discipline—usually Life Orientation). Primary school teachers may consider the teaching of HIV&AIDS education to be appropriate only while they are teaching the range of health issues and the material relevant to social, personal, and physical development in the Life Orientation Learning Programme. To date, Life Orientation is not an examinable subject in all schools and does not enjoy the elevated status of other learning areas such as mathematics (Kollapen et al., 2006). Furthermore, according to the panel who reviewed the National Curriculum Statement (NCS) implementation (Dada et al., 2009) in the Foundation and Intermediate Phases, 'health promotion' should be accommodated under what will be termed 'General Studies'. In General Studies, learners will be taught Health Education in the Foundation Phase for 1 hour per week, and in the Intermediate Phase, 1 hour per week will be used for the teaching and learning of religious and moral education. General Studies will include a wider variety of topics than that considered in Life Orientation because the "personal development and social

L. Theron et al. (eds.), Picturing Research: Drawing as Visual Methodology, 133–146.

development areas of Life Orientation curriculum are part of the general aims of schools" (Dada et al., 2009, p. 43) and need to be infused into the teaching of all subjects. If the recommendations of the panel are implemented, less time will be available for HIV&AIDS education in the primary school curriculum. To extend and improve HIV&AIDS education, it is necessary to encourage teachers to use other options, such as the integration of such education into other subject disciplines. So that teachers can be helped to see that HIV&AIDS education can be integrated into other disciplines, a change in their current mindsets and beliefs about the possibilities of integration is important. Teachers—preservice teachers in particular—need to be comfortable, willing, and able to include HIV&AIDS education in any discipline. Change is never easy and for any such initiative to be taken up, each teacher needs to come to terms with the innovation. For this reason, the beliefs of the individual teacher should be taken into account and developed so that she or he can come to accept the initiative before having to implement integration.

Brock and Salerno (1994) developed a cycle of organisational change that recognises and highlights the fact that accepting change is difficult. According to them, the initial stages in a change cycle are characterised by loss, doubt, and discomfort. When the individual is beginning to consider suggested changes, she or he may be fearful, resentful, or anxious. Furthermore, the person may approach the initiative with caution, scepticism, and confusion. She or he may then be unable to partake in any developmental activities or may become resistant or unproductive. If the change initiative is to succeed, the beliefs of the individuals who are being introduced to the need for change must be addressed. The individual must internalise and take on the challenge of the change before any positive action occurs. Therefore, in this research study of a group of 101 preservice teachers who were registered for a compulsory Primary Mathematics Education module at a faculty of education, it was necessary to initiate possibilities for the integration of HIV&AIDS education in mathematics through an activity that required an active response from each individual. Each preservice teacher was given the opportunity to explain her or his own vision of how this integration might take place by making use of hand-drawn metaphors. The purpose of the drawing activity was to provide preservice teachers with an opportunity to reflect on their beliefs about including HIV&AIDS education in a mathematics classroom. The unique drawings were seen to be a means of providing opportunities for exploring and communicating preservice teachers' initial beliefs about the challenging changes required for this integrated approach.

LOCATING THE STUDY

This chapter describes the use of drawings to investigate possible ways of overcoming the initial fearful, resentful, and/or anxious feelings that preservice teachers experience when they are considering the integration of HIV&AIDS education in mathematics. The work presented in this chapter builds on and then extends research that was previously explored with a group of 7 fourth (final) year preservice teachers in a faculty of education who had volunteered to be part of an integration research project (Van Laren, 2007). In this chapter, work using drawings with an entire group of fourth-year preservice teachers to introduce the possibilities for integration of HIV&AIDS education as part of the requirements for teaching and learning of a compulsory Primary Mathematics Education module is explored.

At the University of KwaZulu-Natal (UKZN), Primary Mathematics Education is a compulsory requirement for preservice teachers registered for the Foundation, Intermediate, and Senior Phase tracks in the Bachelor of Education programme. These preservice teachers are preparing to become Grade R-9 teachers (of children between the ages of 5 and 14 years). Grade R-9 learners spend almost one third of their time at school doing mathematics, so while teaching compulsory mathematics in the school curriculum, these teachers, through integration, are in a favourable position to simultaneously provide the appropriate knowledge, skills, attitudes, and values for HIV&AIDS education. Furthermore, the integration of HIV&AIDS education in mathematics elevates the status of HIV&AIDS education since mathematics is considered to be a high status subject (De Freitas, 2006) in the school curriculum. Using drawing in the high status subject of mathematics to initiate integration is considered to be a deviation from the usual mathematics education requirements.

This research in which the use of hand-drawn metaphors is considered in mathematics education is informed by two theoretical and conceptual frameworks. The first makes use of a 'starting with ourselves' approach through self-study and the second relates to the notion that addressing HIV and AIDS should become the responsibility of all teacher educators and school teachers.

Self-Study

Self-study involves making use of the emerging body of research in teacher education (LaBoskey, 2004; Loughran, 2004, 2007; Pithouse, Mitchell, & Weber, 2009) that emphasises the need for teacher educators to become self-reflective while taking on the challenges of research that is related to social action. Through teacher educator-led responses to the challenges of integrating HIV&AIDS education in mathematics, I explore the use of drawing as a creative, participatory approach to address the fearful, resentful, and/or anxious feelings that teachers experience when they are introduced to unfamiliar curriculum changes.

Pithouse et al. (2009) described seven key characteristics of self-study from the literature that point to the usefulness of self-study methodology for research on integration of HIV&AIDS education by a mathematics teacher educator. My self-study satisfies these seven key characteristics in the following ways: (1) aiming at understanding, describing, and improving the practice of preservice teachers and teacher educators; (2) making use of a variety of methods (including drawings) to promote integration of HIV&AIDS education in mathematics education from a social justice perspective; (3) being inquiry-orientated as my teacher/practitioner research is interwoven with social and/or political issues; (4) including experiences and notions of the 'self' in relation to preservice teachers as 'others'; (5) involving risk taking and gaining critical and reflective suggestions through interactions with preservice teachers; (6) providing opportunities to review what the preservice teachers and I observe in drawings and how we view integration from diverse perspectives; and (7) aiming at social action and changes to my practice, positions, and viewpoints as a mathematics teacher educator.

Tidwell and Manke (2009) showed how self-study methodology, using drawings of metaphors, facilitates reflective practice since the visual representation allows for the in-depth examination of meanings at a particular moment. These authors considered metaphor drawing to be important because of the two linked aspects—the process of drawing and the meanings represented by the drawings. Not only is it possible to explore the meanings expressed in a drawing but the process of developing the metaphoric representation is also significant. Part of the process requires appropriate individual selection of a drawing that best represents the understanding of a concept such as integration of HIV&AIDS education.

Responsibility for the Integration of HIV&AIDS Education

In addition to the teaching and learning of HIV&AIDS education, where the focus is on health issues and social, personal, and physical development, teachers need to develop strategies to integrate HIV&AIDS education into other disciplines or learning areas. In this context, teachers need to address openly and confidently issues of discrimination, misconceptions, and myths surrounding HIV and AIDS. Some teachers may not be comfortable with discussing sex-related HIV&AIDS issues (Baxen & Breidlid, 2004), but all teachers should be HIV-aware and HIV-competent in everyday classroom interactions with learners. Issues related to HIV and AIDS are complex and require teachers to display particular attitudes while interacting with learners to teach a discipline. An interdisciplinary approach that explores HIV&AIDS education has a powerful influence on learners; what teachers know, do, care about, and believe has an important impact on the lives of learners (Hattie, 2003).

In order to integrate HIV&AIDS education into mathematics, preservice teachers need to be competent in the teaching and learning of HIV and AIDS as well as mathematics. In the vast body of literature on mathematics education, there are particular areas of competence advocated for the preservice teacher curriculum. For example, the influential work of Manouchehri (1997) described a range of competences required by preservice teachers who are to teach mathematics. The competencies included Mathematics Subject Content Knowledge (SCK), Pedagogical Content Knowledge (PCK), and Pedagogical Reasoning and Beliefs about teaching and learning. Manouchehri (1997) considered that the teachers' beliefs form an important component since beliefs influence the ways in which teachers develop PCK for classroom presentations. If teachers are introduced to unfamiliar, innovative concepts, they need to believe that the change suggested is possible. Fullan (2001) also pointed out that the acceptance of new beliefs is significant in the development of curriculum innovations. Attending to the beliefs that preservice teachers have about integration into the mathematics discipline is important, and it needs attention when one is promoting the concept of integration of HIV&AIDS education.

The inclusion of one kind of learning within another may be interpreted and used in a variety of ways. In this research, the theoretical framework suggested by Mathison and Freeman (1997) is adopted. They describe integration as an approach in which the crossing of disciplinary knowledge borders introduces a realistic view of knowledge through the use of thematically based activities. In discussing the hand-drawn metaphor activity in the next section, integrated activities for mathematics classroom use will not be explored. The focus of this chapter is on the use of drawings in addressing the initial beliefs of preservice teachers about the integration of HIV&AIDS education in a discipline.

METHODOLOGY

I chose to situate my research within a 'starting with ourselves' framework by selecting my own higher education teaching institution, where I am a mathematics teacher educator, as the research site. Connelly and Clandinin (1988) would have described this form of qualitative study as autobiographical since I investigated my own practice to understand how HIV&AIDS education may be facilitated in mathematics education modules that I teach. I researched my practice to help me see how I could become informed of preservice teachers' beliefs on HIV&AIDS education and its implementation so as to adapt my practice during mathematics education modules. Furthermore, I believe that I need to take action and do something as a teacher educator in relation to addressing HIV and AIDS.

The 'starting with ourselves' methodology is often challenged on the grounds of validity and subjectivity, but because of the interactions with other 'selves' within the lecture room situation, I was able to reflect on how I could study the integration innovation from the inside. Studying one's own practice to articulate it coherently is also demanding and difficult. In self-study, detailed documentation of the research process is a requirement for studying one's actions so as to facilitate reflexive teaching (Bleakley, 1999).

As previously discussed, after having worked with a focus group of 7 final-year preservice teachers who volunteered to work with me while we designed activities to initiate the integration of HIV&AIDS education in mathematics (Van Laren, 2007), I decided to extend this work on making use of drawings to further integration research with the entire group of Bachelor of Education preservice teachers who were registered for a compulsory final-year Primary Mathematics Education module.

Using preservice teachers' hand-drawn pictures and descriptions of metaphors, I explored the beliefs of preservice teachers about the integration of HIV&AIDS education in mathematics. The drawing activity was informed by the metaphor research done by Johnston, Needham, and Brook (1990) and Hobden (1999). Drawings of metaphors are described as a creative way of depicting a situation in order to give a representation of teaching and learning. I explained the concept of a metaphor to the preservice teachers as follows:

> A metaphor may be described as an imaginative way of describing a situation to give a vivid and interesting picture. These descriptions do not exist in real life. For example, we might refer to a caring person as 'having a heart of gold' because we associate something of good quality as consisting of gold.

In the lecture situation, the preservice teachers were given the opportunity to discuss a number of hand-drawn pictures that I provided as examples of metaphors. We explored the metaphors by considering who or what represented the teacher, the learner, the mathematics and the HIV&AIDS education embedded in the mathematics. I then asked the preservice teachers to draw their own personal metaphors. These were not meant to depict actual mathematics lessons but rather to show possibilities for inclusion of HIV&AIDS content into mathematics and facilitate reflection.

Data Selection and Analysis

I collected the drawings of all 101 preservice teachers. The preservice teachers' drawings were not marked or graded for module assessment purposes. I selected interesting, unusual drawings made by 8 of the preservice teachers for further exploration. I asked these female preservice teachers for written permission to use their responses, and they were also asked to discuss their drawings. During these voluntary discussions of their hand-drawn metaphors, each of the 8 preservice teachers was given the opportunity to say more about why she decided on the particular metaphor, how her metaphor explained integration of HIV&AIDS education, and whether she saw herself as the teacher in her drawing. The preservice teachers were not directly asked to comment on their feelings about integrating HIV&AIDS education in mathematics. Instead, by replying to the question about seeing themselves as the teachers in their drawings, respondents were given the opportunity to say whether or not they would be willing to consider integrating.

The learning suggested by the drawing of a metaphor may be classified using Sfard's (1998) two categories: Acquisition and Participation. These categories are based on interpreting the type of learning being represented as an end-product (Acquisition) or symbolically as a process (Participation). This classification may be used to identify types of learning theories: Does the drawing show that the preservice teacher appears to have a teacher-centred or a learner-centred approach to integrating HIV&AIDS education? It was not my intention to classify the types of learning for ranking purposes, but, rather, I wanted to understand the manner in which the participants envisaged integrated teaching. This would enable me to explore the drawing as an initial entry point in the consideration of the possibility of inclusion of HIV&AIDS education in mathematics.

To illustrate the variety of ideas about integrating HIV and AIDS into mathematics, I have used four (Anisha, Celest, Felicity, and Nandi[i]) of the 8 preservice teachers' drawings of metaphors for analysis in this chapter. Anisha, Celest, and Felicity are Foundation/Intermediate (Grade R–6) Phase preservice teachers, and Nandi is an Intermediate/Senior (Grade 4–9) Phase specialist.

The drawing activity and subsequent discussion did not focus on creative ability: It provided a starting point for preservice teachers to help alleviate their fears about integrating HIV&AIDS education into a discipline using an interesting, different—in that it was non-mathematical—activity. During the lecture in which I introduced the concept of the drawing of a metaphor, I emphasised that there was no such thing as a correct or incorrect metaphor drawing or description.

What the Visual Data Revealed

The "Masterpiece" metaphor was drawn by Anisha, who had elected to study English and Life Orientation as major subjects in her Bachelor of Education degree. In her drawing (see Figure 10.1), Anisha shows a painter standing beside an easel that has a painted canvas on it. A palette with paints and a paintbrush are featured next to the easel. The painting is at the centre of the drawing while the artist stands next to it. Her description of the metaphor indicates that the painter represents the teacher who uses mathematics, together with HIV&AIDS education, to develop the learner. The end result is the painted canvas that represents the learner.

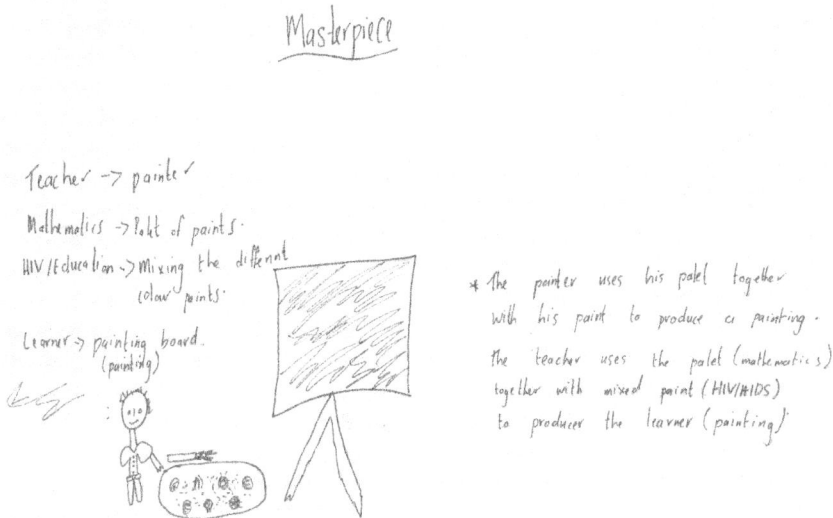

Figure 10.1. "Masterpiece": The metaphor drawn by Anisha (October 2009) with her hand-written explanation of what each part of the drawing represents.

Anisha chose her metaphor drawing of a painter and painting because she thinks that effective integration is achieved though the mixing of different coloured paints. When she described her metaphor drawing of the masterpiece and how integration of HIV and AIDS may take place, she explained that, for her, the painter produces a message or symbol that needs to be interpreted through emotions and feelings in a particular context. The interpretation of the picture that the painter creates depends on the particular viewpoint of the individual interpreter. For Anisha, the learner could then become the painter once the integration of HIV&AIDS education in mathematics has been taught. She believed that each learner could then develop a different interpretation of the knowledge gleaned from the teaching situation.

Celest's major subject is Technology. She interpreted the integration differently and called her metaphor drawing "Chocolate Cake". Her drawing provides a step-by-step description of the various components (see Figure 10.2). The process begins with the baker, who uses ingredients to produce a cake. The cake, together with the icing, is the final product. A slice of the enticing iced chocolate cake is then presented to the learner for consumption.

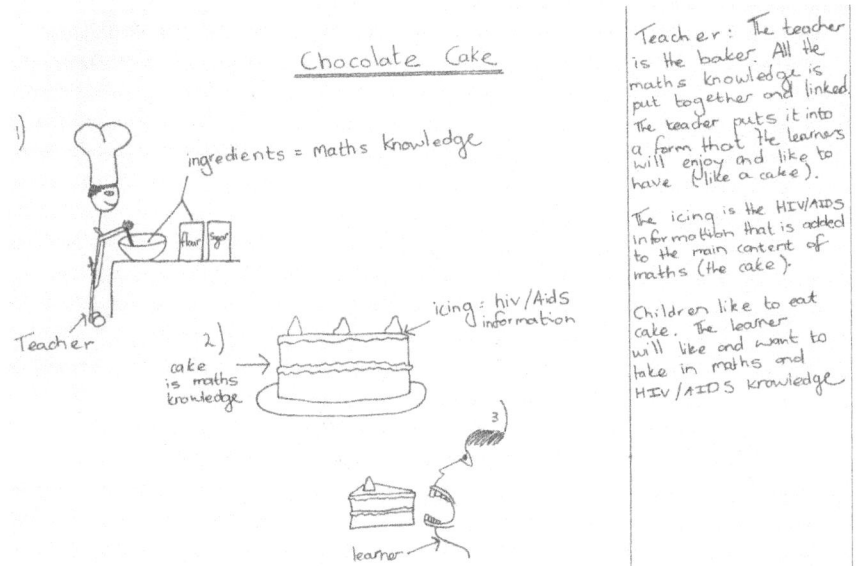

Figure 10.2. "Chocolate Cake": The metaphor drawn by Celest (October 2009) with her hand-written explanation of what each part of the drawing represents.

Celest's metaphor was influenced by what her friends had drawn. In the discussion, she pointed out that the teacher decides what is important when including HIV&AIDS education content. The teacher, represented as the baker, wants the presentation of the content to be in a palatable form. The chocolate cake with icing, then, is a tempting, encouraging way of presenting the mathematics and HIV&AIDS education knowledge. The cake, which consists of mathematics and HIV&AIDS education, is consumed by the learner so that her/his knowledge of mathematics and HIV and AIDS can be taken in.

Felicity's major subject is English. She titled her metaphor, "New Concepts" and drew a central hovering spaceship with a pilot. From the spaceship, rays are shown beaming down to a person standing on the ground (see Figure 10.3).

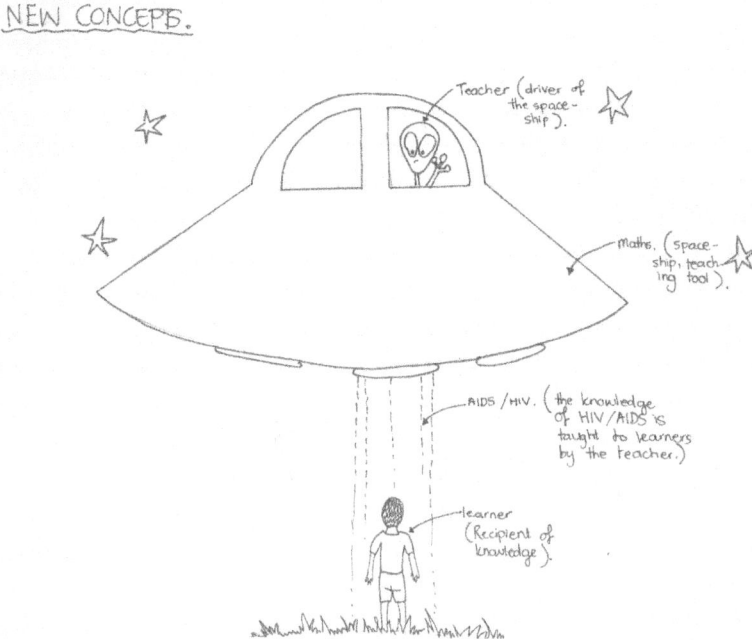

Figure 10.3. "New Concepts": The metaphor drawn by Felicity (October 2009) with her hand-written explanation of what each part of the drawing represents.

Originally, Felicity considered drawing a person planting seedlings to illustrate her metaphor for integrated teaching and learning, but then she decided to draw "something more fun and different", so she drew a scene showing a spaceship interacting with a human. She emphasises that the teacher uses mathematics to deliver the HIV&AIDS education since the learners may not know about the required HIV&AIDS education. In her drawing, the pilot of the spaceship represents the teacher, and the spaceship is the mathematics that is the vehicle used by the teacher to teach about HIV and AIDS. The person on the ground is the learner, who receives the knowledge about HIV and AIDS through the mathematics.

Felicity enjoyed the activity and was excited about the prospect of the integration of HIV&AIDS education into mathematics. Her drawing showed that it is possible to integrate in a manner that is not a forceful bombarding. Integration, then, provides her with opportunities to "slip in" information about HIV and AIDS "smoothly" without using heavy-handed tactics.

Nandi had elected to register for Arts and Culture and Technology as her major subjects. One of her family members was about to get married, so she decided to draw a wedding scene (see Figure 10.4). She wanted to represent "something that is familiar to everyone because we all go to weddings". In her drawing, the bride is the central figure and the groom is presenting a ring to her. The groom in her picture represents the teacher and the whole wedding ceremony is the mathematics teaching and learning. An important part of the ceremony is the handing over of a ring that represents HIV&AIDS education. The centrality of including HIV&AIDS education in mathematics is portrayed in her drawing. The bride is the learner receiving the information about HIV and AIDS. Nandi sees herself as taking the role of the groom in her picture—the one who provides the bride, who represents the learner, with HIV&AIDS education.

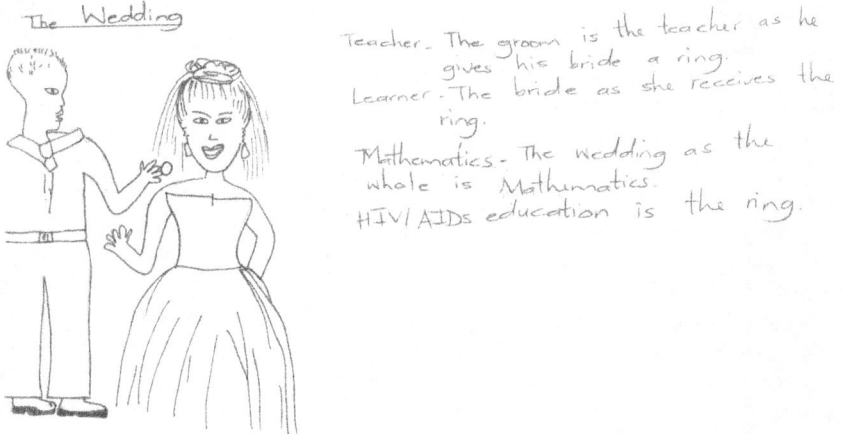

Figure 10.4. "The Wedding": The metaphor drawn by Nandi (October 2009) with her hand-written explanation of what each part of the drawing represents.

DISCUSSION

From the drawings made by Anisha, Celest, Felicity, and Nandi, it is evident that there is an interesting variety of views on how the integration of HIV and AIDS into the mathematics curriculum could be developed. Their views on integration, as displayed in the drawings, should not be seen to be static and unchanging views of teaching and learning. The preservice teachers were given only about an hour during a mathematics education lecture to explore the possibility of integration into mathematics, so their views may change once they have reflected on the possibilities. They will certainly be influenced by the experiences once they qualify to teach in their own classrooms and will probably consider teaching and learning from a different viewpoint by then.

The metaphor drawings and descriptions offered by the preservice teachers showed that all were willing to consider integration processes in mathematics. Yet, Celest openly admitted that she did not see herself as a teacher who had enough knowledge about HIV and AIDS to confidently integrate HIV&AIDS education into a mathematics classroom. All 4 preservice teachers indicated that mathematics education modules could assist with the development of HIV&AIDS teacher education, but it is clear that Felicity would like integration activities in mathematics to be extended to incorporate further information about HIV and AIDS together with concrete examples of how attitudes can be changed. Three of the preservice teachers pointed out that HIV&AIDS education should be considered across *all* disciplines to assist with the preparation of teachers for the management of HIV&AIDS education at classroom level. Celest, however, proposed that "there should be a general module on HIV&AIDS education that shows us how to incorporate it across learning areas, as a lot of us are generalists".

Advantages of Using Drawings

The preservice teachers were not asked to extend their initial integration ideas, as presented in their drawings, to real action in classrooms, but the drawing activity did appear to dispel the initial fears, doubt, and discomfort about the integration innovation. The drawing of a particular metaphor opened up discussion on possibilities for integration of HIV&AIDS education into mathematics without focusing on a correct or incorrect solution to the problem. The drawings allowed for thinking about an innovation in a non-threatening, non-stressful situation. The preservice teachers were given the opportunity to experiment with their own ideas through the drawings. By making integration concepts visible in a hand-drawn metaphor, each preservice teacher gained some insight into coming to terms with integration.

CONCLUSIONS AND IMPLICATIONS

In having them produce hand-drawn pictures, the complexity of integration was customised into a simple form that matched each individual preservice teacher. Individual participation allowed the preservice teachers to consider how each thought about the suggested integration innovation from the inside, through reflection. Although I proposed the innovation as a mathematics teacher educator, this could have been seen to be a change initiative developed by an outsider imposing an unwelcome top-down change strategy. Using personalised hand-drawn metaphors, we could explore individualised understandings of change.

The drawings addressed the initial risks and fears described in the change cycle mentioned above (Brock & Solerno, 1994) and enabled these preservice teachers to move towards the discovery of, and also the understanding of, integration possibilities. By affording each preservice teacher the opportunity to take on the challenge at a simple level using a hand-drawn picture, the preservice teachers would work through the "Danger Zone" (Brock & Solerno, 1994). The drawings provided support for overcoming possible cautiousness, resistance, and confusion and paved the way for creativeness and pragmatic focus on integration strategies. The personalised drawings served as an ice-breaking activity to reduce tension and anxiety so that each preservice teacher could mull over the implications of the intervention. The drawings facilitated their becoming acquainted with the intervention and provided them with opportunities to directly become involved and work to the next step in the process of the integration of HIV&AIDS education. The activity paved the way for the next goal, which could include the development of required integration action through the exploration of classroom strategies.

The metaphor drawings uncovered the initial responses of these preservice teachers to teaching and learning and are not meant to represent a permanent, unchanging, cast-in-stone statement about their beliefs and attitudes. The illustrations suggest that these preservice teachers were inclined to adopt a teacher-centred approach to integrating HIV&AIDS education into mathematics, and this is linked to Sfard's (1998) Acquisition metaphor for learning. This approach could, however, change through further reflection and after classroom teaching experience. In this chapter, the drawings allowed for exploring the 'beginning' ideas. After further teaching and learning experiences, these preservice teachers may want to adapt and/or reconceptualise their drawings. At a later stage in their professional careers, it would be useful and very meaningful to ask them to reconsider or repeat the drawing activity so that we could compare their current beliefs and attitudes about implementing HIV&AIDS education integration with their earlier beliefs and attitudes.

The drawing activity served as the relatively small, yet important, first step towards achieving the vision of integration of HIV&AIDS education into mathematics. It provided the bottom rung of the scaffold—in an explicit manner and with a particular outcome—to address beliefs about integration. Each pre-service teacher who was registered for the Primary Mathematics Education module was willing and able to engage with this first step, which focused on convincing them that the change in the teaching and learning of mathematics is achievable. The relatively new initiative that involved their drawing of a metaphor in a mathematics module encouraged the acceptance of an alternative way of thinking about the teaching and learning of mathematics in a school classroom. Furthermore, the activity highlighted the fact that the preservice teachers at a faculty of education in KwaZulu-Natal, where HIV&AIDS teacher education is mainly considered in the elective Life Orientation module, would not only require but welcome and benefit from more HIV&AIDS education subject content knowledge and pedagogical content knowledge from Life Orientation specialists and from other disciplines.

NOTE

[i] Pseudonyms are used to protect the identity of the participants.

REFERENCES

Baxen, J., & Breidlid, A. (2004). Researching HIV/AIDS and education in Sub-Saharan Africa: Examining the gaps and challenges. *Journal of Education, 34*, 9–29. Retrieved from http://www.uky.edu/~drlane/research/ISLESA/baxen.pdf.

Bleakley, A. (1999). From reflective practice to holistic reflexivity. *Studies in Higher Education, 24*(3), 315–330. doi:10.1080/03075079912331379925.

Brock, L. R., & Salerno, M. A. (1994). *The change cycle: The secret to getting through life's difficult changes.* Washington, D.C.: Bridge Builder Media.

Connelly, F. M., & Clandinin, D. J. (1988). *Teachers as curriculum planners: Narratives of experience.* New York, NY: Teachers College Press.

Dada, F., Dipholo, T., Hoadley, U., Khembo, E., Muller, S., & Volmink, J. (2009). *Report of the Task Team for the Review of the Implementation of the National Curriculum Statement. Final report October, 2009.* Retrieved from http://www.info.gov.za.

De Freitas, E. (2006). *Mathematics education through a socio-cultural lens: Using theories of identity and discourse to examine school mathematics.* Paper presented at the Faculty of Education, McGill University, Montreal, QC.

Fullan, M. (2001). *Leading in a culture of change.* San Francisco, CA: Jossey-Bass.

Hattie, J. (2003, October). *Teachers make a difference: What is the research evidence?* Paper presented at the Australian Council for Educational Research Annual Conference: Building Teacher Quality: What Does the Research Tell Us?, Melbourne, Australia. Retrieved from http://www.educationalleaders.govt.nz.

Hobden, S. D. (1999). *The beliefs of preservice teachers about mathematics teaching and learning.* (Unpublished master's thesis). Faculty of Community and Development Disciplines, University of KwaZulu-Natal, Durban, South Africa.

Johnston, K., Needham, R., & Brook, A. (1990). *Children's learning in science project: Interactive teaching in science – Workshops for training courses.* Leeds, England: Centre for Studies in Science and Mathematics Education, University of Leeds.

Kollapen, J., Chaane, T., Manthata, T., & Chisholm, L. (2006). *Report of the Public Hearing on the Right to Basic Education.* South African Human Rights Commission. Retrieved from http://www.pmg.org.za/docs/2006/061027humanrights.pdf.

LaBoskey, V. K. (2004). The methodology of self-study and its theoretical underpinnings. In J. J. Loughran, M. L. Hamilton, V. K. LaBoskey, & T. Russell (Eds.), *International handbook of self-study of teaching and teacher education practices* (pp. 817–869). Dordrecht, The Netherlands: Kluwer Academic. doi:10.1007/978-1-4020-6545-3_21.

Loughran, J. J. (2004). A history and context of self-study of teaching and teacher education practices. In J. J. Loughran, M. L. Hamilton, V. K. LaBoskey, &T. Russell (Eds.), *International handbook of self-study of teaching and teacher education practices* (pp. 7–30). Dordrecht, The Netherlands: Kluwer Academic. doi:10.1007/978-1-4020-6545-3_1.

Loughran, J. J. (2007). Researching teacher education practices: Responding to the challenges, demands, and expectations of self-study. *Journal of Teacher Education, 58*(1), 12–20. doi:10.1177/0022487106296217.

Manouchehri, A. (1997). School mathematics reform: Implications for mathematics teacher preparation. *Journal of Teacher Education, 48*(3), 197–209. doi:10.1177/0022487197048003005.

Mathison, S., & Freeman, M. (1997). *The logic of interdisciplinary studies.* Paper presented at the Annual Meeting of the American Educational Research Association, Chicago, IL. Retrieved from http://cela.albany.edu/reports/mathisonlogic12004.pdf.

Pithouse, K., Mitchell, C., & Weber, S. (2009). Self-study in teaching and teacher development: A call to action. *Educational Action Research, 17*(1), 43–62. doi:10.1080/09650790802667444.

Sfard, A. (1998). On two metaphors for learning and the dangers of choosing just one. *Educational Researcher, 27*(2), 4–13. doi: 10.3102/0013189X027002004.

South African National Department of Education. (1999). *National policy on HIV and AIDS for learners and educators in public schools and students and educators in further education and training institutions.* [Government Gazette, Vol.410, No. 20372]. Retrieved from http://wced.school.za/branchIDC/special_ed/hiv_aids/National_policy_on_HIV-AIDS.pdf.

South African National Department of Education. (2001). *Education white paper 6. Special needs education: Building an inclusive education and training system.* Retrieved from http://www.info.gov.za.

South African National Department of Education. (2002). *Revised National Curriculum Statement, Grades R–9 (schools): Mathematics.* Pretoria, South Africa: Author.

South African National Department of Education. (2003). *National Curriculum Statement Grades 10–12 (general): Mathematics.* Pretoria, South Africa: Author. Retrieved from http://www.education.gov.za.

Tidwell, D., & Manke, M. P. (2009). Making meaning of practice through visual metaphor. In D. L. Tidwell, M. L. Heston, & L. M. Fitzgerald (Eds.), *Research methods for the self-study of practice* (pp. 135–153). Dordrecht, The Netherlands: Springer Science+Business Media. doi:10.1007/978-1-4020-9514-6.

Van Laren, L. (2007). Using metaphors for integrating HIV and AIDS education in a mathematics curriculum in pre-service teacher education: An exploratory classroom study. *International Journal of Inclusive Education, 11*(4), 461–479. doi:10.1080/13603110701391451.

CHAPTER 11

READING ACROSS AND BACK:
THOUGHTS ON WORKING WITH (RE-VISITED)
DRAWING COLLECTIONS

Jean Stuart and Ann Smith

INTRODUCTION

This chapter is self reflective in that it considers what I[i] can learn about furthering
teacher development by revisiting and bringing together two collections of
drawings that show how young people view HIV and AIDS. These drawings were
produced in the From Our Frames and Youth as Knowledge Producers projects.
These two projects were implemented at the University of KwaZulu-Natal
(UKZN). They explored ways in which arts-based approaches can contribute to
teacher education and development. Although different, each began with the same
brief drawing exercise that asked participants to represent their perspective on HIV
and AIDS in response to the prompt: '*Draw a picture that represents your view of
HIV and AIDS.*' Most of the drawings discussed in this chapter were produced by
preservice teachers who ranged in age from 19 to 35 years, but I will also consider
two drawings produced by teenaged schoolchildren in the From Our Frames
project in response to the same prompt. After describing the projects and the
process of the production of the drawings, I will take a closer look at, and across,
individual drawings so as to demonstrate how the drawings served, and can
continue to serve, as pedagogical and research tools for their producers, and for
me. I want to discuss what possibilities such collections offer for further teaching
and research. To make meaning of the drawings, I will consider what the
participants say they represent and will also consider how much validity there is in
working with 'outsider' semiotic and content analysis.

TWO ARTS-BASED PROJECTS WORKING TOWARDS
TEACHER DEVELOPMENT IN THE AGE OF AIDS

I have been involved in Participatory Action Research (PAR) related to the field of
teacher education and HIV and AIDS since 2003. It is time to think back over two
projects that generated drawings and consider what lessons I have learned that I
can now pass on to other researchers.

L. Theron et al. (eds.), Picturing Research: Drawing as Visual Methodology, 147–161.
© 2011 *Sense Publishers. All rights reserved.*

Project 1: From Our Frames

In the current South African climate of high HIV prevalence, the impact of this pervasive condition is felt in many homes and schools. Teachers are expected to make a significant contribution to schools and communities by educating learners about HIV and AIDS; by handling challenges, such as those related to stigma, with sensitivity; and, overall, by helping learners personally deal with the effects of the epidemic. But teachers need to understand the socially and culturally embedded context of HIV and AIDS and to become fully aware of their own beliefs and concerns before being able to fulfil these expectations (Stuart, 2006). The From Our Frames project took place within a UKZN module for preparing teachers as school counsellors. I launched it in response to the belief that only if teachers actively explore their own understandings, perceptions, and attitudes to HIV and AIDS will they be able to deal confidently with the demands the epidemic places on them as educators. The central purpose of this project was to explore, with 13 preservice teachers, ways in which visual arts-based approaches (such as drawings and photograph-generated HIV- and AIDS-related messages) could contribute to addressing the challenges of HIV and AIDS in relation to education. I wanted to find out what we could learn from these visual representations of HIV and AIDS and what implications these drawn and photograph-generated messages and, very importantly, the associated processes of their production could have on teacher development in the age of AIDS. I chose a visual arts-based approach for the high level of participation it encourages and because of its potential to simultaneously engage the mind, body, and emotions (Weber & Mitchell, 2004).

Swart's (1990) work with street children attests to the fact that drawings can be used to explore perceptions and experiences. Research also shows drawings to be useful in investigating children's beliefs about health, cancer, and risk (Williams & Bendelow, 1998). And, in line with Freire (1972), drawings can also allow for the representation of participants' individual voices, existing knowledge, and ideas on the subject they depict. Given my involvement in preservice teacher training, I chose drawings as an entry point in the From Our Frames project for both the preservice teachers and me to begin thinking about how we see HIV and AIDS and, tentatively, to access each image creator's related perceptions, beliefs, and understandings. A central focus of the preservice teachers' arts-based experimentation in subsequent workshops was their production of photo-stories or photo posters aimed at creating HIV-related messages for their peers (Stuart, 2006). However, it is the supporting drawing exercise on which I will focus here. This drawing exercise took place in the first workshop, serving as an introduction to the From Our Frames project. During the exercise, preservice teachers ascribed their own meaning to the official HIV and AIDS red ribbon logo commonly attached to a wide range of materials and products associated with AIDS awareness and education. They then drew their own representations of HIV and AIDS in response to the prompt mentioned above: '*Draw a picture that represents your view of HIV and AIDS.*' They also wrote about these drawings. At the conclusion of the From Our Frames project, I repeated the drawing exercise as part of a participants' review on what they had learned through the process of using visual arts-based methods to address HIV and AIDS. I have written elsewhere (Stuart, 2007) about the potential for the comparative analysis of these drawings to be used as an aspect of research assessment (as have others, such as Theron, 2008) and have published work on drawings that suggests most clearly that some of the From Our Frames participants' drawings supported their written claim of shifts in their 'before' and 'after' intervention perspectives. For this chapter, I use previously unpublished 'before' and 'after' drawings of four more From Our Frames participants to illustrate the variety of responses evident even among these 4 preservice teachers. Their prompt for the drawings on both occasions was the following: '*In the box above, draw a picture that represents your view of HIV and AIDS.*' It was succeeded by the request: '*Explain why you have chosen this representation.*' The teachers were given space in which to write their explanations of their depictions. The following interpretations of the drawings include reference to the artists' comments as well as my own observations. Below, I begin to compare an 'outsider' analysis with the 'insider' ones presented by the artists themselves.

Nthuseng drew variations of HIV and AIDS as a monster for both her 'before' and 'after' pictures.

Figure 11.1. The virus as monster (before).   *Figure 11.2. The virus as monster (after).*

Although in both drawings she represented the virus as a monster, Nthuseng indicated in writing that she thought her attitude had changed through the project. She said, "Because in the past I thought people living with HIV/AIDS are already dead, but to my discovery I found that PLWA can live for more than ten years as long as they take care of themselves." This 'discovery' was evident in a photo-story she developed later with another student, which depicted a couple who contract and learn to live positively with HIV. The fact that Nthuseng had listened to her peers' points of view in relation to her original ideas explains an interesting difference in the monster representations. In the 'after' drawing, the combination of the rather wry tentative smile on the face of the monster coupled with the open eyes give the face a less menacing look. Also of interest in a comparison of these

149

two pictures is the rectangle in the bottom right of her second drawing. Just what she intended with this I cannot now ask, and her reason was not recorded, but the rectangle appears to be a figure on the cover of a book. Might this suggest something about the student's association of her new knowledge about HIV and AIDS with the epidemic itself? My reading of this rectangle makes sense to me, but would it make the same sense to her? Is it valid, even, for me to suggest this possible extension of the meaning of her drawing? How might my asking Nthuseng about this affect her and possibly change her beliefs and attitudes?

Iris used a crying face in both her drawings to represent the distress of all those affected and infected.

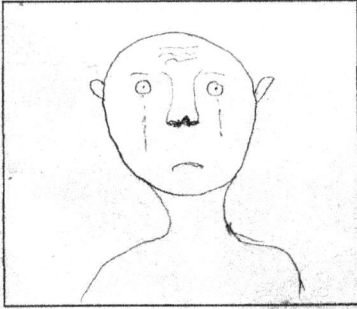

Figure 11.3. Human tears depicting HIV and AIDS (before).

Figure 11.4. Human tears depicting HIV and AIDS (after).

She wrote that she thought that her attitude had not changed through the project. She asserted that "I still feel strongly about HIV/AIDS." Here, we can see that Iris's depiction of HIV and AIDS has not changed much except that her second figure is smaller than her first. It is pictured from further away. Does this indicate that she is withdrawing even further from any engagement with the topic, or does it mean that she now has a clearer—and longer—view of it? Here, again, I suggest, but also question the value of, my own analysis of this difference between the pictures in the absence of any definitive interpretation from the artist herself.

A third participant, Lisa, drew a stick figure under an equals sign for her 'before' drawing and wrote that the infected are "still human beings" and "still equal to human rights".

After producing a photo-story about stigma and discrimination associated with HIV and AIDS, she used only the equals sign for her 'after' drawing, explaining that infected people have been discriminated against and that "the symbol is just to say share the same equal rights with all the people". Her progression from a combination of the figure and the equals sign to only the equals sign may suggest that having worked through the construction and presentation of a photo-story that exposes and explores the effects of discrimination and possible solutions, she is more adamant, and more confident, about addressing AIDS from her particular position. I draw part of this conclusion from an informal discussion I had with her at the end of the session when she and her partner Mamelo told their story. Lisa expressed a sense of agency that resulted from the affirmation she received from her peers' open, supportive response and their interest in the photo-story she produced. Further analysis might lead to the suggestion that Lisa's omission of the human figure in her 'after' drawing points to her recognition that rights are more important than individuals. Equally, we might see in this 'after' drawing the recognition that, to paraphrase the Zulu expression, we are people through other people so it is therefore unnecessary to show any human figures with the equals sign. I wonder if offering my own analysis to a new viewer of Lisa's drawings would enhance or damage Lisa's work? It is this type of question that is central to this chapter.

Figure 11.5. HIV and AIDS
and equal rights (before).

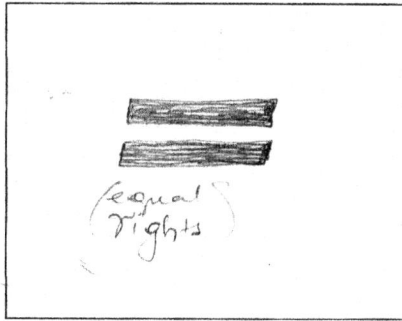

Figure 11.6. HIV and AIDS
and equal rights (after).

Nokuthula visually indicated her awareness of HIV and AIDS in relation to the family and wrote about her perception of "children who are suffering and so many orphans".

Figure 11.7. Children and
HIV and AIDS (before).

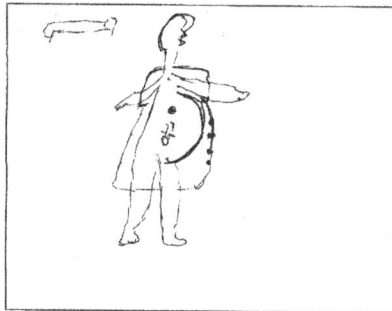

Figure 11.8. Children and
HIV and AIDS (after).

The photo-story she and Nonhlanhla subsequently produced is about protecting a pregnant woman who has the courage to find out her HIV status. Nokuthula's 'after' drawing—that of a pregnant woman with a visible baby in her uterus—reflects that she has thought through one way of addressing the suffering of children. She explained that this was the image of a woman who did not find out her status and whose baby would die by contracting the virus in her or his mother's breast milk. Nokuthula thought her attitude had changed after participating in the project: "Because I thinking that there was nothing we can do to fight against it but now I see I can do a lot."

Had I not spoken to Nokuthula about her 'after' drawing I would have assumed that the pregnant woman depicted in it is a symbol of hope! After all, I might have thought, in the 'before' picture the child is already labelled as being HIV positive but in the 'after' picture the child is not yet born so still susceptible to HIV prevention interventions like Nevirapine. Here is a clear example of how my own analysis would have contradicted that of the artist at the most fundamental level of interpretation. For me, on the one hand, this sounds a warning bell in relation to the ascription of meaning to the drawings of others and points to the necessity of discussion with each participant. This is not to say that the researcher should offer no input, but it is to insist that the artist's interpretation must be seen to be paramount. On the other, a discussion with Nokuthula about the hopefulness in my interpretation of the symbolism of the pregnant woman might well have opened up fruitful discussion about other ways in which she can, indeed, "do a lot".

I am interested in how I could increase the validity of the interpretation of these 'before' and 'after' drawings. If I used the same drawing exercise again and was interested in using the drawings to contribute to understanding how the participants think their views might have changed, I would add in time for them to compare and comment on differences in their own drawings. I might consider offering them my interpretations so as to provoke further discussion; yet, this might influence them into agreeing with me even if they do not. This sharing of my understandings presents the biggest of the challenges given my position of authority, and I realise that I would have to do this very carefully and thoughtfully.

Reading across the From Our Frames drawings. Small though the database is, the application of a basic content analysis (Rose, 2001) in relation to common discourses about HIV and AIDS across the four 'before' and 'after' drawings just discussed and the rest of the From Our Frames preservice teachers' drawings illustrates, thought-provokingly, that even though in this small group the preservice teachers held a variety of views on HIV and AIDS, they all invoked popular images of the epidemic. This raises the question of how we might use this familiarity with these discourses to help teachers deal with HIV and AIDS in educational and other settings. The most frequently recurring image is that of a monster and appears in various forms in seven of the 22 drawings (see Figures 11.1 and 11.2). There are many discourses around HIV that may have contributed to the prevalence of this image. The HIV virus is also depicted visually as a ball covered with spikes—a diagrammatic representation of the virus under a microscope. HIV is also spoken about as a 'killer' and we are urged to join the fight against it. The spiked ball and the notion of a killer are both linked to the monstrous. These students personified HIV as the enemy and put a particularly frightening face to it. But, although dominant, these menacing monsters are not the only depictions of HIV that the preservice teachers drew. The embodiment of HIV was also shown repeatedly through representations of the human body (see Figures 11.3, 11.4, 11.5, 11.7, and 11.8). This is hardly surprising given the raw evidence of HIV and AIDS on the body. This links back, of course, to the notion of the monstrous killer disease. Human feelings were depicted as women's tearful faces in two pictures (see Figures 11.3 and 11.4). Five of the drawings contained iconic representations of emotion symbolised by tears and broken hearts. The feminisation of HIV and AIDS is a powerful discourse and one that is internalised at an unconscious level in the lived experience of most women in South Africa. The stick figures, some looking at the HIV monster described elsewhere (Stuart, 2006) and others that include a sexless stick figure bowed with affliction, invoke, perhaps, the depersonalised nature of the virus. The affected family, particularly a child and a baby, and a pregnant woman (see Figures 11.7 and 11.8) invoke, perhaps, the awareness of HIV and AIDS as a burden on families and households. A drawing of clasped hands brings to mind religious discourses of suffering and hope. Human death was represented by coffins and grave stones, and this invokes the powerful, though, of course, misleading, discourse of HIV and AIDS as being, necessarily, an immediate death sentence, a scourge. Human rights discourses were reflected in the recognition of the need for equal treatment for all—illustrated with an equals sign (see Figures 11.5 and 11.6).

Interpreting the content of these drawings in relation to common discourses of HIV and AIDS provides us as researchers and lecturers with the opportunity of using the commonalities between and among them to help inservice and preservice teachers work with learners in projects that will empower them towards a critical consciousness of their own responses to what is involved in living with HIV and AIDS, whether as infected or affected people. Using common discourses about the epidemic—like the red ribbon logo, for example—as the starting point for projects that involve drawing and other arts-based and visual methodologies makes this participatory work more accessible and more immediate to the participants and the researchers. What might happen if we encourage preservice teachers, like Iris in particular, to see HIV and AIDS in a different light? If we suggested, in a follow-up draw-and-write activity, that Iris use a 'Living Positively' discourse instead of, say, the 'Killer' one to inform her representations of how she views HIV and AIDS, would the act of drawing and writing in such a guided way help to change her attitudes and beliefs, or would this simply drive them underground?

Project 2: Youth as Knowledge Producers

The Youth as Knowledge Producers project began in 2007 on the UKZN campus—3 years after the completion of the From Our Frames project—and will continue until 2011. One of its aims is to explore how arts-based methodologies can be used with young people in rural schools to create a more youth-focused and learner-centred approach to knowledge production and behaviour change in the age of AIDS. Towards this end, a new group of preservice teachers, already committed to HIV education through a campus peer education programme, volunteered to explore how arts-based methods such as forum and image theatre, hip hop, photovoice, collage, and video making can contribute to HIV education in schools. As part of an introductory workshop, the preservice teachers were invited to draw their representations with exactly the same prompt as that given to the From Our Frames group. However, in contrast to the From Our Frames drawings, which were viewed initially only by their creators and later by the researcher, participants in the Youth as Knowledge Producers workshop shared their drawings with the group as they introduced themselves to each other. A selection of these drawings, which I chose for their diversity, is shown below together with participants' written comments on their own drawings. No 'after' drawings have been created to date since the project is not yet finished.

I will present all the drawings first and will then discuss how they might be (re)used to further the training and development of the preservice teachers.

Figure 11.9. Teaching about HIV and AIDS.

Nadia explained her representation of a teacher standing in front of four learners and pointing to the words on a chalkboard thus: "It clearly shows that people need to be taught about HIV/AIDS virus in order to know about it, it's shown about people gathered and someone is teaching."

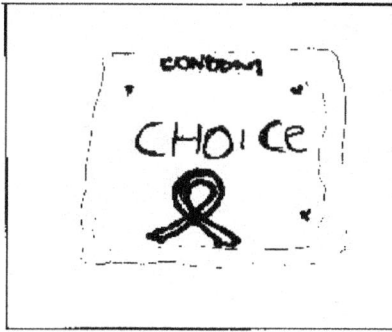

Figure 11.10. Condomise to prevent AIDS.

Nonhlahla wrote that she chose a drawing of a condom "because I want to represent the image that aids can be prevented by, being faithful, abstinence, even condomising if you fail to do the above".

Figure 11.11. HIV and AIDS and knowledge.

Sbu's image included the words "lack of knowledge" below the image of a person made up of three letters: H, I, and V. Sbu described the drawing as follows: "The image represents a skinny victim of HIV/AIDS after he discovered that he is HIV positive. A person didn't take his ARV's that is why his CD4 count went down until he got sick and became skinny."

Zama's explanation of his drawing also suggests that knowledge of HIV is of crucial importance:

The tree that have branches symbolise life although there is HIV which is trying to disturb or enter the roots. People are effectively fighting winnable war. The other tree is dying because the roots are having HIV and people are not aware of what is going on in the roots of the tree.

155

Figure 11.12. Life through HIV knowledge.

Reading across the Youth as Knowledge Producers drawings. My comments here draw only from the Youth as Knowledge Producers drawings shown in this chapter. It will also be clear that my interpretation of them reflects my interest in working with preservice teachers to develop a wide range of methods suited to the socio-cultural embeddedness of the 'disease'. For me, a consciousness of the role of knowledge about, awareness of, and education on HIV and AIDS comes through very strongly in all the Youth as Knowledge Producer drawings depicted in the previous section. The teacher standing in front of the children (see Figure 11.9) is quite explicit in educational intent as she draws attention with her pointer to the question "What is AIDS?", and the preservice teacher who drew this picture emphasises this with her explanation that "people need to be taught" about the epidemic. The drawing of the condom posits prevention through the mantra of the ABC approach; the term 'choice' suggests that those who want to avoid infection have control over their sexual encounters by abstaining, being faithful, or condomising.[ii] The remaining two drawings (Figures 11.11 and 11.12) call attention to the importance of self-knowledge in relation to the virus: one by depicting a person who lacks CD4 count knowledge and the other by presenting both a thriving and a dying tree as a metaphor for the effect that self-awareness and HIV&AIDS awareness and their opposites, respectively, have on people. But although a commitment to HIV&AIDS education is clearly depicted in these drawings, there is a striking absence of evidence that these preservice teachers understood while drawing that providing such education requires more than teacher-led knowledge transmission. However, my interests and knowledge affect my interpretation of the drawings; therefore, throwing open the reading to the preservice teachers themselves would likely reveal their foci and could be used, along with my analysis, to generate discussion on, for example, the role of the educator in HIV&AIDS education.

Since completing these introductory drawings, the preservice teachers of the Youth as Knowledge Producers project have completed workshops on using arts-based methods to address HIV- and AIDS-related challenges for educators. For example, they have worked with collage, hip-hop, and image theatre to envisage solutions to negotiating sex within relationships. Then, accompanied by experienced educators, they worked to translate what they had learned into classroom lessons. It was a complex challenge, and researchers noted the tendency of the young preservice teachers to become didactic. This was discussed in debriefing sessions attended by both researchers and the young teachers.

Based on what I have concluded from work in the From Our Frames project about the value of participants themselves looking across drawing collections, in this second project, I still have the opportunity to test out what emerges when the Youth as Knowledge Producers preservice teachers work to interpret those introductory drawings they produced on their views of HIV and AIDS. I hope that thinking together about didacticism will be productive in the light of my interpretations of the drawings as well as theirs. For example, in Figure 11.9 there is no sign of any interaction occurring between the learners and the teacher. The teacher is more carefully drawn than the learners, and her image includes a lot of detail. She wears a patterned skirt with a plain top. She has an AIDS ribbon pinned to her top, and her hair style is shown in some detail. The learners, however, are little more than blobs sitting in front of her. They have no distinguishing features or characteristics and differ only in terms of height, ranging from biggest to smallest. This may well further indicate that the artist sees herself, as teacher, to be more important than her learners. Presenting this possible interpretation to Nadia might well encourage her to rethink her views on teaching as didactic knowledge transmission.

Nonhlahla's lack of awareness about what constitutes choice within the ABC model of HIV prevention may well be linked to her notion of teacher as agent of knowledge transmission and pointing this out as a possible interpretation of her drawing may well encourage new ways of thinking in this preservice teacher.

Along with the discussion that my interpretations of their drawings might lead to, I plan to invite the preservice teachers to compare their depicted views of HIV and AIDS with the schoolchildren's drawings presented in the next section. In this way, I hope to increase the preservice teachers' critical consciousness about what it is to be a learner and what is involved in the intimate relationship between the HIV-positive learner and her or his infection.

COMPARISONS BETWEEN AND ACROSS DRAWINGS

Several months after the completion of the From Our Frames workshops, on the occasion of the Faculty Open Day, the preservice teachers' HIV-related messages (which they had constructed in the form of photo-stories or photo posters) were exhibited to an audience of schoolchildren interested in future enrolment as trainee teachers. The preservice teachers offered the schoolchildren the opportunity to comment on what they considered to be the best HIV&AIDS photo messages, and the children were also invited to justify their choices. Included on the pages given to them to record their comments was an invitation to draw their own representations of HIV and AIDS. This drawing exercise was exactly like the one

157

that the beginning teachers had taken part in before constructing their photo messages. Although many schoolchildren commented on the photo messages, only three turned the page over to do a drawing in response to the same prompt used for the preservice teacher groups: '*Draw a picture that represents your view of HIV and AIDS.*' One of the children drew a stick figure of a girl and wrote, "This is me helping." The other two schoolchildren's drawings are shown next.

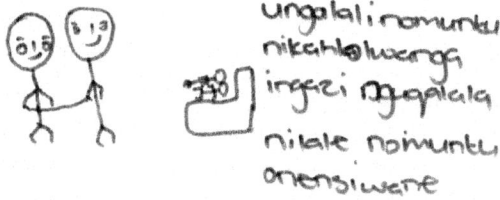

Figure 11.13. Sexual engagement and HIV and AIDS.

The schoolgirl who drew this picture wrote an explanation in isiZulu beside it: "Do not sleep with a person without having a blood test first—in case you sleep with an infected person" is the literal translation.

Figure 11.14. HIV and AIDS and its impact on the community.

The young person who produced this drawing did not write an explanation to accompany it. He or she presented a sequence of four scenes. In the absence of the artist's written comment, my semiotic interpretation follows. In the first scene, two adults—one male, judging by the appearance of the ears and hair, and one female, who is clearly pregnant—and two children stand in front of two small buildings, perhaps their home. Their smiles and close proximity to each other signify, for me, a happy family group. Each adult holds the hand of one of the two children, and the free hand of the male adult figure is extended towards the other child. The second scene, in contrast, is filled with sadness, showing a female figure with down-turned mouth lying on a bed. This figure has hair similar to that of the woman in the first scene. She is dying. This is clearly indicated in a speech bubble: "My baby died yesterday and soon I am also dying." The impression that this is the same woman is intensified by the fact that she is pregnant in the first scene but is not pregnant in the second scene. The repeated use of "R.I.P." and the dates on the eight rectangles indicate unequivocally that the third scene is of a graveyard. If the dates on the tombstones indicate dates of birth and death, simple arithmetic shows that the scene refers to the deaths of young people. The fourth scene shows three figures standing in front of two buildings similar to those in the first scene. Their down-turned mouths and the tears on the faces of the smaller figures portray misery. Reading across the four scenes, I interpret the unhappiness of these three figures to relate to the absence—perhaps, death—of the fourth member, the mother figure of the group in the first scene.

Having the Youth as Knowledge Producers preservice teachers engage with these pictures drawn by schoolchildren could be enormously productive in that each of these drawings shows far more awareness of HIV and AIDS than do any of the adults' pictures. The two people about to have sex in Figure 11.13 have what might be described as lascivious, or at least knowing, looks on their faces. This may be a function of teenaged preoccupation with sex but may equally be the recognition that sex is, both in its inevitability and in the inevitability of HIV transmission if it is unprotected sex, an issue that has to be confronted. The preservice teachers' drawings show little awareness of the relationship between sex and HIV transmission: Only the mention of 'condomise' draws attention to this relationship. The pregnancy evident in the first scene of the four-part drawing done by a schoolchild speaks directly to (unprotected) sex.

As researchers, we need to ask why this is the case. Are these preservice teachers living out a notion that appropriate behaviour in teachers excludes overt reference to sex? Sbu's words, "The image represents a skinny victim of HIV/AIDS after he discovered that he is HIV positive. A person didn't take his ARVs that is why his CD4 count went down until he got sick and became skinny", indicate that for him the issue is one of treatment adherence. There is no indication that prevention is part of his awareness and no indication that sex is likely to have played its part in the infection of the depicted person.

Careful management of a comparison of these pictures, along with a discussion between us, as researchers, and these preservice teachers, may lead to the recognition that transmission style teaching is not going to help address the issue of learners coming to terms with the problems and challenges of HIV and AIDS. What teachers need is the awareness shown by, for example, the anonymous artist of the four-part drawing, who accurately and poignantly tackles the situation.

Perhaps, in this way, I will be able to use all the drawings as pedagogical and research tools for their producers in relation to how they and others have viewed them as well as how I have interpreted them. And if this process of revisiting these drawings can include an external auditor, my personal bias as the researcher might be addressed, if not actually reduced, so that the drawings can become more powerful, potentially, as tools.

ACKNOWLEDGEMENTS

Jean Stuart wishes to thank her research colleagues and all the participants involved in the Youth as Knowledge Producers project for their enthusiastic participation and ongoing contribution to HIV&AIDS education; the National Research Foundation (NRF) for funding the project research (Stuart, J., Mitchell, C., Pattman, R., De Lange, N., Moletsane, R., & Buthelezi, T. [2007–2008]. *Youth as Knowledge Producers: Arts-based approaches to HIV and AIDS prevention and education in rural KwaZulu-Natal.* NRF study); all the student participants in the From Our Frames project who tackled the exploration of arts-based methods with her; and her PHD supervisor Professor Claudia Mitchell, who taught her how to write about her experiences.

NOTES

i   Because this is a reflective piece, it is written in the first person voice of the first author who did the research. The second author functioned as what Creswell (2009) calls an "external auditor" (p. 192) in providing alternative critical readings of the data. The analysis of the drawings in this chapter and the critical questions posed represent a confluence of the first author's reflections and the second author's critical contemplation of the data, which then doubles back to meeting the first author's reflections and so on.

ii *The South African National HIV Prevalence, Incidence, Behaviour and Communication Survey, 2008: A Turning Tide Among Teenagers?* (Shisana et al., 2009) draws attention to the many complex reasons why such control is not possible.

REFERENCES

Creswell, J. W. (2009). *Research design: Qualitative, quantitative, and mixed methods approaches* (3rd ed.). Thousand Oaks, CA: Sage.

Freire, P. (1972). *Pedagogy of the oppressed.* Harmondsworth, England: Penguin Books.

Rose, G. (2001). *Visual methodologies: An introduction to the interpretation of visual materials.* London, England: Sage.

Shisana, O., Rehle, T., Simbayi, L., Parker, W., Zuma, K., Bhana, A., . . . Pillay, V. (Eds.). (2009). *The South African national HIV prevalence, incidence, behaviour and communication survey, 2008: A turning tide among teenagers?* Cape Town, South Africa: HSRC Press. Retrieved from http://www.hsrcpress.ac.za

Stuart, J. (2006). From our frames: Exploring with teachers the pedagogic possibilities of a visual arts-based approach to HIV and AIDS. *Journal of Education HIV/AIDS, 38*(3), 67–88.

Stuart J. (2007). Drawings and transformation in the health arena. In N. de Lange, C. Mitchell, & J. Stuart (Eds.), *Putting people in the picture: Visual methodologies for social change* (pp. 229–240). Rotterdam, The Netherlands: Sense.

Swart, J. (1990). *Malunde: The street children of Hillbrow.* Johannesburg, South Africa: Witwatersrand University Press.

Theron, L. C. (2008). "I have undergone some metamorphosis!" The impact of REds on South African educators affected by the HIV/Aids pandemic. A pilot study. *Journal of Psychology in Africa, 18*(1), 29–40.

Weber, S., & Mitchell, C. (2004). Visual artistic modes of representation for self-study. In J. J. Loughran, M. L. Hamilton, V. K. LaBoskey, & T. Russell (Eds.), *International handbook of self-study of teaching and teacher education practices* (pp. 979–1037). Dordrecht, The Netherlands: Kluwer Academic.

Williams, S. J., & Bendelow, G. (1998). Malignant bodies: Children's beliefs about health, cancer and risk. In S. Nettleton & J. Watson (Eds.), *The body in everyday life* (pp. 103–123). London, England: Routledge.

HOW TEACHER-RESEARCHER TEAMS SEE THEIR ROLE IN PARTICIPATORY RESEARCH

Liesel Ebersöhn, Ronél Ferreira, and Bathsheba Mbongwe

BACKGROUND TO DRAWING-BASED INQUIRY

STAR Project

Our investigation forms part of a broader study that commenced in 2003. Supportive Teachers, Assets and Resilience (STAR) is an ongoing collaborative project between South African primary and secondary school teachers from three provinces and educational psychology researchers from the Unit for Education Research in AIDS and the Department of Educational Psychology at the University of Pretoria. The STAR intervention emerged from a number of studies (Ebersöhn, Ferreira, & Mnguni, 2008; Ferreira, 2007, 2008; Ferreira, Ebersöhn, & Loots, 2008; Ferreira, Ebersöhn, & Odendaal, 2010; McCallaghan, 2007) in a longitudinal study on resilience in schools. All these studies constituted the pilot phase of the STAR intervention project. For the pilot phase, researchers partnered with female teachers (n=10) at a primary school in an informal settlement community in the Eastern Cape. The aim of the participatory reflection and action partnership was to investigate how resilience in a school could be addressed by teachers' psychosocial support actions.

During further phases of the STAR project, similar partnerships have been set up with teachers (n=30) in three other schools in two other South African provinces (Ebersöhn, 2006, 2007; Ebersöhn & Ferreira, 2009; Loots, Ebersöhn, Ferreira, & Eloff, 2009; Olivier, 2009). During 2007–2009, 30 of these teachers were trained as STAR facilitators. Currently, the project is in a dissemination research phase in which STAR facilitators are implementing STAR with teachers in neighbouring schools (Ebersöhn, 2008, 2009). In all, teachers (n=74) from eight additional schools are being trained by STAR facilitators, with researchers fulfilling a monitoring and evaluation, as well as a supportive, role.

In this chapter, we report on the way in which we used drawings to elicit teacher-researchers' experiences of being involved in the STAR intervention. Specifically, we explore teacher-researchers' experiences from a feminist standpoint perspective so as to reflect on power and roles in a longitudinal participatory inquiry.

L. Theron et al. (eds.), Picturing Research: Drawing as Visual Methodology, 163–176.

CHAPTER 12

DRAWING PARTNERSHIP EXPERIENCES

Purpose and Rationale of the Inquiry

The purpose of our feminist qualitative research is explanatory and descriptive by nature (Babbie, 2005) since we endeavour to elucidate on partnership dynamics and mechanics, and on power relations and dynamics, as experienced by co-researchers, with the aim of informing Participatory Reflection and Action (PRA) methodology. Despite an understanding of the importance of partnership in community asset-based projects, existing knowledge, in terms of practical issues that emerge during the process of community research collaboration, remains limited (Altman, 1995; Baum, Santich, Craig, & Murray, 1996; Guldan, 1996). As Willms (1997) states, "Research should be understood as a process of rediscovering and recreating personal and social realities" (p. 7).

Therefore, our inquiry does not merely involve the creation of knowledge for the purpose of expanding an academic discipline (participatory methodology) but is also about making it possible for individuals (participating teachers) to understand their own realities. Even though traditional academic research may allow for academics to pursue intellectual endeavours, community-based research creates opportunities for marginalised individuals to better understand their own realities and seek to recreate these because this will help them understand these realities from a different perspective in ways that might benefit them. In essence, our study describes what transpires when co-researchers are brought together to explore 'working as partners' in participatory research with university researchers.

(POWER-FULL) THINKING ABOUT PARTNERSHIP

Feminist Standpoint Theory and Gaventa's 'Power Cube'

Our interest in power relations, partnership, and feminist theory led us to investigate what might become visible if a feminist lens was applied to partnerships and power relations in participatory research. Specifically, we situate our study within feminist standpoint theory because of our interest in local sites of power, particularly the locations in which power is exercised, and look at how the relevant discourses might include and exclude privileges and issues of knowledge (Halbert, 2006). A feminist standpoint can provide insight into power, knowledge, and social structures (Brookfield, 2001; Jacques, 1992; Ritzer, 1992). Feminism has conceptualised power as a resource to be (re)distributed as domination and as empowerment, both at an individual and collective level (Belenky, Clinchy, Goldberger, & Tarule, 1986). Through this study, we could thus formulate a method of articulating voices of participants as they experience power relations, collaboration, the authority of knowledge, and experiences of enablement.

We selected Gaventa's (2006) 'power cube' as our analytical framework to analyse three dimensions of power: spaces, forms, and levels. Gaventa (2006) stated that many of the sides of a cube may be used as a first point of power analysis. He argued that any successful change in power relations requires each of

164

the pieces on each dimension of a cube to align with each other simultaneously. In order to understand power relations, we need to ask how the spaces of power for participation have been created—with whose interest in mind and with what terms of engagement (Gaventa, 2006).

In terms of the first dimension of power, continuums of space exist in three types (Gaventa, 2006). First, the notion of 'closed spaces' concerns the question of whether or not decisions are made by a set of actors behind closed doors: Do researchers make decisions and provide services 'to the people' without the need for consultation or their involvement? Secondly, the notion of 'invited spaces' is concerned with the type of people invited by various authorities to participate. These spaces, as ways of consultation, can range from ongoing to more transient. Thirdly, 'claimed/created spaces' are often claimed by the less powerless actors from the power holders.

The second dimension of power concerns the level at which power operates and the interrelationship of the various potential levels (Gaventa, 2006). These levels can include power interplay on local/regional levels, national levels, or in the global arena. Organisations and encounters from a range of levels can influence power relations in a direct or indirect manner.

Finally, the last dimension of Gaventa's (2006) power cube involves the forms of power, which are referred to as the dynamics of power that shape the inclusiveness of participation within each space. The forms of power involve three dimensions. 'Visible power' refers to an observable form of decision making (strategies that entail the 'who', 'how', and 'what'). 'Hidden power' entails power forms in which certain powerful people and institutions maintain their influence by controlling who makes decisions and what is included on the agenda. Lastly, 'invisible power' is an insidious form of power because it shapes the psychological and ideological boundaries of participation: Certain problems and issues are kept not only from the decision-making table but also from the minds and consciousness of the different players involved. This might influence how individuals think about their place in the world; it might shape people's beliefs, their sense of self, and their acceptance (or refusal) of the status quo. Invisible power influences the construction of 'voices' in invited spaces: Participants may merely echo what the power holders who shape places want to hear (Gaventa, 2006).

LOCATING DRAWINGS IN PARTICIPATORY REFLECTION AND ACTION (PRA)

PRA is a methodology for interacting with local people, understanding the context in which they live, and learning from their experiences. It involves a set of principles, a process of communication, and a menu of methods that seek local people's participation in putting forward their points of view to make use of such learning. It initiates a participatory process and aims to sustain it. PRA is a means of collecting different kinds of data; identifying and mobilising intended groups; evoking their participation; and opening ways in which intended groups can participate in decision making, project design, execution of actions, and monitoring of progress and outcomes (Chambers, 2005; Mukherjee, 1993).

Based on its participatory nature, PRA is a useful methodology through which to focus attention on people, their livelihoods, and their inter-relationships with socio-economic and ecological factors. To fully explore an in-depth experience of co-researchers as partners in research with particular reference to power relations, our study rests on a PRA design. Because PRA can be categorised as an innovative approach to data collection, we have continually sought for unique ways of inquiry that could illuminate information on participants' experiences in terms of power relations in research partnerships.

Within the broad methodological framework of PRA, we used drawings as a visual data collection method to help explain how co-researchers view themselves as participating teams in a participatory research project. Educational researchers (see, for example, Richards, 1996, 1998), particularly those employing qualitative methods, often express interest in using visual approaches as a form of inquiry (see, for example, Banks, 2001; Emmison & Smith, 2000; Janesick, 2004; Pink, 2001; Prosser, 1998; Rose, 2007; Van Leeuwen & Jewitt, 2001). Visual method interpretation as a form of data provides the alternative opportunity to explain phenomena in a rich manner, interpreting experiences (Coffey & Atkinson, 1996). "Making a picture is a form of thinking" (Ernst-daSilva, 2001, p. 4) that might be used as a vehicle for promoting self-exploration, reflection, and personal discovery. Following post-positivist research, social scientists have often connected photographs, videos, drawings, paintings, and film with narrative description to help illuminate societies' cultures and behaviours (Denzin & Lincoln, 2005) in an attempt to understand people's thinking and experiences (Clifford & Marcus, 1986; Flick, 2002; Pink, 2001).

METHODOLOGY

We conveniently selected 20 teachers (2 men and 18 women) who participated in a colloquium[i] as participants in this inquiry. Table 12.1 outlines the schools, the provinces the schools represent, and the number of teacher-participants from each school at the colloquium. For the drawing activity, teachers worked together in teams. Because of their numbers, the participants from School 1 were divided into two teams for the drawing activity. For the purpose of our study, we did not differentiate between the perceptions and experiences of male and female teachers, regarding the data holistically in terms of the groups in which the participants worked.

Table 12.1. Teacher-researcher participants.

School and Province	Role in STAR phases	Members at colloquium	Teams
1, Eastern Cape	STAR pilot school, STAR facilitators, disseminated STAR to 2 schools	8	A & B
2, Eastern Cape	Trained in STAR by School 1 STAR facilitators	2	C
3, Eastern Cape	Trained in STAR by School 1 STAR facilitators	2	D
4, Mpumalanga	Trained in STAR	4	E
5, Gauteng	Trained in STAR	4	F

We requested the teacher-researcher teams to draw a symbol of their experience as partners in the ongoing STAR project. Following the drawing exercise, each team chose a representative to present its drawing to the colloquium audience (see Figures 12.1 and 12.2). We audio-recorded these presentations and transcribed them later as verbatim accounts. We also visually documented the drawings as photographs (see Figures 12.3–12.8).

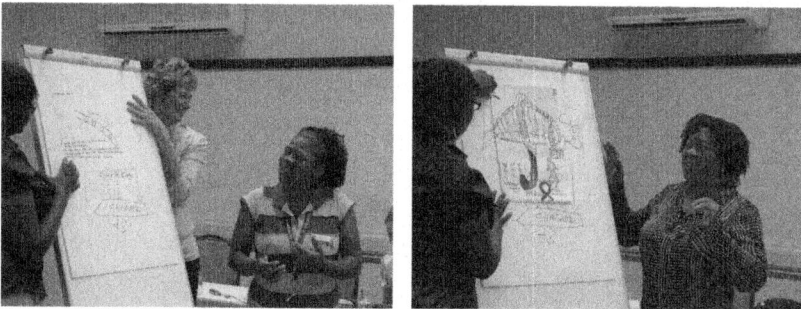

Figures 12.1 and 12.2. Presenting drawings to the colloquium audience.

Prior to the colloquium, we asked all participants if we had their informed consent to include inputs during the colloquium in our research database. As part of the STAR project, teacher-participants elected not to remain anonymous but to be identified (by name and visually in photographs) in any reports and publications as co-creators of knowledge flowing from the project. For this reason, we explained the purpose and processes that we would follow at the colloquium in order for them to be able to make an informed decision about whether or not they wanted to participate in this phase of the project. We also reminded all participants that they could withdraw (themselves or their contributions) from the process at any time if they wished to do so. Since the participants had been involved in the STAR project for several years, they were all familiar with research ethics and the application of the relevant ethical principles. In our employment of PRA principles, we continually followed an open approach through which participants were involved in and informed about the research process, ensuring that we were not misleading or deceiving them in any manner. Finally, we attended to the ethical principle of accuracy by reporting on the data we obtained during the colloquium in an accurate manner when disseminating it (Babbie, 2005; Denzin & Lincoln, 2005).

We thematically analysed both the visual images of the drawings (see Figures 12.3–12.8) as well as the verbatim transcripts of the drawing-presentations. We made use of multiple coders during thematic analysis. Participant validation formed part of both data generation and subsequent data analysis.

Drawings of Teacher-Researcher Teams

Figure 12.3. Team A: Cow.

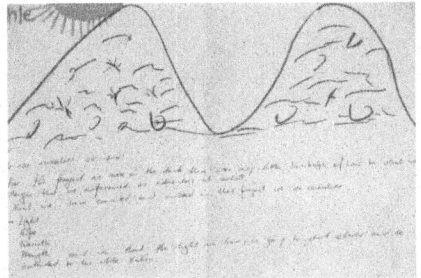

Figure 12.4. Team B: Sun.

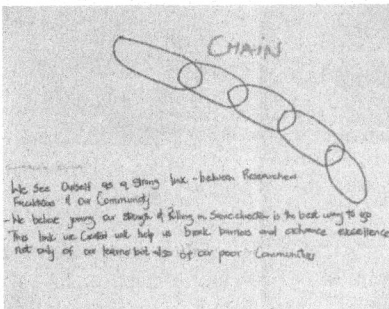

Figure 12.5. Team C: Chain.

Figure 12.6. Team D: Sun.

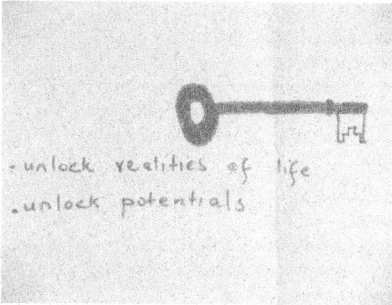

Figure 12.7. Team E: Key.   *Figure 12.8. Team F: Umbrella.*

RESULTS

Thematic Analysis

Table 12.2 presents an overview of raw data (drawings and transcribed participant comments) from the presentation of the various teams' drawings. In the last column of the table, we present a first-level interpretation of our understanding of the drawings in conjunction with participant comments.

Table 12.2. Drawings, participant comments, and first-level meaning-making.

School and Team	Drawing	Comment	First Interpretation
1, Team A	Cow	*"Learners and community are suckling from us as well as members in our school .... As you see we are fat and we have big udders."*	We nurture
1, Team B	Sun	*"The sun gives light to everyone. It gives hope, warmth as well as strength."* *"We ... go and expand whatever we have received back to the nation."*	We give hope

2, Team C	Chain	*"We see ourselves as a strong link between researchers and learners in the community. We believe joining our strength and in the same direction is the best way to go."*	We link
3, Team D	Sun	*"We give warmth to learners, educators and our community with the sunrays. The light, which we receive from the researchers here, we apply it back to our community and our school."*	We give warmth
4, Team E	Key	*"We are seeing our self as a key that can unlock realities of life to the community .... And we are also unlocking their potential .... They did things they never thought of doing before."*	We unlock
5, Team F	Umbrella	*"It encompasses all the things that we gained from the workshops. We gained passion, enthusiasm, motivation."*	We integrated our support

Three themes (each with categories) emerged from our thematic analysis of both the drawings and verbatim transcriptions. The teachers indicated, first, that they had obtained power from researchers during the participatory project. Second, teachers seemingly equated their experience of power in the participatory project with providing a service. Finally, the teachers expressed commitment to extend the power they experienced.

The power that teachers mentioned as being obtained from researchers during participatory research was reflected in terms of (1) acquired capacity, as signified by Team F's teachers expressing that "we are renewed" and adding that they had an "umbrella shape" encompassing their newly acquired competencies. Similarly, Team A expressed their feelings of capacity by stating, "As you see we are fat and we have big udders." The reported gained power was further mirrored in (2) future expressions of hope, optimism, and expectancy. In this regard, teachers articulated that they "gained passion, enthusiasm, motivation" (Team F); they commented on "the light, which [they] receive from the researchers" (Team D); they decided to "expand whatever [they had] received" (Team B); and they spoke of "unlocking their potential" (Team E).

Teachers seemed to equate power with service provision, particularly in two areas. First, teachers felt that the power they experienced afforded them the necessary means to provide or unlock new information and different perspectives on life for others. In this regard, Team E stated that "[they could] unlock unrealities of life" and that "people should know that HIV&AIDS is there and it kills" whereas Team D suggested that "the information [they] have will be a remedy" (Team D). Correspondingly, Team C felt that the teachers' role as chain "helps [them] break barriers and achieve excellence". Second, teachers linked their power to the ability to provide care and support, signified in statements such as "the sunrays, we use it, because it gives warmth, health and life" (Team D); "we are nurturing" (Team A); "it gives hope, warmth as well as strength" (Team B); and "these kids will get help from the clinic, the vegetable diet, and then they will be taken care" (Team F).

Teachers' commitment to spread their gained power was, on the one hand, indicated by teachers reportedly targeting audiences whom they (as teachers) considered relevant for service provision (power). Such recipients include various school-related systems, as illustrated by the following vignette from Team D:

> We give warmth to learners, educators and our community with the sunrays. The light, which we receive from the researchers here, we apply it back to our community and our school. The researchers' light will not fade, we will take it with us back to our communities, to our school and everybody who needs it …. We have street children back home.

Other excerpts relating to identified recipients of teachers' power include, on the one hand: "learners and the community are suckling from us as well as members in our schools" (Team A); "unlock realities … to the community" (Team E); "whatever we have received back to the nation …. It starts slower and then it's going to extend to the community" (Team B); "we see ourselves as a strong link between researchers and learners and the community" (Team E); "not only to our learners but to our poor community" (Team E)"; and "these kids will get help" (Team F).

On the other hand, teachers' commitment to spread their gained power is implied by their dedication to the belief that "the researchers' light will not fade" (Team D), that "we are motivated and encouraged to go and work harder" (Team F), and that "we take ourselves to go and expand whatever we have received" (Team B). In addition, Team C summarised their selected way of giving life to their dedication: "Joining our strength and in the same direction is the best way to go."

POWER-SHARING INSIGHTS

Situating Our Results within Gaventa's 'Power Cube' Model

According to the teacher-participants' experiences (as reflected in the themes that emerged), the dynamics of power in a participatory project could be influenced by dimensions of power. It seems as if the type of space available in this scenario is that of an ongoing invited space where people (teachers, target audiences, researchers) are invited to participate by various authorities (teachers, target audiences, researchers). In addition, the ongoing invited space seems to become a claimed or created space as teachers take over some of the roles in a participatory project (determining the nature of power and also targeting audiences for power).

Based on the results we obtained from this study, we posit that teachers might perceive power in a participatory project to operate on the interrelated levels of national and local arenas. This is indicated by these locations of power seemingly being influenced by both the purpose of local civil society organisations (specific health, nutrition, and education needs of local community members) as well as broader national-level debates (poverty and HIV prevention as examples). Regarding the form that power can take, the teachers in our study highlighted that the inclusiveness of participation is often shaped by visible power as expressed by teachers' belief in observable decision making concerning strategies of what power constitutes as well as who would be holding the power and how power would be executed.

Drawing Insights from Drawings: Perspectives on Power, Partnerships, and Participatory Methodology

Figure 12.9 illustrates our meaning-making based on the findings presented.

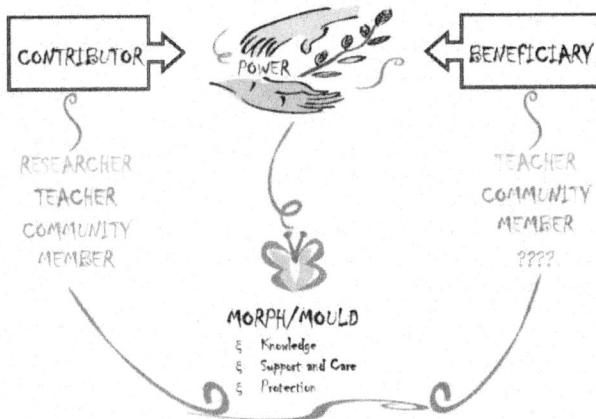

Figure 12.9. Insights on power, partnerships, and participatory methodology.

Based on these findings, we posit that during participatory studies contributors and beneficiaries collaborate (take hands) to develop a chain of power. We theorise that each contributor decides on (1) the nature of power (care, support, knowledge, hope) and (2) the target audience (beneficiary) of power (teacher, learners, school, community). In subsequent phases of participatory research, the beneficiary becomes the contributor. In this way, we argue that power changes or morphs during participatory inquiry.

We therefore found that for teacher-participants, *power* in a participatory project could be visible and mirror local and/or national level debates while fusing ongoing invited space with created/claimed space. Likewise, in terms of power, teacher-participants apparently experienced themselves, among other roles, as co-researchers. In this regard, in participatory methodology, teacher-participants might experience *joint roles* of the initial *beneficiary* of power and the subsequent *contributor* of power. In the participatory process, the teacher-participant in the role of contributor and/or researcher would then mould *power* by deciding on the new beneficiary as well as the nature of power to contribute. In this way, power is morphed by whoever is fulfilling the role of contributor at a given time.

Our theorising of power in participatory research as voiced by the co-researchers (teachers) in our study remains flawed. We are left wondering what role contributors might play and when, in further stages of participatory endeavours, the beneficiary will assume the role of contributor. Do contributors subsequently become obsolete in the participatory research investigation? Or do contributors merge into the background landscape of research, becoming observers of processes? Or do they remain contributors, but as secondary, adjutant ones to a newly designated primary contributor? Other possible hypotheses include the possibility that future cycles of participatory research could assign contributors the roles of useful advisors, superfluous voyeurs, or redundant outsiders.

Our study aims to add insights to the field of participatory research methodology, particularly within an asset-based intervention approach, by positing the above understandings of power relations in partnerships in PRA. Subsequently, the findings of our study might inform best practices and future participatory projects.

POWERFUL PICTURES

The Difference Drawings Made in This Inquiry

Using drawings to elicit experiences proved valuable in this inquiry. Teachers were able to express experiences of their team's perspective on a phenomenon (being participants in a collaborative project) without the barrier of language encumbering their expression. In addition, the drawing activity provided a space for teachers to collectively articulate their experiences. In this way, the process of drawing was opportune in creating a space for participants from schools to unify their shared experiences of participation. The process of drawing (teachers co-deciding what their experiences were, what to draw, who would draw, who would present the drawing to the group at large) thus became a shared-power space in the story of collaborative research. Similarly, the drawings provided a way of measuring experience in a culturally appropriate way. First, teachers could interpret the drawing request among themselves in their mother tongue. Then, they could draw on their communal histories to single out a contextually and culturally meaningful metaphor to signify their experience. In this way, then, the suns, cow, umbrella, and chain arguably became cultural artefacts of lived experience revealed as data generation.

The drawings were similarly appropriate as a data collection method in a participatory project. Teachers easily negotiated around the interactive, group-based nature of being requested to draw; discussing and drawing in groups; interacting with researchers facilitating the data generation among groups; and finally, reporting back to the various groups regarding their individual team drawings. In the same way, the drawings (as data generation product) seemed to become interview schedules, since the drawings facilitated discussions that subsequently took the form of interviews, guided by certain questions.

During each team's presentation (reporting back) of the drawing, the team members used the drawing to structure their verbal meaning-making of joint experiences. During this process, the drawings had the added advantage of serving to increase trustworthiness. In this regard, the drawings and verbal accounts provided means of representing authentic participant expressions during dissemination (as with this chapter). Similarly, the presentations of the drawings led to a first round of participant validation as participants shared their meaning-making of the drawings with a broad audience, thus allowing them the opportunity to clarify uncertainties and questions that subsequently arose.

NOTES

[i] Partners in Education Research and Practice: Collaboration Between Teachers and Education Researchers colloquium, March 1–3, 2009, Amanzingwe Lodge, South Africa.
[ii] Funder prefers to remain anonymous.

REFERENCES

Altman, D. G. (1995). Sustaining interventions in community systems: On the relationship between researchers and communities. *Health Psychology, 14*(6), 526–536. doi:10.1037/0278-6133.14.6.526.
Babbie, E. R. (2005). *The basics of social research*. Belmont, CA: Thomson Wadsworth.
Banks, M. (2001). *Visual methods in social research*. London, England: Sage.
Baum, F., Santich, B., Craig, B., & Murray, C. (1996). Evaluation of a national health promotion program in South Australia. *Australian and New Zealand Journal of Public Health, 20*(1), 41–49. doi:10.1111/j.1467-842X.1996.tb01334.x.
Belenky, M. F., Clinchy, B. M., Goldberger, N. R., & Tarule, J. M. (1986). *Women's ways of knowing: The development of self, voice, and mind*. New York, NY: Basics Books.
Brookfield, S. D. (2001). Unmasking power: Foucalt and adult learning. *The Canadian Journal for the Study of Adult Education, 15*(1), 1–23.
Chambers, R. (2005). *Ideas for development*. London, England: Earthscan.

Clifford, J., & Marcus, G. E. (Eds.). (1986). *Writing culture: The poetics and politics of ethnography.* Berkeley: University of California Press.

Coffey, A., & Atkinson, P. (1996). *Making sense of qualitative data: Complementary research strategies.* Thousand Oaks, CA: Sage.

Denzin, N. K., & Lincoln, Y. S. (2005). *The SAGE handbook of qualitative research* (3rd ed.). Thousand Oaks, CA: Sage.

Ebersöhn, L. (2006). *School-based HIV&AIDS project.* Unpublished research report for M&SS Trust.[ii]

Ebersöhn, L. (2007). *Teachers supporting vulnerable children in the context of HIV&AIDS.* Unpublished research report for Toyota Albert Wessels Trust.

Ebersöhn, L. (2008). *Teachers supporting vulnerable children in the context of HIV&AIDS.* Unpublished research report for Foschini Group.

Ebersöhn, L. (2009). *Teachers supporting vulnerable children in the context of HIV&AIDS.* Unpublished research report for Foschini Group.

Ebersöhn, L., & Ferreira, R. (2009, March). *Teachers and researchers piloting a PRA intervention: Asset-based psychosocial support in the context of HIV&AIDS.* Paper presented at Partners in Education Research and Practice: Collaboration Between Teachers and Education Researchers colloquium, Magaliesburg, South Africa.

Ebersöhn, L., Ferreira, R., & Mnguni, M. (2008). Teachers' use of memory-box-making to provide psychosocial support in their pastoral role. *Journal of Psychology in Africa, 18*(3), 305–315.

Emmison, M., & Smith, P. (2000). *Researching the visual: Images, objects, contexts and interactions in social and cultural inquiry.* London, England: Sage.

Ernst-daSilva, K. (2001). Drawing in experience: Connecting art and language. *Primary Voices K–6, 10*(2), 2–8.

Ferreira, R. (2007). Community-based coping: An HIV/AIDS case study. In N. Duncan, B. Bowman, A. Naidoo, J. Pillay, & V. Roos (Eds.), *Community psychology: Analysis, context and action* (pp. 380–391). Cape Town, South Africa: UCT Press.

Ferreira, R. (2008). Culture at the heart of coping with HIV&AIDS. *Journal of Psychology in Africa, 18*(1), 97–104.

Ferreira, R., Ebersöhn, L., & Loots, T. (2008). Batemobilisering as strategie vir die hantering van MIV/VIGS. *Acta Academica, 40*(3), 142–162. Retrieved from http://www.up.ac.za/dspace/bitstream/2263/9738/1/Ferreira_Batemobilisering%282008%29.pdf.

Ferreira, R., Ebersöhn, L., & Odendaal, V. (2010). Community-based educational psychology intervention to enhance teachers' support competencies in the HIV&AIDS realm. *Education as Change, 14*(2), 103–113.

Flick, U. (2002). *An introduction to qualitative research* (2nd ed.). Thousand Oaks, CA: Sage.

Gaventa, J. (2006). Finding the spaces for change: A power analysis. *IDS Bulletin, 37*(6), 23–33. doi:10.1111/j.1759-5436.2006.tb00320.x

Guldan, G. S. (1996). Obstacles to community health promotion. *Social Science & Medicine, 43*(5), 689–695. doi:10.1016/0277-9536(96)00114-1

Halbert, D. (2006). Feminist interpretations of intellectual property. *American University Journal of Gender, Social Policy & the Law, 14*(3), 431–460. Retrieved from http://www.wcl.american.edu/journal/genderlaw/14/halbert3.pdf.

Jacques, R. (1992). Critique and theory building: Producing knowledge "from the kitchen". *Academy of Management Review, 17*(3), 582–606. doi:10.2307/258724.

Janesick, V. J. (2004). *"Stretching" exercises for qualitative researchers* (2nd ed.). Thousand Oaks, CA: Sage.

Loots, T., Ebersöhn, L., Ferreira, R., & Eloff, I. (2009, February). *Optimism and adversity as the two faces of teachers' psycho-social support within the context of HIV and AIDS.* Paper presented at HIV and AIDS Research Indaba, Centre for Study of AIDS, University of Pretoria, Pretoria, South Africa.

McCallaghan, M. (2007). Die gebruik van liggaamsportrette deur opvoeders in die vervulling van hulle pastoral rol (Master's thesis, University of Pretoria, Pretoria, South Africa). Retrieved from http://upetd.up.ac.za.

Mukherjee, N. (1993). *Participatory rural appraisal: Methodology and applications.* New Delhi, India: Concept.

Olivier, H. A. (2009). 'n Fenomenografiese ondersoek na verhoudinge binne die bategebaseerde benadering (Doctoral dissertation, University of Pretoria, Pretoria, South Africa). Retrieved from http://upetd.up.ac.za.

Pink, S. (2001). *Doing visual ethnography: Images, media and representation in research.* London, England: Sage.

Prosser, J. (Ed.). (1998). *Image-based research: A source book for qualitative research.* Philadelphia, PA: RoutledgeFalmer.

Richards, J. C. (1996). Creating self-portraits of teaching practices. *The Reading Professor, 18*(1), 4–19.

Richards, J. C. (1998). Self-portraits of teaching practices. In M. Milton (Ed.), *Reconceptualizing teacher education: Self-study in teacher education* (pp. 34–44). London, England: Lanier Press.

Ritzer, G. (1992). *Contemporary sociological theory* (3rd ed.). New York, NY: McGraw-Hill.

Rose, G. (2007). *Visual methodologies: An introduction to the interpretation of visual materials* (2nd ed.). Thousand Oaks, CA: Sage.

Van Leeuwen, T., & Jewitt, C. (Eds). (2001). *Handbook of visual analysis.* London, England: Sage.

Willms, D. G. (1997). You start your research on your being. In S. E. Smith, D. G. Willms, & N. A. Johnson (Eds.), *Nurtured by knowledge: Learning to do participatory action-research* (pp. 7–12). New York, NY: The Apex Press.

LEARNING TOGETHER:
TEACHERS AND COMMUNITY HEALTHCARE
WORKERS DRAW EACH OTHER

Naydene de Lange, Claudia Mitchell, and Jean Stuart

INTRODUCTION

Vulindlela is a rural district in the lower foothills of the Southern Drakensberg, a district in South Africa ravaged by the HIV&AIDS pandemic. In one area of the district, a vibrant clinic addresses the health issues of the surrounding community as best it can. Adjacent to the clinic is the ever-expanding Centre for the AIDS Programme of Research in South Africa (CAPRISA). The Centre is committed to finding a medical solution to the pandemic, especially for the benefit of this particular community. The many schools in the area are an indication of the large number of young people living in the community, all eager to learn and to make progress in life. However, these same young people are also the most affected by the pandemic. Worldwide, young people between the ages of 15 and 24 account for 40% of all new infections, with young women between the ages of 15 and 19 being the most vulnerable (UNAIDS, 2008). In 2007 in South Africa, 13% of females and 4% of males in the 15–24 age range were living with HIV (UNICEF, 2009). In the context of Vulindlela, the young people reflect these same statistics. In a sense, the clinic, with its community healthcare workers, and the neighbouring schools, with their educators, have a shared vested interest in keeping these young people alive and healthy. In this chapter, we focus on an 'entry point' intervention in which we asked community healthcare workers and teachers to draw pictures of each other. In order to contextualise the relationship between AIDS and young people, we provide a lengthy background to the very complex issue. We focus on how the use of drawings, as a participatory visual method, served to evoke discussion and, at the same time, offered a window into key issues to be addressed in multi-sectoral work. The chapter ends with a consideration of some critical concerns about using drawings as a research method in working with adults.

KEEPING YOUNG PEOPLE ALIVE IN THE AGE OF AIDS

Given the magnitude and complexity of issues of youth and sexuality in South Africa in the age of AIDS, no single intervention or sector can address all of the central factors such as poverty and the high rates of gender-based violence. Moreover, although several sectors might be focusing on the same target population, they might not actually be working in tandem; indeed, they might even

L. Theron et al. (eds.), Picturing Research: Drawing as Visual Methodology, 177–189.
© 2011 *Sense Publishers. All rights reserved.*

be working at cross purposes (De Lange et al., 2003). If communities are to play an effective role in AIDS prevention and care among youth, they need to consider ways of integrating the efforts of those working in various sectors: health, safety/security, community development, education, etc. However, although an integrated multi-sectoral approach to HIV&AIDS intervention may be key, community, school, and healthcare workers often lack a space in which to explore tactics and strategies and to share lessons learned. Hence, despite greater recognition by healthcare and community workers of the importance of schools in addressing the health of young people, attempts to date to deliver integrated sexual and reproductive health education in schools have often been hampered by the divisions that exist in the public service, such as the separation of Education, Health, and Social Services departments. A good example of this (and indeed the inspiration for our work in the first place) could be seen in a three-day conference in 2003 at what was then the University of Natal. The conference was on school-based approaches to healthcare and included primarily policy makers and practitioners from health and social services. However, almost no one involved in education attended, even though schools were being targeted as the entry point for service delivery. Oddly enough, cutting through the various bureaucratic layers to ensure that nurses were available to visit schools seemed to be viewed as the most important outcome. Instead, they should have realised that having all the support services available, such as well-trained healthcare professionals, age-appropriate materials, and transportation is only the beginning! The context of the school site, the particularities of the community, and classroom interactions are often overlooked as important features of program delivery. However, it is well established in fields such as pedagogy and curriculum development that these features are at the very heart of the teaching–learning process.

There is a possibility that both healthcare workers and educators run the risk of being demonised because of their work with young people. On the healthcare side, access to counselling and care through public health clinics is often very uneven for girls and young women in rural areas (Delius & Walker, 2002; Kelly & Parker, 2000). Equally problematic, however, are the attitudes and gendered assumptions by healthcare workers about young women seeking information related to safer sex practices. As Wood, Maforah, and Jewkes (1998) pointed out, attitudes of community healthcare workers often reinforce harmful stereotypes, and young women may even be made to feel ashamed of their requests for information. Although there is an emerging body of literature about youth-friendly clinics (Mitchell, 2004), these recommendations are still to be put into practice in most rural districts in KwaZulu-Natal. In addition, it is important to note that some of the more successful youth-friendly clinics outside South Africa (as in the case of Mozambique) are attached to schools (Mitchell, 2004). A study by Senderowitz (1999) confirmed the negative experiences of young people who seek HIV testing, pregnancy testing, and information on safer sex practices. Ninety-five percent of the respondents stated that the attitude of healthcare staff was the reason for their avoiding local clinics. Another study, by Vetten and Bhana (2001), suggested that the response of staff in rape crisis centres is particularly problematic since staff members often lack basic training, especially regarding the link between HIV and AIDS and gender-based violence. This is supported by Wood et al. (1998), who noted that health practitioners often feel inadequately equipped to converse with young people.

The importance of the school as a site for integrating services is of prime concern because it is both part of the solution and often a central part of the problem. Schools can serve as key points for delivery of services since they are community-based in terms of governance, and even 'out-of-school youth' are defined in terms of school units. However, schools are a particularly vulnerable site for affecting change in relation to HIV and AIDS. A study of the devastating effects of AIDS on the teaching population in KwaZulu-Natal clearly illustrates this point (Kahn, 2005; UNAIDS, 2006). It could be argued that teachers might not be in the best position to speak with young people about HIV and AIDS. Not only are teachers also vulnerable, but learners regard them as lacking both personal credibility and 'street cred' when it comes to discussing issues of sexuality. Indeed, as noted in a study by ActionAid regarding the challenges faced by schools in Tanzania and Kenya in implementing HIV prevention programs (Boler, Adoss, Ibrahim, & Shaw, 2003), the teachers felt that not only did they lack expertise in HIV&AIDS issues, education, and so on but that they often felt that they lacked the support of the parents to deal explicitly with issues of sexuality in the classroom. Furthermore, the teachers simply did not have the time to consider HIV&AIDS education because of their involvement in various curricular activities; they struggled to fit it into the content that they were obliged to cover. In some schools reported in the ActionAid study, teachers did not even participate in sexuality lessons provided by Community Based Organisations (CBOs) because it was thought that their presence could inhibit student participation. In other studies, teachers are the very predators who are responsible for putting young women at risk in the first place (De Lange, 2008; Human Rights Watch, 2001). Notwithstanding the crisis of AIDS, schools in many districts are still often barely functional when it comes to offering even basic education services such as providing textbooks and ensuring school attendance.

If schools have not necessarily played a key role to date in combating the AIDS crisis, they remain, as noted above, at the nexus of service delivery and also bring to the table a particular knowledge base in relation to youth, gender, and pedagogy. Indeed, even if the implementation of a learner-centred pedagogy still remains only a goal of the new curriculum and not an actuality, it should nevertheless be pursued. At the same time, and as is well-established in the research literature, AIDS is a result of a multiplicity of social, economic, pedagogical, and medical factors that extend beyond the knowledge base of any one professional group. Public nurses, for example, may have a more sophisticated medical knowledge about AIDS than teachers, even if teachers have a much better understanding of what pedagogy to use in discussing the pandemic and what is age-appropriate for the classroom. Those working in communication, particularly in relation to health promotion, are likely to understand the complexity of issues at play in trying to get the message across. Community and social welfare workers are likely to have a much more sophisticated understanding of the links between and among such factors as poverty and human security. Even from the perspective of the school itself, AIDS is not just a curricular area (for example, Life Skills) but also a management issue, one of human rights and protection and so on. It cannot be addressed easily through fragmentary one-off and disparate information sessions conducted by groups outside the school setting.

PICTURING EACH OTHER THROUGH DRAWINGS

Clearly, teachers and healthcare workers in rural settings need to understand each other. We, as researchers, were interested in how participatory methodologies could be used to bring together the various sectors and partners working in the area of gender, youth, and HIV prevention and care in one community. We wondered how we might first enable the community healthcare workers and the teachers to begin to understand each other's work and then to collaborate in addressing HIV and AIDS. In this context, we turned to art or, more specifically, drawings as an entry point for exploring professional identity. As a number of researchers have noted, drawing, although often associated with work with children, can be a very effective research tool with adults, particularly when it is framed within discussion and not in a competitive mode (Combrinck & Van Wyk, in press; D'Amant, 2009; Weber & Mitchell, 1995, 1996). Teachers from three senior secondary schools and community healthcare workers from the nearby clinic were invited to participate in the Learning Together project.[1] A group of 18 teachers and 18 community healthcare workers volunteered. They were all isiZulu-speaking. Half were male and half were female. Very simply, we asked the participants to draw how they saw each other (i.e., how the teachers 'saw' the community healthcare workers and how the community healthcare workers 'saw' the teachers).

It was arranged for the participants to meet at the local district clinic one afternoon after working hours. Once the participants were introduced to each other and told the purpose of the project, we engaged them in the 'entry point' drawing activity. They were given 15 minutes to work with the prompts: 'Teachers, draw how you see the community healthcare workers' and 'Community healthcare workers, draw how you see the teachers' Each participant was given an A4 sheet of white paper as well as a stick of charcoal. No further instructions were provided. Once their drawings were completed, the participants were invited to share their drawings with all the participants, if they so wished. In a follow-up discussion, later in the session, participants were divided into smaller groups composed of both teachers and healthcare workers. They shared more thoughts on their drawings and went on to compile questions they wanted to ask each other. Having obtained the participants' consent, the drawings were retained for analysis. The entire session was recorded on video.

To analyse the participants' perceptions of each other and the way drawings facilitate the emergence of these perceptions, we made use of the 'products', or material drawings, and, where possible, the associated sharing 'process' as captured on video. The process of analysing drawings always raises the issue of bias. At the first level of analysis, the participants' own interpretations were prioritised, voiced, and presented, with the participants sharing 'how we see each other' and formulating questions towards deeper understanding.

Now, several years after the event, we turn once again as researchers to the evidence in order to consider what the data reveals and to identify some critical issues in the methodology itself. Our analysis here draws first on the artists' own interpretations of their drawings and then on our reading of the drawings. Fortunately, most of the drawings have some text or captions anchoring potential interpretation and revealing the participants' points of view. Not all participants were captured on video presenting their drawings, yet where a participant's point of view was not clear to us in the drawing, we went back to the video recording to check against the participants' presentations and explanations of their drawings.

Altogether, we worked with 36 drawings by the participants and also with the video footage of the two-hour session. We began by scrutinising the visual and verbal content of the set of drawings, using a process of close reading (see, for example, Moletsane and Mitchell, 2007, on working with a single photograph) and a system of open coding to identify units of meaning and categories (Tesch, as cited in Creswell, 1994). In so doing, we began to identify emerging themes in the two sets of images.

EMERGING PERCEPTIONS

Starting with the images of the teachers produced by the healthcare workers, we saw positive depictions and less than positive depictions. On the positive side, the healthcare workers identified such points as "teaching for a better life", "bringing light", "respect[ing] each other", "good speaking", "expanding knowledge", "prevention through condom use" and "safe sex" in addressing HIV and AIDS. They also spoke about "caring and supportive" teachers acting as parents and sympathising with children. On the negative side, they noted that teachers "abuse children" with the stick, and sexually. Interestingly, they also noted that teachers drive nice cars.

Teachers depicted community healthcare workers in a variety of mostly positive ways. For example, the teachers said that "money is not the motivating factor". They also said that the healthcare workers' "heart is in the people they work with". They said that the healthcare workers are "dedicated", "supportive", "sympathetic, accepting, loving", and "hard working from early till late". However, they also stated that they can be "impatient, angry, and ill-treating". They identified the "caregiver role" and "drawing on skills and knowledge from books and experience" as well as the use of "injections, tablets, medication, bandages, first aid box", "nutrition", and that "gloves are their priority". Finally, the teachers' images of healthcare workers spoke of "giving hope" and made reference to the fact that they too need "love and protection from the community".

The themes just referred to are useful as indicators that show how both groups were viewed from a variety of perspectives with both positive and negative elements emerging for sharing and discussion. For closer scrutiny of how drawings can represent perceptions, we consider two drawings of teachers in which the image of a stick is central.

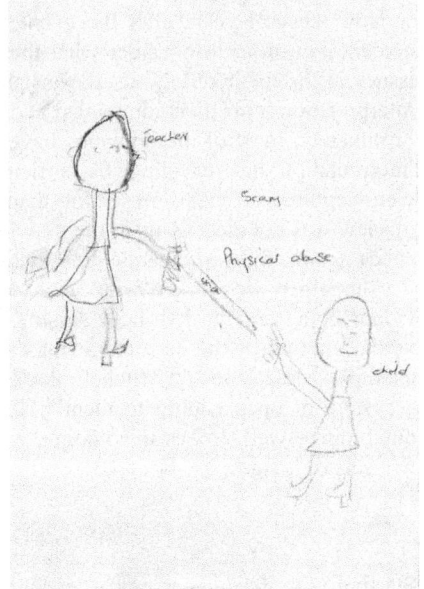

Figures 13.1 and 13.2. Community healthcare workers' drawings depicting teachers.

Figure 13.1 is a drawing of a male teacher by a healthcare worker. It is significant that the teacher is centred in the middle of the page since this placement displays the power he has in the classroom. The healthcare worker who drew the picture confirmed that this was indeed a central focus of the drawing and emphasised two aspects of the picture: the stick and the teacher's words. The teacher is raising a stick to point to alphabetical lettering on a chalk board. A speech bubble shows his didactic delivery, which has him commanding the learners to "Say it. These are small letters." The absence of hands on this teacher is intriguing and may possibly be interpreted as significant. However, nothing was mentioned in this regard.

In Figure 13.2, a stick appears again in the hands of a teacher and is prominent because of its central placement. However, in this case, its usage is more sinister because it is pointing directly at a child, and the words 'scary' and 'physical abuse' clarify the situation. The healthcare worker's presentation of this drawing made clear that it was the teacher's physically abusive nature that was being emphasised. Interestingly, the emphasis is on corporal punishment rather than on the teacher's delivery of knowledge. Also, the teacher is given large hands but no mouth, and the child is depicted with only one arm to ward off the 'scary' stick and 'physical abuse'. Unfortunately, without a further opportunity for elaboration from the healthcare worker, we can only guess if this was done consciously or not. However, for us as researchers it intensifies the impression of unequal power relations between child and teacher. During this study, it emerged that the healthcare workers felt that the teachers were better equipped to lead a discussion group than they were. Hence, it is noteworthy that in these drawings they depict teachers with a different and not necessarily admirable style of leadership. Their drawings bring a contentious subject, such as abuse, to the table.

Although the recurrence of themes across drawings was not examined, teachers were less inclined than healthcare workers to represent their subjects in a negative role. In fact, only one teacher's drawing depicted a healthcare worker negatively. It showed her being impatient, angry, and treating patients unkindly. The teacher depicted this worker with an unhappy face. Yet, even in this drawing the representation is balanced with a 'happy face' image and the words "love—listens, accepts and care[s]". Figures 13.3 and 13.4 are typically representative of the teachers' perceptions of healthcare workers.

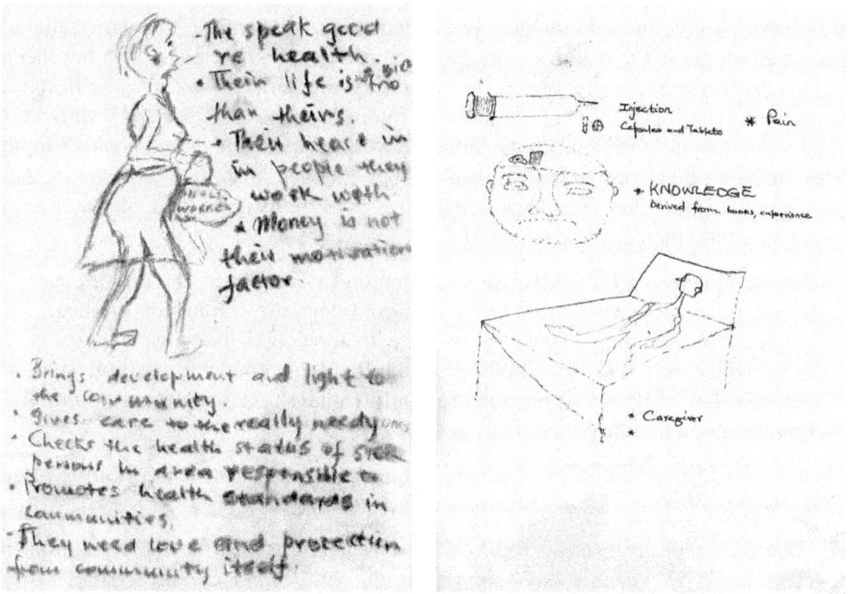

Figures 13.3 and 13.4. Teachers' drawings depicting community healthcare workers.

In Figure 13.3, we are presented with the side view of a female healthcare worker apparently in motion as indicated by the positioning of her feet, the forward thrust of her upper body, the way she holds the 'health worker' bag in front of her body with arm bent at a right angle to the ground, and the way in which her face is lifted and a prominent eye shows that her gaze is focused outside of the frame. The female figure is barefoot and her clothes are functional rather than decorative.

183

Overall, then, this figure signifies to us someone who is on a mission and who is unconscious of herself. On video, the artist/teacher presenting this drawing said that he had tried to list next to the figure all the things that a healthcare worker does, and this list seems to reinforce the reading of the figure as being in action beyond herself rather than being in any way self-interested. He portrays the perception of healthcare workers as people (specifically a woman, in this case) whose "heart is in the people they work with", for whom "money is not their motivation", who "speak good re health", who "bring development and light to the community", who "give care to the really needy", who "check the health status of sick persons in area", and who "promote health standards in communities". Because such people are obviously busy, it is unsurprising that the figure is in action, but the last bullet point below the drawing indicates the teacher's perception of the vulnerability of this community role player: "They need love and protection from community itself." This is an observation from the perspective of the teacher that our recorded data does not explain.

In Figure 13.4, the active nature of healthcare workers is also represented but this time purely through images associated with three roles: the pain reliever (depicted through the syringe and pills), a carrier of knowledge that has been gained partly through experience (conveyed by the serious-looking head), and a caregiver (signified by the bedbound figure). Although teachers' drawings predominantly showed dedicated healthcare workers in an active and positive light, the teachers' questions in the mixed groups showed that they also had other perceptions since they began to challenge possible stigma and shortcomings associated with their methods. One of the teachers observed:

> The acceptance of HIV/AIDS is not common to everybody, we are not sure about the acceptance of this thing ok—confidentiality. Some of the health workers, maybe they expose, you come to them and they just expose—I mean whispering with somebody or backbiting that somebody has got AIDS yet you don't know you are talking confidentially, yet people are pointing fingers at you that this person has got AIDS.

Healthcare workers' questions generally sought answers from teachers in relation to learner needs. One of the healthcare workers commented:

> Why do teacher refuse to use health worker if you want to talk the youth at the school? Do teacher have time to teach children about HIV&AIDS? If there is a student being abused by a teacher do he get help from other teacher? How do you take a situation like that?

As can be seen, various interesting (and contentious) issues emerged through participants' drawings and questions, and these allowed them and us insight into their understanding of each other. Using their drawings and discussions about their perceptions of each other, we were in a better position to develop a 'research as intervention' strategy in this rural community (see Mitchell, De Lange, Moletsane, Stuart, & Buthelezi, 2005).

SOME CRITICAL ISSUES IN THE DRAWING PROCESS

What Are the Power Dynamics and the Power of Play?

When we are engaging in participatory research with a social change focus in a community, it is necessary for us to be aware of possible power dynamics, not only between researchers and participants but also among the participants themselves. In this research, the participants were community healthcare workers and teachers. The community healthcare workers were ordinary village people who had been recruited to be trained in basic healthcare service delivery, in particular to address HIV and AIDS in their rural community. Most had only a Grade 12 qualification. The teachers recruited into this group were all senior secondary school teachers. Some lived in the community but most commuted from the nearby city, and some had university training. We were therefore sensitive in our attempts to create a space in which the participants could learn about, and from, each other, and we envisaged that using drawing could be a 'playful' tool to create this space. Ultimately, drawing led to photovoice work, and both activities were done in a very low-key and playful way: This supported a climate of collaboration.

Who Gets to Speak and Write?

One of the related challenges in the drawing activity, which also involved writing captions and later engaging in brainstorming activities on flip-chart paper, came out of small group work involving mixed groups of teachers and community healthcare workers. Community healthcare workers often deferred to the teachers when it came to writing on the flip-charts or reporting back to the whole group. "You are the teachers", they said. In fact, the drawing activity had very little to do with level of education or writing ability, but the deference displayed was a reminder that as researchers we need to take notice of perceived differences among the participants.

Who Has Access to Resources and What Are They Doing with These Resources?

As noted above in the analysis of the drawings, the drawing activity that started out in a somewhat uncritical, admiring way with each group recognising the strengths of the other, also created a space for a more honest appraisal by each group. The teachers, for example, who come to work in taxis every day, noted that the community healthcare workers have access to clinic vehicles to travel around the rural area to visit their patients. The community healthcare workers, most of whom would not be able to afford a vehicle, commented that teachers often have nice cars. Their perceptions of each other were often not quite accurate, but what they signalled was a deeper mistrust. Yet, it was not just the material differences they noted. Community healthcare workers noted that teachers are often not doing their job when it comes to educating children about sexuality and, further, that they may be guilty of sexually abusing children.

What Are the Dynamics of Interpretation Using the Drawing, the Caption, and the Artist's Explanation?

One of the advantages of having recorded the whole process on video is that we were able to go back over the session and bring back, in a sense, the moment. In addition, we were also able to see if there were aspects of the process that we had perhaps overlooked at the time. A review of the video-taped proceedings in which the healthcare workers shared the drawings of the stick-wielding teachers (see Figures 13.1 and 13.2) shows that although there was much laughter, there was also almost a sense of daring on the part of the healthcare workers in depicting their perceptions. In replaying the video, we also observed how a male teacher led every mixed group feedback session while a female healthcare worker stood quietly by, often, it appeared to us, exhibiting body language associated with unease and discomfort. It is quite surprising that through the drawings, the healthcare workers were able to expose some challenging issues. At the risk of over interpreting the interpretive process of teachers and healthcare workers working together, we acknowledge that the video footage offers additional data that is not that apparent in what was drawn or said.

Whose Interpretation? Engaging Participants Themselves in the Interpretive Process

One of the limitations of our work with this particular set of drawings in the data production stage was that the participants worked primarily with their own individual drawings or the drawings in their small mixed groups. What would have happened if we had set up an exhibition of all 36 drawings in the clinic and had given the group as a whole the opportunity of engaging in a 'walk about' in order to view the collection? We ask this question because in subsequent projects involving drawings this is one of the steps that we have added, and, indeed, groups have collaborated in creating a curatorial statement and a title for the exhibition (see Chapter 4 in this volume).

We draw attention to these critical issues because they highlight the pedagogical space afforded by the 'drawing each other' activity, a space that is far from being trivial, and, as in several other studies involving adults drawing (see, for example, Weber and Mitchell's [1995] work with beginning teachers), the participants enthusiastically took up the drawing activity. We had no sense that this was something they regarded as being 'just for children'. This is important to note because in methodology courses when we first refer to drawing as an activity to carry out with adults, we are frequently met with concerns from our university students and colleagues that they would feel uncomfortable asking adults to draw. Our response to this is to engage new researchers (and ourselves) in drawing. Students then tend to come around to seeing this as an appropriate activity for adults as well as for children.

At the same time, the drawing activity should not be romanticised. The whole point of engaging in this kind of 'learning together' work in this particular project came out of the fact that teachers and healthcare workers were not learning together when a shared focus on the sexual health of the young people in the area was needed. And it would be a mistake to think that possible suspicions would simply go away with one drawing activity. Significantly, as a team, we had to be prepared to ensure that discussion and genuine exchange was possible during the drawing workshop and in the subsequent sessions.

We also caution against reading too much into any one drawing, but rather, as noted above, we advocate considering the emerging discussion as the most critical component of the activity.

CONCLUSIONS

This chapter has highlighted what we can learn when we get two different groups of adults who work with children and young people to begin to work together. The foundation of this is a variation on the 'starting with ourselves' agenda (Kirk, 2005) focusing on 'how we see each other'. We think that this is a particularly appropriate and relatively easy way to begin to get groups talking to each other. From teachers and parent groups to healthcare workers and agricultural extension workers to the present example of teachers and healthcare workers, there is a rich potential for various government departments and civil society groups to be working together and learning together. For example, in the latest plans for rolling out HIV Counselling and Testing in South Africa, it is key that health and education officials work together. HIV and AIDS cannot be understood solely as a health issue or solely as an issue in the education sector (Motsoaledi, 2010). This was evident when we first started this work in 2004. Now that it is the beginning of a new decade, the demands for healthcare workers and educators to work together, especially in rural areas, are even greater. But South Africa is not alone in suffering the consequences of the silo effect of government departments and of splits between civil society and government departments. As is explored in Chapter 16 in relation to storyboarding in Rwanda, bringing groups together to draw solutions is yet another way in which drawing, as a relatively simple and inexpensive tool, can be a highly participatory and a potentially powerful force for policy and social change.

ACKNOWLEDGEMENT

The authors gratefully acknowledge the National Research Foundation's (NRF's) funding and support of the work discussed in this chapter. The views, findings, and conclusions expressed herein are those of the authors.

NOTE

[1] The project titled "Learning Together: Towards an Integrated Participatory Approach to Youth, Gender and HIV/AIDS Interventions in Rural KwaZulu-Natal Schools" (2004–2006), with N. de Lange, T. M. Buthelezi, M. N. Mazibuko, C. Mitchell, R. Moletsane, J. Stuart, and M. Taylor, used

various visual participatory methodologies in addressing gender and HIV&AIDS issues in a district in rural KwaZulu-Natal.

REFERENCES

Boler, T., Adoss, R., Ibrahim, A., & Shaw, M. (2003). *The sound of silence: Difficulties in communicating on HIV/AIDS in schools.* London, England: ActionAid. Retrieved from http://www.actionaid.org/assets/pdf/HIVSoundofsilence.pdf.

Combrinck, M., & Van Wyk, M. (in press). Developing of a professional practicum through a collaboration of in-service and novice teachers: Experiences and expectations. In F. Islam, C. Mitchell, N. de Lange, M. Combrinck, & R. Balfour (Eds.), *School-university collaborations for educational change in rural South Africa: Particular challenges and practical cases.* New York, NY: Edwin Mellen Press.

Creswell, J. W. (1994). *Research design: Qualitative and quantitative approaches.* London, England: Sage.

D'Amant, A. (2009). *Teachers in transition: Becoming inclusive practitioners.* (Doctoral dissertation, University of KwaZulu-Natal, Durban, South Africa). Retrieved from http://hdl.handle.net/10413/1183.

De Lange, N. (2008). Visual participatory approaches to HIV and AIDS research as intervention in a rural community setting. *Journal of Psychology in Africa, 18*(1), 181–186.

De Lange, N., Buthelezi, T. M., Mazibuko, M. N., Mitchell, C., Moletsane, R., Stuart, J., & Taylor, M. (2003). *Learning together: Towards an integrated participatory approach to youth, gender and HIV/AIDS interventions in rural KwaZulu-Natal schools.* National Research Foundation proposal.

Delius, P., & Walker, L. (2002). AIDS in context. *African Studies, 61*(1), 5–12. doi:10.1080/00020180220140046.

Human Rights Watch (HRW). (2001). *Scared at school: Sexual violence against girls in South African schools.* Retrieved from http://www.hrw.org/reports/2001/safrica.

Kahn, T. (2005, June 9). AIDS stalks teachers in state schools. *Business Day.* Retrieved from the Health Systems Trust website: http://www.hst.org.za/news/20040843.

Kelly, K., & Parker, W. (2000). *Communities of practice: Contextual mediators of youth response to HIV/AIDS. Beyond Awareness Campaign report.* Pretoria, South Africa: Department of Health. Retrieved from http://www.cadre.org.za/node/106.

Kirk, J. (2005). Starting with the self: Reflexivity in studying women teachers' lives in development. In C. Mitchell, S. Weber, & K. O'Reilly-Scanlon (Eds.), *Just who do we think we are: Methodologies for autobiography and self-study in teaching* (pp. 231–241). New York, NY: RoutledgeFalmer. doi:10.4324/9780203464977_chapter_20.

Mitchell, C. (2004). HIV/AIDS in health, education and participation: An action space for youth involvement in the SADC region. *Youth Development Journal, 15*, 22–38.

Mitchell, C., De Lange, N., Moletsane, R., Stuart, J., & Buthelezi, T. (2005). Giving a face to HIV and AIDS: On the uses of photo-voice by teachers and community health care workers working with youth in rural South Africa. *Qualitative Research in Psychology, 2*(3), 257–270. doi:10.1191/1478088705qp042oa.

Moletsane, R., & Mitchell, C. (2007). On working with a single photograph. In N. de Lange, C. Mitchell, & J. Stuart (Eds.), *Putting people in the picture: Visual methodologies for social change* (pp.131–140). Rotterdam, The Netherlands: Sense.

Motsoaledi, A. (2010, March). *Taking responsibility: Reflections on HIV and AIDS in higher education.* Keynote address by the Minister of Health at the HEAIDS Conference, Sandton Sun, South Africa.

Senderowitz, J. (1999). *Making reproductive health services youth friendly.* Washington, D. C.: FOCUS on Young Adults/Pathfinder. Retrieved from http://www.pathfind.org/pf/pubs/focus/RPPS-Papers/makingyouthfriendly.PDF.

UNAIDS. (2006). *Report on the global AIDS epidemic.* Geneva, Switzerland: Author. Retrieved from http://www.unaids.org.

UNAIDS. (2008). *Report on Global AIDS epidemic.* Geneva, Switzerland: Author. Retrieved from http://www.unaids.org.

UNICEF. (2009). *The State of the World's Children special edition: Celebrating 20 years of the Convention on the Rights of the Child.* New York, NY: Author. Retrieved from http://www.unicef.org.

Vetten, L., & Bhana, K. (2001). *Violence, vengeance and gender: A preliminary investigation into the links between violence against women and HIV/AIDS in South Africa.* Johannesburg, South Africa: Centre for the Study of Violence and Reconciliation. Retrieved from http://www.csvr.org.za/docs/gender/violence.pdf.

Weber, S., & Mitchell, C. (1995). *'That's funny, you don't look like a teacher': Interrogating images and identity in popular culture.* London, England: Falmer Press. doi:10.4324/9780203453568.

Weber, S., & Mitchell, C. (1996). Drawing ourselves into teaching: Studying the images that shape and distort teacher education. *Teaching and Teacher Education, 12*(3), 303–313. doi:10.1016/0742-051X(95)00040-Q.

Wood, K., Maforah, F., & Jewkes, R. (1998). "He forced me to love him": Putting violence on adolescent sexual health agendas. *Social Science & Medicine, 47*(2), 233–242. doi:10.1016/S0277-9536(98)00057-4.

DRAWING THE BIGGER PICTURE:
GIVING VOICE TO HIV-POSITIVE CHILDREN

Eliza M. Govender and Sertanya Reddy

INTRODUCTION

South Africa is home to the largest number of people infected with HIV and living with AIDS (UNAIDS, 2008). Children, in particular, represent one of the most vulnerable groups exposed to the harsh consequences of HIV and AIDS. In 2007 alone, 270,000 children died from AIDS (UNICEF, 2010), and at the same time, 280,000 children were living with HIV (UNICEF, 2009). In addition to the large number of children infected by and dying from the pandemic, many are affected by the loss of parents and guardians, which, in turn, results in child-headed households and a significant number of orphans (Richter, Foster, & Sherr, 2006; UNICEF, 2009).

South Africa is therefore confronted with many challenges regarding these children. One of the most important is to ensure that children who are infected by HIV receive treatment through proper health-care systems and are educated and correctly informed about treatment adherence and well-being. This will play a pivotal role in preventing the progression of the virus into AIDS or at least prolonging the progression. Inconsistent treatment adherence can have serious repercussions; the virus multiplies and causes further deterioration of the immune system. As a response to the concerns of doctors and others that HIV-positive children often experience difficulties with treatment adherence, we developed an intervention called "Hi Virus".

The Hi Virus intervention is discussed in this chapter in order to illustrate the role that drawings can play in educating HIV-positive children about treatment literacy and treatment adherence. We discuss, too, the role of the young artists and their drawings in the compilation of a storybook that consists, in part, of these drawings and that serves as a vehicle of information transfer within the wider community in its attempt to spread awareness and knowledge of HIV and AIDS and treatment adherence among South African children. The storybook serves as a record of the thinking of these children as translated through their drawings. The focus is on how drawing can function as a form of participatory art to impart accurate information to HIV-positive children about consistent treatment adherence. In exploring drawings as a tool to foster awareness, knowledge sharing, and knowledge transfer, we focus on both the educational *and* the entertaining nature of drawing: Drawing is unveiled as a participatory form of Entertainment Education (EE).

L. Theron et al. (eds.), Picturing Research: Drawing as Visual Methodology, 191–204.

DRAWING FROM THE VISUAL

From the initial HIV&AIDS interventions in the early 1980s through to the late 1990s, television and radio transmission were the predominant mass media communication strategies used to inform and educate. The escalation in the effects of the epidemic, however, begged for a reassessment of how prevention, treatment, care, and support could be more effectively and appropriately communicated at an interactive and participatory level, primarily for children. Africa, especially, needs to consider more active participation as a possible remedy to the many failures of HIV prevention strategies (Govender, 2010). Despite the transition from the didactic, top-down communicative processes for knowledge transmission to what appears to be more participatory initiatives, the real voices of people infected and affected by HIV are still pervasively silenced. Children, in particular, lack the opportunity to express themselves or openly discuss the realities of living with HIV and AIDS. Diane Melvin explained, in regard to the Phila Impilo! Project, that although children are disproportionately affected by HIV infections, their voices and views are often not sought or heard (as cited in Kruger, 2008).

The question, then, is this: How can participation and dialogue among children be encouraged, and can drawing play a role in this active child engagement? A model developed by Harry Shier (2001) illustrates that child participation involves providing children with platforms from which their voices can be heard and opportunities for their opinions to be discussed. Amid the many potential platforms and opportunities that exist, visual art has been researched widely as a means of encouraging expression among children (Mitchell, 2008; Mitchell, De Lange, Moletsane, Stuart, & Buthelezi, 2005; Rao et al., 2009; Wallace-DiGarbo & Hill, 2006). In particular, art has proven to be effective in addressing sensitive issues with children, such as trauma, abuse, and HIV and AIDS (Gerteisen, 2008; Hrenko, 2005; Pifalo, 2007). In this chapter, however, the focus is on how drawings were used to implement an HIV&AIDS educational and participatory intervention to encourage awareness and knowledge sharing related to the particular challenge of treatment literacy and treatment adherence. Although drawing was consciously used as a participatory tool in the Hi Virus intervention, an unintended aspect of drawing also emerged: The process of drawing proved to be not only participatory but, more specifically, a participatory form of Entertainment Education (EE).

This chapter is written within an interpretative paradigm reflecting the first author's[i] workshop experiences, participant observations, journal notes, and informal group discussions over an 18-month period. The methodologies explored were used to take the children through a process of discovery and learning through telling their stories, sharing their experiences, learning together, and taking action to live more positively.

BACKGROUND TO THE 'HI VIRUS' INTERVENTION

The Hi Virus initiative was introduced by the Centre for HIV/AIDS Networking (HIVAN), established by the University of KwaZulu-Natal in 2001. The project formed part of the Children's Resource Book series, created by HIVAN'S Highly Effective Art programme (HEART), which focused on using participatory art approaches with children to address HIV and AIDS. The Hi Virus initiative was conducted by facilitators[ii] from HEART with a group of 7 children between the ages of 11 and 14 years from a care centre for HIV-positive children in Durban, KwaZulu-Natal. Hi Virus workshops were conducted over three weekends during which the children were taken away from their rural environments to a camp site to address issues of treatment literacy and treatment adherence. The workshops were child-centred and focused on involving the children in the entire process of knowledge sharing and learning in order to develop a deeper understanding and practical application of treatment adherence.

WORKING FROM THE GROUND: METHODOLOGICAL CONSIDERATIONS

Participatory Action Research (PAR) was adopted as the methodological approach for Hi Virus because it entails a process in which the children engage in collective, action-based projects that reflect their own knowledge and mobilise their desired actions (Vio Grossi, 1980; Wadsworth, 1998). The facilitators and children worked together to define the most practical and feasible ways for them to participate, with the majority of the children choosing art-based methods as the medium they wished to work with for the three workshops. In this context, participation was, as McIntyre (2008) put it, a choice, and not an imposition. The workshops took an inductive approach: We worked from a position of discovering possibilities towards empowerment. Hi Virus exhibited characteristics of a grounded theory approach since it allowed for building from the patterns, discussions, and observations during the workshop toward establishing some of the theoretical considerations of using art-based methodology for HIV&AIDS knowledge sharing.

It is useful to conceptualise PAR not as one particular research method but rather as a diversity of approaches that include elements of participation, action, and research (Spaniol, 2005). The participation element ensured that the children were given a space to engage in all levels of the project using art-based methods that they selected. The action aspect allowed for critical dialogue and discussion that translated into the children becoming more aware of the importance of treatment literacy and treatment adherence. The research element was a co-generation of knowledge and ideas from the children and facilitators in relation to the various issues discussed.

The complete workshop process took place over a period of 18 months, commencing with weekly meetings with the children and their guardians to share collectively the challenges attendant on the lack of treatment adherence. Ongoing meetings were conducted with the children for almost 6 months prior to the workshops so that we could understand what they knew about adherence and also decide collectively on how to approach the problem of inconsistent treatment adherence. The workshop programme was discussed with the children's care-givers, counsellors, social workers, and psychologists and strategically designed in consultation with the children. Through discussion groups and play activities, these children became more enthusiastic about drawing, painting, and making things as a way of learning about HIV and AIDS. The workshops were conducted over a 2-month period, with follow-up sessions held once per week during which the children could review their drawings and make desired revisions.

The Workshop Journey

During the workshop weekends, participants had the opportunity of engaging in a variety of creative activities, including participatory games, role-playing, storytelling, puppet making, collage, drawing, and fabric painting, to help them engage in dialogue about specific issues around treatment adherence. Central to the workshop process was engaging the children in this participatory process. Drawing is both a means of communication as well as a problem-solving tool through which children can see what they are thinking and play around with and transform their ideas (Brooks, 2009). Creativity emerged strongly during the drawing process in the Hi Virus workshops. According to Prescott, Sekendur, Bailey, and Hoshino (2008), drawing can be a useful tool in providing a distraction from dealing with painful circumstances and can also provide the opportunity to reshape reality and formulate future goals.

First, through a role-play process, the children shared detailed stories of their experiences of diagnosis, treatment literacy, and some of the challenges of adherence to treatment. The role-play session was based on the children's knowledge about HIV, and any misinformation was corrected with the help of the facilitator as the role plays developed. The children developed storylines, decided on the characters, and made innovative use of various materials and basic clothing to create their own props for their characters. The role plays about their lived experiences were then documented through a process of drawings. The children drew pictures of the characters they had created for the role plays as well as pictures of scenes from them, such as a meeting between a doctor and an HIV-positive character. The purpose of these drawings was, first, to serve as a tool for knowledge sharing among the members of the group because as the children drew, this created a space for dialogue about the challenges of treatment adherence. Second, the drawings functioned as a tool for knowledge transfer; the drawings were used later as the illustrations in an educational storybook for other children.

The children clearly had common experiences with HIV&AIDS treatment. Through the role plays, they were able to express some of the difficulties they face with treatment adherence. When the children began drawing pictures of scenes from the role plays of their lived experiences, they began to express visually their challenges with treatment adherence. These drawings later precipitated ongoing formal discussions, initiated by the facilitator, about the challenges the children faced with treatment adherence and treatment literacy, and informal discussions about their drawings and lived experiences among the children after the workshop. One child shared with the group that he took all his pills everywhere in a Cal-C-Vita container. The immediate response of another child was to question how he knew which pills to take since they were all mixed together in one container.

The drawings were a significant tool to allow the children to go through a process of conscientisation and critical dialogue about their lived experiences. According to Brooks (2009), children can bring something into consciousness more clearly through drawing, and we saw this happening. Eventually, the children's drawings were pieced together by the children and the facilitators in order to begin to form a visual storyboard for a storybook. The children collectively decided that the storybook would be used as an educational tool to teach other children about the importance of treatment adherence. The book's storyline was derived from the transcribed role plays and the children's ongoing informal discussions about their drawings. The dialogue from both of these was recorded and later transcribed by the facilitators so that the children's own words could be used in the storybook. This made the entire process participatory since the children were active participants from the commencement to the end of the project, collectively designing an arts-based approach to addressing their issues, developing the creative content, and translating this content into an educational resource book for other children.

The drawings enabled the children to take the focus away from their own lived experiences and collectively reflect on their shared experiences of treatment literacy and treatment adherence. Through this process, the children collectively identified, in the group discussions, that their drawings reflected a common challenge, allowing them therefore to both problematise their issues as well as move on to discuss how they could address these. As is clear here, artistic activity is consistent with the tenets of PAR because it is, by definition, action-oriented. Drawing was used as the action component of the PAR process with the knowledge that art making lends itself to participation since it often involves people working collaboratively to identify issues and solutions (Spaniol, 2005).

The discussion in the next section reflects some of the theoretical considerations that emerged during the process of using art-based methodologies in working with the children. It is divided into two main sections. The first explores how drawings were used in the Hi Virus project to encourage dialogue and participation among the children in order to facilitate greater awareness and knowledge sharing regarding treatment literacy and treatment adherence. The second section discusses briefly how the drawings can be considered to be a participatory form of EE working towards knowledge transfer.

DRAWING TO PARTICIPATE: CATALYSING 'CRITICAL CONSCIOUSNESS'

The facilitators conceptualised and implemented the Hi Virus project with a participatory orientation clearly in mind. Hi Virus aimed to cater to the particular needs and interests of the children. This is, of course, one of the first pivotal components of participatory development (Bessette, 2004; Servaes, 1999). The process of participation was maintained since the children had ongoing opportunities, through informal discussions and group work, to describe some of their positive and negative experiences with treatment adherence. As these dialogues about challenges and problems developed, they assumed the characteristics of Paulo Freire's participatory pedagogy. Freire (2002) criticised the conventional approach to education, the 'banking method', in which information is transmitted to so-called ignorant people by an external authority. In opposition to this, Freire advocated a 'problem-posing' approach in which people learn through active participation and dialogical exchange with others (see also Shor, 1987; Wallerstein, 1987).

Although Hi Virus created a useful resource for other children in the form of an educational storybook, the significance of the project process was the children's independent selection of drawing as a medium to explore their issues with treatment literacy and to share this knowledge. Once the children had discussed the problems and possible solutions to treatment adherence, they expressed these ideas by drawing pictures. For example, one of the children described how intimidated he felt by taking the ARVs each time he visits the doctor. This fear and intimidation was expressed when he drew his pill bottles as disproportionately big, in comparison to himself, possibly suggesting the overwhelming nature of treatment adherence. This suggests the power of art to help young people to express ideas, reflect on these ideas, and expand them—all in a manner that requires their active involvement (Brooks, 2009). The children also shared their experiences of the challenges of taking their pills since adherence to a cocktail of drugs is often very complex. As a result, they collectively decided that they needed more information about treatment adherence as well as a system that could help them adhere to their complex treatment. The picture illustrating the large medication bottles, drawn by one of the children, led to a discussion about better ways of adherence. The fact that the children identified their problems as a challenge common to HIV-positive children and that they selected drawing and other participatory means of learning was reflective of the power of the intervention to give voice to children through providing a space in which to make their own choices. This is often not a common experience for many children. The drawings, therefore, created a space for critical dialogue about the need for adherence and led later to the development of a pill box. This dialogical exchange occurred as the children collectively discussed the complexity of adhering to the cocktail of treatment while opening up some of the pill containers to show the facilitators and other children the number and variety of pills that had to be taken on different days of the week. Many of the children were not able to explain which pills should be taken at the appropriate times, thus identifying adherence as a problem common to many members of the group. All the children were excited about the possibility of having more discussions about better treatment adherence through a process of drawing. Knowledge sharing is a key characteristic of Freirean problem-posing education because it involves people learning through interaction with others. The children were able to generate suggestions for treatment adherence because they were able to work creatively with their facilitators and each other.

In addition to functioning as a means of dialogue and expression, the drawing also proved to be a method of empowerment for the children. After the children collectively expressed their anxieties with treatment adherence through the various drawings, they discussed possible ways of dealing with the complexities of adhering to treatment at different hours of the day. Many did not own watches or know how to read time. One of the children suggested he needed a 'pill diary', which later became known to the group as a 'pill schedule', and, sometimes, a 'pill box', which would 'remember' to take the pills. The others chuckled at the idea of a pill diary, indicating that they could not stick the pills into the book. With the help of facilitators, they individually developed and decorated pill boxes, with drawings of the sun to indicate the time for the morning treatment and drawings of the moon and stars to indicate the time for the evening treatment. Through drawings and sketches, the children were able to depict the times of the day when certain treatment had to be taken, thus demonstrating their ability to become empowered in taking ownership of their problems. From this, it is clear that drawing has the potential to bring children together so that they can share common experiences and problems and engage in joint learning: "Through expressive arts activities children learn how to solve problems with peers, negotiate and share" (Hutinger, Betz, Bosworth, Potter, & Schneider, 1997, p. 5).

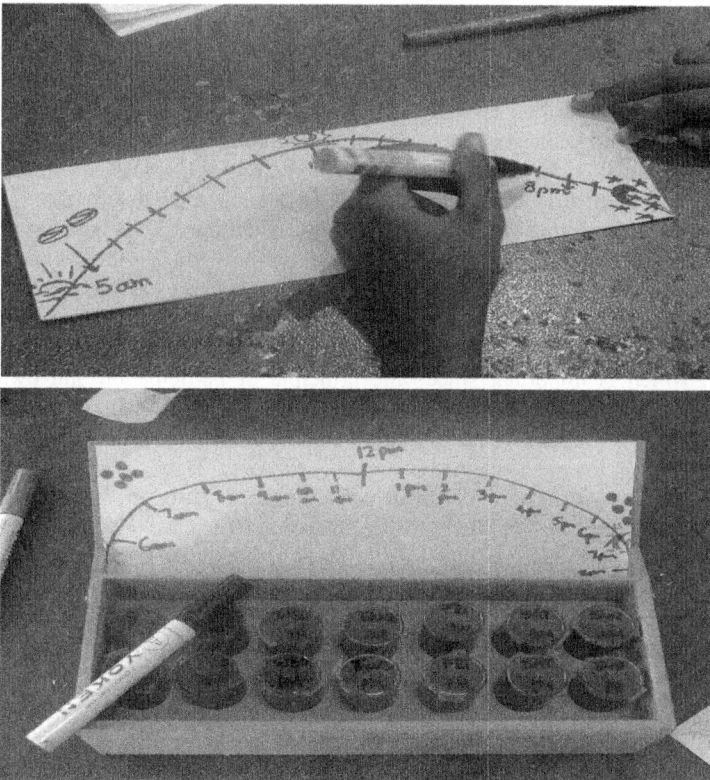

Figure 14.1. Children using drawings to depict sunrise and sunset as pill-taking times.

One of the key components of Freire's (2002) participatory pedagogy is the concept of 'critical consciousness', which involves people becoming more aware of their own abilities and competencies and actively using these to engage with the world around them (see also Nain, 2001; White, 1994). Such critical consciousness became evident when the participants of Hi Virus began to think independently and to develop a sense of self-confidence. The initial days of working with the children prior to the workshop were the most challenging because the children, clearly, were used to being passive learners and were hesitant to participate. During the workshop, however, the act of drawing dissolved the boundaries that existed between the children and the facilitators. As the children progressed in drawing images of themselves and of their lives, as they visually expressed their experiences with medication and doctors, they gained a greater sense of identity and self-esteem.

This new-found self-confidence became evident when the participants assumed control of how their drawings were to be used. The children initially thought that photographs of themselves at the workshop would be used for the images in the storybook. A few approached their facilitators since they were not comfortable with their photos being used in such a book. Here, they demonstrated that they were confident enough to challenge and question the development of the book project and the book's contents. The book development process was discussed and the children were thrilled to discover that their drawings, rather than photos of themselves, would be used in the book. By questioning and identifying their role in the book production, they were developing into activist artists. When Mitchell et al. (2005) conducted an innovative study using photographs to address HIV and AIDS, they realised that "the photos work best when the participants are engaged in selecting, commenting on and deciding on how their views can best be represented visually" (p. 265). Similarly, with the Hi Virus project the drawings worked best when the children felt in control of how their drawings would be used and represented. As they assumed control, they began to take ownership of the project, which is important since "the principle of participation and ownership acknowledges that change is more likely to be successful and permanent when the people it affects are involved in initiating and promoting it" (Thompson & Kinne, 1990, p. 46).

The Freirean concept of critical consciousness, however, extends beyond dialogical processes and problem-posing education to a sense of feeling competent and empowered to transform one's social reality and that of others. The process of drawing, as a result, extended beyond knowledge sharing between and among the children about their lived experiences to knowledge transfer: The knowledge gained through the 18-month intervention was transferred to other children through the production of the educational resource book. Central to this process of positive change was the use of drawings: "Visual images are particularly appropriate to drawing in [relation to] the participants themselves as central to the interpretive process" (Mitchell, 2008, p. 374). Hi Virus developed the children's capacity to the stage at which they were empowered enough to use their experiences and identities as HIV-positive individuals to educate others about treatment literacy. This critical consciousness process was achieved through drawings that served as a vehicle for knowledge sharing and knowledge transfer.

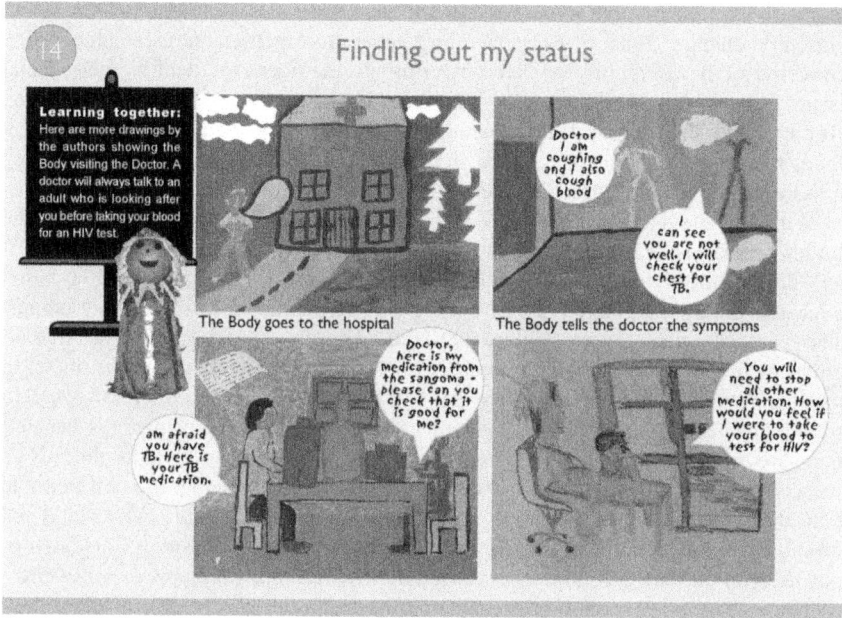

Figure 14.2. Through collective dialogue, the children drew pictures to represent their lived experiences.

EDUCATING THE ENTERTAINING WAY

Through the participatory process of art making, the Hi Virus workshops and the book development phase emerged as an interesting example of participatory Entertainment Education (EE) in practice. In recent years, EE has been used increasingly to communicate pro-social messages (Moyer-Gusé, 2008). As a communication strategy, EE combines both educational and entertainment aspects into communication messages based on the premise that people are more receptive to social messages and learn more effectively when they are enjoying themselves (Coleman, 1999; Singhal & Rogers, 1999). The entertainment aspect captures and maintains the audience's attention whereas the educational aspect focuses on conveying information about a particular social issue. EE has proven to be effective in public health communication, especially in the field of HIV and AIDS (Moyer-Gusé, 2008; Tufte, 2003).

Despite the potential power of EE, it has often been criticised for following a mass media approach, one in which television and radio were the predominant ways of presenting educational messages in an entertaining way. However, over time, EE has evolved to embrace more participatory, grassroots approaches (Tufte,

2005). Tufte divides the field of EE into three generations: the first generation focuses on the significance of social marketing for HIV prevention; the second on bridging paradigms originating in the modernisation-oriented paradigm with elements of the participatory paradigm; and the third focuses on empowerment and structural change (2005, p. 173). The third generation focuses on understanding the concerns of a community and empowering its members to identify their social issues and problems and then to address them in a participatory way. Similar to the way in which the field of development communication evolved from a mass media focus to a more participatory approach, the strategy of EE progressed to embracing grassroots activity and local involvement.

Whereas television programmes and radio dramas were considered to be the traditional forms of EE, drawing started to function as a more participatory form of EE during the Hi Virus project. The children were entertained while being educated about treatment literacy during the participatory art-based workshops. The way characters were depicted by the children often became a source of amusement and led to seemingly endless discussions among the group members. In particular, amusement arose when the children drew pictures of a *sangoma* (a traditional healer) and a Western doctor. Children often face challenges because they are given both traditional medicines by a *sangoma* as well as the ARVs prescribed by doctors. However, through the process of drawing, the children had educational discussions about the importance of taking only the ARVs and not mixing this treatment with any from a *sangoma*. Seemingly endless discussions occurred among the group members when the children drew pictures of *sangomas*.

These drawings expressed the reality of the children's lives; most of them have had treatment adherence experience dealing with both traditional and Western medicine. The entertainment component was evident when the children implemented their own competition to identify who could produce the best drawn *sangoma*. In many cases, the *sangoma* was drawn dressed in fashionable outfits, which contradicts the reality of their usual culturally appropriate attire and which perhaps demonstrates the thrill many children experienced in carrying out the drawing task. Many commented that drawing a *sangoma* is not a common experience (most of them had never drawn one before), and they found depicting the *sangoma* an entertaining process as they discussed the various images and identified the best drawings. Throughout the process, they also explained to each other, as they worked, why certain images were drawn in a particular way. The entertainment aspect of the drawing compelled even the most introverted children to share a smile and a laugh as they explained their drawings to each other.

Figure 14.3. Drawing of a sangoma as part of the depiction of the conflict between traditional and western medicine.

The potential for drawings to serve an educational function expanded from knowledge generation and knowledge sharing to knowledge transfer. The storybook created by the children during the Hi Virus workshops served as the vehicle for this transfer. At the final stages in the workshop process, the drawings were placed together to form a storyboard—a step towards creating a storybook for knowledge-transfer beyond the small group of children who participated in Hi Virus.

How much education took place relative to the amount of entertainment? Although the process can sometimes seem to be more entertaining than educational for children, the art-based methods provided them with a space in which to engage in both creative and entertaining artistic reflection and expression and to develop a critical consciousness of the possibilities of change regarding their treatment adherence behaviour.

EE initiatives often attribute their success to the entertainment aspect, capturing participants' attention first, so that they can then be educated. As Hutinger et al. (1997) observed, artistic activities have the ability to engage, amuse, and eventually educate those involved. The Hi Virus project, however, drew on the importance of active participatory engagement that the children suggested should be manifested through drawings. In the exploration of the educational and knowledge-sharing level of treatment literacy, entertainment became an explicit benefit of the intervention. Hi Virus drew on the power of art to gain and maintain the children's interest in the issues under discussion, and this led to their being entertained, as well.

CONCLUSION

The unique feature of Hi Virus is that it drew simultaneously on participation, Entertainment Education, and art to help children learn more about HIV and AIDS. By being part of participatory action research, the children engaged in Freirean critical thinking, dialogical knowledge sharing, and knowledge transfer. The PAR approach encouraged open, egalitarian learning, and the entertaining process furthered this enjoyable environment in which learning could occur.

Although EE is often thought of as having to do exclusively with mass media, the Hi Virus intervention suggests that drawing can function as an innovative form of participatory EE. The richness of the entertainment component of drawings can be effectively adapted to educate children about HIV issues, and we should be thinking about how to do this. Successful EE initiatives could be created by harnessing the effectiveness of drawings to encourage participation and dialogue and to stimulate greater awareness and critical thinking about a particular issue. In turn, these drawings could be developed further and used to develop participatory, child-friendly storybooks on a range of challenging topics. The significance of the Hi Virus initiative is not only that the drawings were used as educational tools among the participants but also that the participants became 'activist artists' by helping to form a book around their drawings in order to spread greater awareness of the importance of treatment literacy and treatment adherence.

Mitchell et al. (2005) argued that photographs can be used as a tool of inquiry, a tool of representation, and a tool for taking action, and, in arguing thus, they suggested the scope of possibility available to anyone working with visual methods. Hi Virus revealed the multiple functions of drawings as an art form, serving as a tool of expression, documentation, knowledge sharing, and, to a large extent, as an agent of change, or what we might call a catalyst for change. Drawing was a means of expression; the children were able to explore their lived experiences and feelings in a non-verbal context. Drawing was a tool for documentation; the children were able to record and reflect on the challenges of adhering to treatment. It worked as a tool for knowledge sharing; the children were able to use their drawings to discuss with other children some of the obstacles to proper and consistent treatment-adherence. It worked, too, as a tool to effect social change; the children created a storybook to educate other children about HIV and AIDS.

ACKNOWLEDGEMENTS

Thanks to the Stephen Lewis Foundation, Voluntary Service Organisation, and Carnegie Corporation for funding, through The Centre for HIV/AIDS Networking (HIVAN), this study and thanks to the Graduate Programme in the Centre for Communication and Media and Society at the University of KwaZulu-Natal for the time allocated to this project. We are grateful to Bren Brophy and Emma Durden for their contribution throughout the research, design, and implementation phases.

Disclaimer: The opinions expressed herein are those of the authors and do not necessarily reflect the views of any of the previously mentioned funders.

NOTES

[i] The first author has undertaken extensive research on Entertainment Education and participatory communication within an HIV context. Numerous workshops and interventions were developed as a result of this research. The second author has experience working with participatory arts-based methodologies with youth through her work with an NPO that uses art to educate and advocate for peace and reconciliation. Therefore, the past experience of both authors stimulated the interest in writing this chapter focusing on art and HIV/AIDS with children.

[ii] The workshop was designed and facilitated by Eliza Govender, Lauren Cobham, and Bren Brophy.

REFERENCES

Bessette, G. (2004). *Involving the community: A guide to participatory development communication.* Penang, Malaysia: Southbound; Ottawa, ON: International Development Research Centre.

Brooks, M. (2009). Drawing, visualisation and young children's exploration of "big ideas". *International Journal of Science Education, 31*(3), 319–341. doi:10.1080/09500690802595771.

Coleman, P. L. (1999). The enter-educate approach for promoting social change. *Journal of Development Communication, 11*(1), 75–81.

Freire, P. (2002). *Pedagogy of the oppressed.* New York, NY: Continuum.

Gerteisen, J. (2008). Monsters, monkeys, & mandalas: Art therapy with children experiencing the effects of trauma and Fetal Alcohol Spectrum Disorder (FASD). *Art Therapy, 25*(2), 90–93. Retrieved from http://home.gci.net/~junebug/EJ797303.pdf.

Govender, E. M. (2010). HIV and AIDS communication: An African context. *African Communication Research, 3*(2), 205–234.

Hrenko, K. (2005). Remembering Camp Dreamcatcher: Art therapy with children whose lives have been touched by HIV/AIDS. *Art Therapy, 22*(1), 39–43. Retrieved from http://www.eric.ed.gov/PDFS/EJ682612.pdf.

Hutinger, P. L., Betz, A., Bosworth, J., Potter, J., & Schneider, C. (1997). *ArtExpress, a curriculum for young children with disabilities.* Macomb: Macomb Projects, Western Illinois University.

Kruger, J. (2008). *Live life! Children advocate best practices for healing.* Overport, South Africa: Young Insights for Planning. Retrieved from International Children's Palliative Care Network website: http://www.icpcn.org.uk.

McIntyre, A. (2008). *Participatory action research.* London, England: Sage.

Mitchell, C. (2008). Getting the picture and changing the picture: visual methodologies and educational research in South Africa. *South African Journal of Education, 28*, 365–383. Retrieved from http://ajol.info.

Mitchell, C., De Lange, N., Moletsane, R., Stuart, J., & Buthelezi, T. (2005). Giving a face to HIV and AIDS: On the uses of photo-voice by teachers and community health care workers working with youth in rural South Africa. *Qualitative Research in Psychology, 2*(3), 257–270. doi:10.1191/1478088705qp042oa.

Moyer-Gusé, E. (2008). Toward a theory of entertainment persuasion: Explaining the persuasive effects of entertainment-education messages. *Communication Theory, 18*(3), 407–425. doi:10.1111/j.1468-2885.2008.00328.x.

Nain, Z. (2001). From pedagogy to praxis: Freire, media education, and participatory communication. In M. Richards, P. Thomas, & Z. Nain (Eds.), *Communication and development: The Freirean connection* (pp. 209–224). Cresskill, NJ: Hampton Press.

Pifalo, T. (2007). Jogging the cogs: Trauma-focused art therapy and cognitive behavioral therapy with sexually abused children. *Art Therapy, 24*(4), 170–175. Retrieved from http://www.eric.ed.gov/ PDFS/EJ791441.pdf.

Prescott, M. V., Sekendur, B., Bailey, B., & Hoshino, J. (2008). Art making as a component and facilitator of resiliency with homeless youth. *Art Therapy, 25*(4), 156–163. http://eric.ed.gov/ PDFS/EJ825771.pdf.

Rao, D., Nainis, N., Williams, L., Langner, D., Eisin, A., & Paice, J. (2009). Art therapy for relief of symptoms associated with HIV/AIDS. *AIDS Care, 21*(1), 64–69. doi:10.1080/09540120802068795.

Richter, L., Foster, G., & Sherr, L. (2006). *Where the heart is: Meeting the psychosocial needs of young children in the context of HIV/AIDS.* The Hague, The Netherlands: Bernard van Leer Foundation.

Servaes, J. (1999). *Communication for development: One world, multiple cultures.* Cresskill, NJ: Hampton Press.

Shier, H. (2001). Pathways to participation: Openings, opportunities and obligations. *Children & Society, 15*(2), 107–117. doi:10.1002/chi.617.

Shor, I. (1987). Educating the educators: A Freirean approach to the crisis in teacher education. In I. Shor (Ed.), *Freire for the classroom: A sourcebook for liberatory teaching* (pp. 7–32). Portsmouth, NH: Boynton/Cook.

Singhal, A., & Rogers, E. M. (1999). Lessons learned about entertainment education. In A. Singhal & E. M. Rogers (Eds.), *Entertainment-education: A communication strategy for social change* (pp. 205–227). Mahwah, NJ: Lawrence Erlbaum Associates.

Spaniol, S. (2005). "Learned hopefulness": An arts-based approach to participatory action research. *Art Therapy, 22*(2), 86–91. Retrieved from http://www.eric.ed.gov/PDFS/EJ688457.pdf.

Thompson, B., & Kinne, S. (1990). Social change theory: Applications to community health. In N. Bracht (Ed.), *Health promotion at the community level: New advances* (2nd ed., pp. 45–65). London, England: Sage.

Tufte, T. (2003). Edutainment in HIV/AIDS prevention: Building on the Soul City experience in South Africa. In J. Servaes (Ed.), *Approaches to development: Studies on communication for development* (pp. 1–12). Paris, France: UNESCO.

Tufte, T. (2005). Entertainment-education in development communication—Between marketing behaviours and empowering people. In O. Hemer & T. Tufte (Eds.), *Media & glocal change: Rethinking communication for development* (pp. 159–174). Buenos Aires, Argentina: CLACSO Books. Retrieved from http://bibliotecavirtual.clacso.org.ar/ar/libros/edicion/media/14Chapter9.pdf.

UNAIDS. (2008). *Report on the global AIDS epidemic.* Geneva, Switzerland: Author. Retrieved from http://www.unaids.org.

UNICEF. (2009). *Children and AIDS: Fourth stocktaking report.* New York, NY: UNICEF, UNAIDS, WHO, and UNFPA. Retrieved from http://www.unicef.org/publications/index_51902.html.

UNICEF. (2010). *Nutrition and HIV/AIDS.* Retrieved from http://www.unicef.org/nutrition/ index_HIV.html.

Vio Grossi, F. (1980). The socio-political implications of participatory research. In F. Dubell, T. Erasmie, & J. de Vries (Eds.), *Research for the people—research by the people: Selected papers from the international forum on participatory research in Ljubljana, Yugoslavia* (Rev. ed., pp. 69–80). Linköping, Sweden: Linköping University, Department of Education.

Wadsworth, Y. (1998). Paper 2: What is participatory action research? *Action Research International.* Retrieved from http://www.scu.edu.au/schools/gcm/ar/ari/p-ywadsworth98.html.

Wallace-DiGarbo, A., & Hill, D. (2006). Art as agency: Exploring empowerment of at-risk youth. *Art Therapy, 23*(3), 119–125. Retrieved from http://www.eric.ed.gov/PDFS/EJ777007.pdf.

Wallerstein, N. (1987). Problem-posing education: Freire's method for transformation. In I. Shor (Ed.), *Freire for the classroom: A sourcebook for liberatory teaching* (pp. 33–44). Portsmouth, NH: Boynton/Cook.

White, S. A. (1994). The concept of participation: Transforming rhetoric to reality. In S. A. White, K. S. Nair, & J. R. Ascroft (Eds.), *Participatory communication: Working for change and development* (pp. 15–34). London, England: Sage.

WITH PICTURES AND WORDS I CAN SHOW YOU: CARTOONS PORTRAY RESILIENT MIGRANT TEENAGERS' JOURNEYS

Catherine Ann Cameron and Linda Theron

BACKGROUND TO THE DRAWING-BASED INQUIRY REPORTED IN THIS CHAPTER

Our research[i] with adolescents highlights the necessity of projecting the voices of youth in order to come to understand and share their experiences fully (Cameron & Creating Peaceful Learning Environments Team, 2002a, 2002b). Teenagers have powerful statements to make about their own situations. Their narratives are powerful: They are insightful; they are veridical; they are deeply engaging; and, most importantly, youths have stories that can inform theory and practice. In listening to the voices of youth, we have previously applied a wide range of methodological approaches (as reported in Cameron, 2004), but we have never asked youths to cartoon their experiences.

Recently, the first author collaboratively developed a methodology for the international investigation of developmental thriving that involved filming a *day in the life*[ii] of children in their home environments (Gillen & Cameron, 2010; Gillen et al., 2007). Subsequently, this methodology was adapted for the Negotiating Resilience Project (NRP) to accommodate the 'habitus', or socio-cultural milieux, of resilient adolescents in transition by using multiple converging methodologies: NRP community youth advocates recruited NRP teenagers for us to interview about their thriving. We filmed them for an entire *day*, they participated in a photo-voice project, and iteratively engaged in reflection on their lived experiences

This project afforded participants the opportunity to reflect on the roots of their resilience from many vantages. Bronfenbrenner's (1979) perspective of observing youth in micro- to macro-contexts informed this research by enhancing endeavours to identify the nature of their 'growing up well', their resilience, which is defined as their thriving in the face of hardship (Ungar et al., 2007). When we recruited the adolescents, we informed them they had been recommended to us as youths who were unusually well adapted and that we were interested in understanding their sources of strength, both personal and social.[iii]

One of our adolescent NRP participants, a female Mexican immigrant to Canada, informed us that she had participated in a community programme for immigrant youth wherein they cartooned to communicate their relocation experiences (Heraty, 2008). She shared her cartoons with us. They revealed socio-emotional and discursive aspects of her migration experiences that we had not

L. Theron et al. (eds.), Picturing Research: Drawing as Visual Methodology, 205–217.

previously noticed or been able to appreciate. We invited her to cartoon other experiences that contributed to her resilience and she readily agreed. We then asked another of our cooperative participants, a boy in Thailand who had migrated from Bangkok to the north of his country and who was also an avid artist, if he would cartoon as well. Our analyses of the value-added information we gained from this youth expression are the subject of this chapter.

CARTOONING

According to McCloud (1993), cartoons, which have been around since at least 1300 BC, are "juxtaposed pictorial and other images in deliberate sequence, intended to convey information and/or to produce an aesthetic response in the viewer" (p. 9). McCloud reported that sequentially arranged images drawn in Egyptian antiquity were precursors to a pre-Columbian pictorial manuscript and to the Bayeux Tapestry depicting the Norman invasion of England (pp. 10–18). There has been a long and intricate history to the use of images to enhance the depiction of narratives, wherein sequences of graphic representations explicate events or experiences. Ontogenetically, children scribble and make markings before mature writing representations develop (Pinto, Accorti Gamannossi, & Cameron, 2010); primitive combinations of drawing and writing are encouraged in the education of children in their early years. Emergent readers respond enthusiastically to picture books and cartoons during their transitions to independent literacy and more accomplished graphic representational skills. An enormous body of children's literature in such hybrid forms of written and graphic communication appeals to the interest of children and youths. McCloud (1993) acknowledged the somewhat restricted domains captured by cartoons, and their more impelling attraction for young mainstream males, and proposed, in 2000, the expansion of cartooning genres to attract a broader diversity of interested readers and creators.

We note, but do not explore, discussions of whether cartoons are a 'low' or 'high' form of art, and we observe that there is a current upsurge in interest in their analysis as expressive media reflecting political observation, ethnic representation, gender balance, genre diversity, life narratives, and humour (Gordon, 2003; McCloud, 2000, 2006; Shaw, 2007). Cartooning as a literary and artistic form of autobiographical reflection is increasingly noted and lauded. We will not examine the developing skills of young children either to comprehend cartoons (Takahashi & Sugioka, 1988; Sobel & Lillard, 2001) or produce them. In fact, there is a paucity of research on children's cartoon productions, even though cartooning is a favourite activity of many children and youths and deserves further exploration.

'Autographics' or richly illustrated sequential graphical and verbal productions have become popular mechanisms for representing adult 'life journeys' (Hui, 2009; Watson, 2008). Integrating illustrations and text creates powerfully direct communications media that appeal to an increasingly large audience. Tackling difficult topics not easily addressed in either words or pictures alone is rendered less onerous by the combination of the two communication channels (Macias, Wilson, Hui, & Heyman, 2010).

The goal of this chapter is to examine how two youths give voice in cartoons to their experiences of surpassing challenges. We seek to achieve a deeper understanding of the transitional experiences of these youth by involving them integrally in joint representations of their experiences. We expected our encouragement of cartooning to afford the youths an opportunity to reveal their perceptions while reflecting on their lives.

The Journeys of Idzel and Pond

We turn now to the cartoons produced by the two participants.

Idzel in Canada. Idzel was 14 years old when she was introduced to us as a middle school student who was doing well in her new community in spite of certain radical changes in her life circumstances. Idzel and her family (maternal grandmother, mother, father, and her younger sister) had recently emigrated from Mexico to Canada with support from the Mormon Church. None of the family members spoke English confidently on arrival, and it was the Mormon community who scaffolded many family needs, both practical and spiritual. Further, the family protected Idzel and her sister from many of the immigration status insecurities they were facing.

Idzel's cartooning. Idzel indicated that she was keen to illustrate for us her experience of becoming a Mormon young woman.[iv] She had told us during discussion of her *day* that she is expected to rise at 05:30, five mornings a week, in order to take part in the Mormon studies for girls between the ages of 15 and 18 years, which provide precepts to help them enact their faith. In her cartooning reflections, Idzel indicated finding that those religious studies increasingly enhance her religious practices, providing her with comportment guides on how to make "good decisions". She said that those decisions made her happy.

Initially, she indicated not knowing how to draw faces and thought that this put her work at a disadvantage. She was concerned that her individual frames might not fit together as a cohesive narrative. Her own favourite cartoons are *Garfield*, *Peanuts*, and *Calvin and Hobbes*, and she reflected that even though her narrative would not be as funny as these, she would not want to produce cartoons that were not at least somewhat engaging. She reported seeking her mother's advice on how to frame the vignettes so as to represent personal challenges while maintaining the interest and sympathy of the reader.

Once she had her narrative strategy in place and reassurance that figurative skills were not as important as the underlying message, she reported being fine to proceed, genuinely wanting to share her stories of learning to be a Mormon young woman with a wide audience:

I would not draw a [cartoon] if it is not something that is important to me but I do not want it to be boring. If people read it and understand it, it will be worth it. They might think, "Being a Mormon is difficult" as a first impression, but then, if they think, "she must have a good reason if she can go through all that", [her goal would be accomplished].

In a sense, this suggests transformation of Idzel's personal struggles into social/political action. She proceeded to depict in her cartoons 4 *days in her life* during which she is subjected to a range of interactions in which her personal practices (grounded in Mormonism) are misunderstood: Thursday and Friday in school and Saturday and Sunday at home and out and about. When we interviewed her, Idzel reflected on her experience of her peers seeing her as unusual and reported not minding being thought "weird". She drew the line, however, at what she sees as ignorant derision directed toward her religion. For example, when she chooses to make "good decisions", she does not mind if classmates deride her. However, if they say negative things about her church (for example, a teacher said in class that members of her church were polygamists and not Christian), she becomes distressed (Gordon, 2003).

In her first cartoon, "Thursday" (see Figure 15.1), Idzel depicts her early rise to attend her seminary class. The opening frames of religious instruction serve as a backdrop and set the stage for the ensuing cartoons. She shows herself proceeding to school where she resists temptation to skip classes as invited by her classmates to do. Later in the day, she refuses a free cup of coffee saying that she only puts healthful substances into her body, in keeping with her Mormon beliefs.

Figure 15.1. "Thursday": The experiences of a young Mormon woman.

Idzel shows, via a "Friday" cartoon, her physical education class in which her teacher misattributes extra credits to her. She confesses to her teacher that she deserves four not six points, maintaining integrity even if her classmates do not comprehend her need to do so. Later in the day, Idzel defends her decision to not have burned songs sent from her friends for her birthday party to a CD because they contained 'inappropriate' content.

In her "Saturday" cartoon, Idzel shops for a dress for her birthday party with her mother and sister. Four hours and 70 stores later, they find a dress that is not too short and that has no immodest touches. She observes in an aside text bar that shopping is sometimes difficult as it is hard to find clothes that are appropriately modest. After shopping, she goes to a local community centre and strives to seek out companions who do not use coarse language. She returns home to watch TV but turns it off at midnight so as to observe the Sabbath with piety. In "Sunday", Idzel attends Sunday school, where her efforts of the week are reinforced. She spends the rest of the day with her family as can be seen in Figure 15.2.

Figure 15.2. "Sunday": The Sabbath day of a young Mormon woman.

Idzel, in depicting examples of her standing tall in spite of possibly being misunderstood, reported taking pride in defending what she believes in, emphasising how many of her church friends do not admit in school that they are Mormons due to fear of derision. However, she feels strongly that so long as classmates only see her as "weird" she is strong enough to tolerate that: It is a small price to pay for enacting the principles that guide her life.

She does not explicitly depict some of these subtle reflections in the cartoons; these reflections were the result of nuanced exchanges between researchers and artist and not previously explored without her comic strips as prompts. Further, she reported vacillating between concern that readers might either not understand her message that these small indignities are worth the price of peer alienation, thus creating an overly empathetic reaction that she would not welcome, or perceive the slights to be so trivial as not worth mentioning. Unless one is a Mormon, she feels, one may not really understand.

Pond in Thailand. Pond was 13 years old when we first interviewed him. He lived in Chiang Mai, Thailand, with his father at the time; he had been in that northern capital only for 3 to 4 months. The move had been difficult for Pond since his mother and older sister still lived in Bangkok. Pond's artist father had opened a noodle shop in Chiang Mai to support the family, but he also encouraged Pond to spend time each week exercising his considerable graphic skills.

Pond sketched for 1 hour during the filmed *day* of observation, using sketchpads, graphite, and a straight edge ruler, copying from books of traditional Thai drawings. He reported being interested in cartooning and had many models to use, some of which included English text. He reported reading cartoons, when not playing video games, and accepted with alacrity our invitation to cartoon about his daily experiences.

Through his cartooning, Pond confirmed concretely that what we witnessed during the filmed *day* could be deemed the significant routines of his daily landscape. He could have sketched stylised Thai themes or cartoon action characters that he draws on a regular basis and could have ignored the mundane activities of his days, but instead, he not only enacted his values in showing us his daily routines when we filmed his *day* but also showed that these activities are enduring and noteworthy as cartoons that reflect the strengths of his daily life.

See Figure 15.3 for Pond's 'regular day' cartoon. At the start (in the first row), he wakes up (bed/pillow) and then his father takes him to school (motorcycle). A plate, a fork, and a spoon depict lunch break. He buses home from Chiang Mai Gate. At home he showers (showerhead), eats (plate/fork/spoon), does homework (notebook and pencil), and plays games (computer). On Saturday (see the second row), there is a tutoring class (book). After class, Pond helps his dad (noodle shop), returns home (bus), plays games (computer) and sometimes goes to a friend's house, then does homework (notebook), showers (showerhead), and goes to bed (bed/pillow). On Sunday (see the third row), he gets up (bed/pillow), sometimes goes biking with his father (bicycle), watches TV (television), eats (plate/fork/spoon), does homework (unclear), washes dishes (stack of plates), sweeps the house (broom), mops the floor (mop), and plays games (computer).

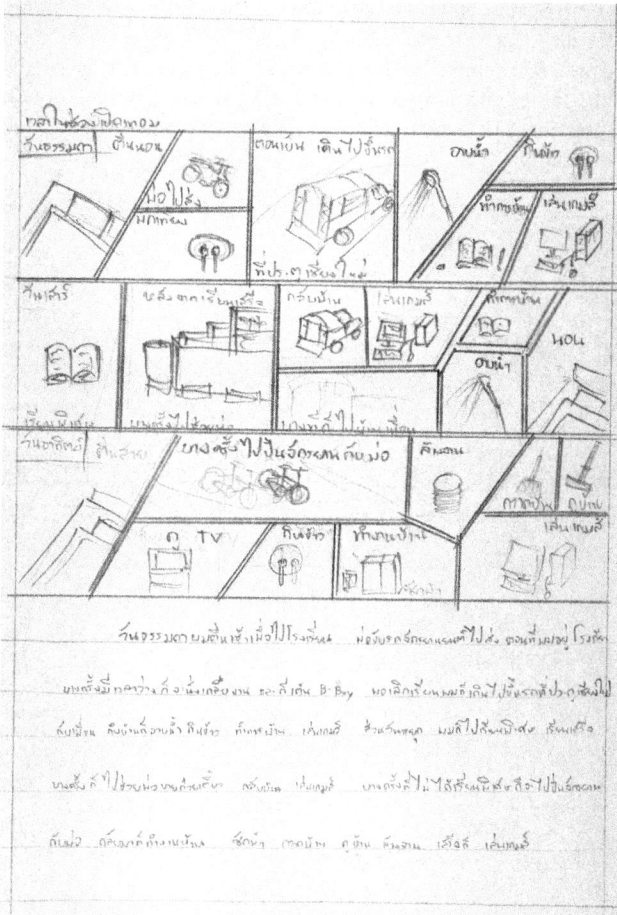

Figure 15.3. Pond's regular day routines.

The text at the bottom of the page elucidates the three rows of pictures:

On schooldays, I get up early to go to school. Dad takes me to school on his motorcycle. While at school when I have some free time, I try to clear away my work and practice B-Boy Dance. After school, I walk with my friends to Chiang Mai Gate to get on a bus. Upon arriving home, I shower, eat, do my homework, and play games. During weekends, I go to special tutoring class. After class, I sometimes go to help my dad sell noodles, then go home, play games. Some days, when I don't have to go to tutoring class, I go biking with my dad. I do homework when I return home, do my laundry, sweep, and mop the floor, wash the dishes. After finishing my chores, I play computer games. (English translation)

211

In Figure 15.4, Pond depicts holiday *days in his life*. (Many images are common to the 'regular day' cartoon pictured in Figure 15.3.) At a nearby temple, hungry dogs abound as represented in the middle of the second row of the following cartoon. Pond's father encourages his son to take scraps from the noodle parlour to feed them. They enact Buddhist values of compassion and respect for living things routinely in this daily ritual.

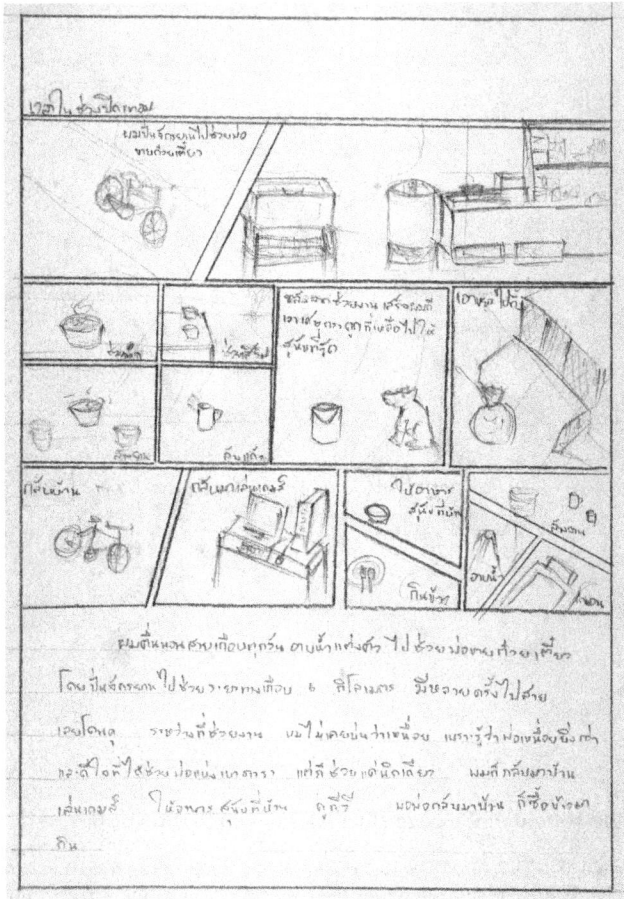

Figure 15.4. Pond's holiday day script.

Pond's drawings and texts are veridical, careful, and almost architectural. He drew the frames and gutters of his cartoons with precision and innovation (some gutters were drawn diagonally to accommodate all the ideas he wanted to incorporate), and it was clear that he had worked out in advance how to fit everything into the days' cartoons.

Pond's cartooning reflects his enduring dedication to his home life. He details the minutiae of his days—from mopping the floor and disposing of the garbage to serving noodles and washing up afterwards to taking a shower and reading cartoons and playing on his computer. His reflections on his cartoons leave no doubt that his routines are a source of some comfort to him in this transitional period of his life.

CONCLUSIONS

Cartoons Contributing to Theory

From a theoretical perspective, teen expressions are critical to the development of an understanding of teenagers' 'habitus' or natural mode of life (Goodnow, 1997, 2002). If we are to know youth in the many roles they wish to share with us, or on the many levels on which they operate, reflective interviews, photo elicitations, and filmed *days in their lives* are all rich contenders for grounded theoretical analyses, but the value added from cartooning opens unprecedented doors for extended reflections, complementing our existing lengthy engagement with these youths. Encouraging this sort of exchange provides a welcome forum that enlists deeper practical and theoretical insights.

Despite the relative brevity of the cartoons, several themes instrumental to the understanding of doing well in the face of adversity emerge in the cartoons and in the reflective discussions following the production of the cartoons. Themes of religious pride and allegiance to rigorous moral and cultural codes, along with dedication to home life, become vivid. Although the NRP findings depict (among others) traditional cultural values and strengths (Theron, Cameron, Lau, Didkowsky, & Mabitsela, 2009), the place of cultural pride and human capital in youths' perceptions of their own resilience (Brooks, 2009, 2010), emotional security (Cameron, Tapanya, & Gillen, 2006), and the protective functions of family responsibilities (Didkowsky, 2010), cartoons embellish these themes in graphic reflection.

Our very outgoing participating youth, Idzel, took us, in her cartoons, outside the frameworks she had created in her interviews, photographs, and filmed *day*. She provided us with a rather individualistic landscape of personal thoughts and emotions about the challenges her religious precepts posed to the development of her femininity and about her courage in being different from her school peer group. Pond, who was more reserved, focused on externals that could reflect a collectivist perspective. His care and attention to his detailed cartooning as well as his inclusion of more information than he knew we had previously obtained provided a forum for dissemination to a wider audience. The cartooning choices of these teenagers brought new dimensions to the pictures we were framing of them and encouraged our belief that we should listen to their perspectives in many media but perhaps especially when they had a chance to engage with words and pictures together.

Cartooning as Methodology

After examining and discussing the cartoons of these two resilient youths, we see that there are distinctly different graphic approaches that teenagers might take when asked to create cartoons, but whichever paths they choose, these artefacts of their contemplations enhance both their and our reflections on their strengths. Idzel's cartoons afford glimpses of the inner terrain of her experiences played out in emotionally vivid dialogues, captions, and sketches. The small dramatic incidents afford us insight into the trials she faces more vividly than words or pictures alone could do. Cartooning the challenges she faced in confronting the gap between what she wished to express as a developing Mormon young woman and what she was prepared to tolerate in social disrespect generated for Idzel and for us valuable information on her sophisticated insights into these challenges: Accepting a personal slight is different from accepting attacks on her church. Further, she carefully considered how to develop a cartoon that presented her challenges in the light she wanted, exposing her metacognitive and social awareness of the importance of portraying her faith practices in a favourable yet truthful light. In Pond's case, his cartooning was less emotive and more documentary; he chronicled the details of his daily routine with precision and care. He gave expression to the emotional security that his daily routine conveys in this close attention to detail.

In both instances, reflective discussions deepened the meaning embedded in their cartoons. The interview we held with Idzel added rich information to our interpretation of the visual material. It was, further, the source of increased appreciation of the depth of her contemplations of her roles in her family as a faithful child; her roles with peers, as an atypical teen but one admired for her strength of character; and her interactions with some teachers who ridiculed her religious allegiances. She said of cartooning: "I have to search into my life."

In the case of the not so loquacious Pond, it is interesting to note that he was more verbally responsive when we asked him to describe and reflect on his cartoons than when we invited him simply to talk about his filmed *day*. This might have related to his pride in his graphic skills: When we asked him to draw and comment on his cartooning, he was carefully but much more richly informative. For example, in reflecting on his drawings, he verbalised his hesitation about complaining to his father about work: He reported that he felt that his father was more entitled to complain of exhaustion than he was. During his reflections on his cartoons, Pond emphasised his respect for what his father sacrifices for the family in their noodle shop.

The value of the reflective interviews suggests that although the cartoon products themselves are of interest for their integrative contents and dedication to communicate important life narratives, they are also perhaps even more valuable as engagements in the construction process, eliciting reflections that lie beneath a simple expression of an experience. The drawings and texts were just the beginning; the teenagers' descriptions of the roots of their scenarios were equally rich as they afforded informative nuances and alternative views.

A possible caveat to using cartooning as a method of generating data is that we worked with youths who took pride in their drawing and who were greatly interested in reading cartoons. Although the youths chose different graphic technical approaches, they both most willingly engaged in the activity. It would be unwise to expect that youth who are less comfortable with these media might find this as enjoyable an activity or one so easy to complete.

Despite her proclivity for cartooning, Idzel sought reassurance that the quality of her drawing was secondary to its communicative value. This suggests that researchers should be sensitive to putting youth who engage in drawing activities at ease, even when participants enjoy comics and are familiar with drawing as a medium of expression.

Our participants also clearly sought feedback on their artistic and storytelling skills. They valued appreciation of their efforts. The youths were keen not just for us to reflect on the work they did but to make sure that others would see their cartoons and gain an appreciation of lives like theirs. This should remind researchers that visual data deserve more popular dissemination. Both participants were not only happy to share their work for this chapter but were willing to have the cartoons go on display so a wider audience might grasp the tenor of their lives. They felt it would be exciting to have exhibitions or poster sessions displaying a wide variety of comic strips that reflected the various particularities of the mundane but that also showed the daily rounds of other such resilient teenagers. We agree and feel that their unique reflections, which are at the same time common reflections of indomitability, would be informative.

Final Thoughts

Both the act of cartooning and reflecting on this act encouraged deeper understanding of our participants' resilience: It was a forum for our participants to express, richly, perspectives on their lived experiences. When they had trouble finding words for an experience, they could represent it graphically, and when they felt they could not draw something, they used words.

Of course, cartooning would not appeal to all teenagers, but since cartoons are so widely appreciated by many youths, it would be of some value to explore further the potential of using this method to elicit narratives that remain as yet untold.

Their artefacts, and reflections on them, would both provide additional valuable knowledge for our information set from a divergent perspective and offer a new methodology, a revealing standpoint on these teenagers' experiences and their sensitive perceptions of them.

NOTES

[i] This project is an extension of the multi-method Negotiating Resilience Project funded by the Social Sciences and Humanities Research Council of Canada (410-2007-0427). The Principal Investigator is Michael Ungar and the Co-Investigators are Catherine Ann Cameron and Linda Liebenberg. We thank Cindy Lau and Rakchanok Chayutkul for dedicated research assistance, and we are especially

grateful to the participating teenagers without whom we could not have conducted this research so satisfactorily. Corresponding author: Catherine Ann Cameron, Department of Psychology, University of British Columbia, Vancouver, BC, V6T 1Z4, acameron@psych.UBC.ca.

ii The words 'day in the life' and variations of this formulation such as 'day' are italicised when they are used to describe participants' actions and experiences as well as events that were captured on video during the application of this specific visual methodology.

iii Locally determined institutional ethical approvals were obtained with particular respect to the potentially invasive visual methodologies and the anticipation of some 20 hours of voluntary teenager participation.

iv She was simply asked to depict her experiences as cartoons and was given a month to create the cartoons. We visited her once to see her work in progress, and a second meeting involved a detailed discussion of her cartoons, primarily obtaining her reflections on her goals and on the processes she had drawn upon in enacting the productions.

REFERENCES

Bronfenbrenner, U. (1979). *The ecology of human development*. Cambridge, MA: Harvard University Press.

Brooks, C. (2009, June). *Resilience through our eyes: Urban Aboriginal youth negotiate self-identity*. Paper presented at Protective Factors During a "Day in the Life" of Resilient, Relocated Adolescents in Eight Communities around the Globe symposium at the annual meeting of the Jean Piaget Society, Park City, UT.

Brooks, C. (2010, March). *Urban Aboriginal youth's visions of resilience and social capital*. Paper presented at Adolescents' Negotiating Resilience during One 'Day in Their Lives' symposium at the annual meeting of the Society for Research on Adolescence, Philadelphia, PA.

Cameron, C. A. (2004). Schools are not enough: It takes a whole community. In M. L. Stirling, C. A. Cameron, N. Nason-Clark, & B. Miedema (Eds.), *Understanding abuse: Partnering for change* (pp. 269–294). Toronto, ON: University of Toronto Press.

Cameron, C. A., & Creating Peaceful Learning Environments Team. (2002a). *Worlds apart ... coming together: Part 1: 'She said, he said'* [Community facilitator training video]. Fredericton, NB: Muriel McQueen Fergusson Centre for Family Violence Research.

Cameron, C. A., & Creating Peaceful Learning Environments Team. (2002b). *Worlds apart ... coming together: Part 2: Together we can* [Community facilitator handbook]. Fredericton, NB: Muriel McQueen Fergusson Centre for Family Violence Research.

Cameron, C. A., Tapanya, S., & Gillen, J. (2006). Swings, hammocks, and rocking chairs as secure bases during A Day in the Life in diverse cultures. *Child and Youth Care Forum, 35*(3), 231–247.

Didkowsky, N. (2010, March). *The relationship between contribution to community-wellbeing and resilience for youth in transition between cultures and contexts*. Paper presented at Adolescents' Negotiating Resilience During One 'Day in Their Lives' symposium at the annual meeting of the Society for Research on Adolescence, Philadelphia, PA.

Gillen, J., & Cameron, C. A. (2010). *International perspectives on early childhood research: A day in the life*. Basingstoke, England: Palgrave Macmillan. doi:10.1057/9780230251373.

Gillen, J., Cameron, C. A., Tapanya, S., Pinto, G., Hancock, R., Young, S., & Accorti Gamannossi, B. (2007). 'A day in the life': Advancing a methodology for the cultural study of development and learning in early childhood. *Early Child Development and Care, 177*(2), 207–218. doi:10.1080/03004430500393763.

Goodnow, J. J. (1997). Parenting and the transmission and internalization of values: From social-cultural perspectives to within-family analyses. In J. E. Grusec & L. Kuczynski (Eds.), *Parenting and children's internalization of values: A handbook of contemporary theory* (pp. 333–361). Hoboken, NJ: Wiley.

Goodnow, J. J. (2002). Adding culture to studies of development: Toward changes in procedure and theory. *Human Development, 45*(4), 237–245. doi:10.1159/000064984.

Gordon, S. B. (2003). The Mormon question: Polygamy and constitutional conflict in nineteenth-century America. *Journal of Supreme Court History, 28*(1), 14–29. doi:10.1111/1540-5818.00053.

Heraty, P. (2008). Every picture tells a story. *Vancouver Foundation newsmagazine, 1*(1), 8–11. Retrieved from http://www.vancouverfoundation.ca/documents/VFmag-june2008_000.pdf.

Hui, J. (2009, October). *Shanghai Daily: Travel collage. Graphic memoir on pacific Canada and diaspora.* Paper presented at the annual meeting of the Canadian Asian Studies Association, Vancouver, BC.

Macias, Y., Wilson, A., Hui, J., & Heyman, V. (2010, April). *Reflections on the life of a story: Engaging, creating, and dialoguing with Holocaust testimony.* Paper presented at the 2010 Holocaust Conference: Bearing Witness: Memory, Representation, and Pedagogy in the Post-Holocaust Age, Shenandoah University, Winchester, VA.

McCloud, S. (1993). *Understanding comics: The invisible art.* New York, NY: HarperCollins.

McCloud, S. (2000). *Reinventing comics: How imagination and technology are revolutionizing an art form.* New York, NY: HarperCollins.

McCloud, S. (2006). *Making comics: Storytelling secrets of comics, manga, and graphic novels.* New York, NY: HarperCollins.

Pinto, G., Accorti Gamannossi, B., & Cameron, C. A. (2010). Notational systems. In J. Gillen & C. A. Cameron (Eds.), *International perspectives on early childhood research: A day in the life* (pp. 114–136). Basingstoke, England: Palgrave Macmillan.

Shaw, M. J. (2007). Drawing on the collections. *Journalism Studies, 8*(5), 742–754. doi:10.1080/14616700701504716

Sobel, D. M., & Lillard, A. S. (2001). The impact of fantasy and action on young children's understanding of pretence. *British Journal of Developmental Psychology, 19*(1), 85–98. doi:10.1348/026151001165976.

Takahashi, N., & Sugioka, T. (1988). The developmental study of children's understanding of animated cartoons. *Japanese Journal of Educational Psychology, 36*(2), 135–143. Retrieved from http://ci.nii.ac.jp/naid/110001897477.

Theron, L., Cameron, C. A., Lau, C., Didkowsky, N., & Mabitsela, M. (2009, August). *A day in the lives of four resilient youth: An investigation of the cultural roots of resilience.* Paper presented at the annual conference of the Psychological Society of South Africa, Cape Town, South Africa.

Ungar, M., Brown, M., Liebenberg, L., Othman, R., Kwong, W. M., Armstrong, M., & Gilgun, J. (2007). Unique pathways to resilience across cultures. *Adolescence, 42*(166), 287–310. Retrieved from http://www.resilienceproject.org.

Watson, J. (2008). Autographic disclosure and genealogies of desire in Alison Bechdel's *Fun Home. Biography, 31*(1), 27–58. doi:10.1353/bio.0.0006.

BEFORE THE CAMERAS ROLL: DRAWING STORYBOARDS TO ADDRESS GENDERED POVERTY

Claudia Mitchell, Naydene de Lange, and Relebohile Moletsane

INTRODUCTION

"Girls Can Make It" is the title of a storyboard created by a small group of adult participants during a workshop in Kigali, Rwanda, on using visual participatory methodologies in addressing gendered poverty in Rwanda. Their title is an optimistic one and is in harmony with the United Nations Millennium Development Goals (MDGs). The challenge, of course, is whether girls can actually "make it", given that their voices are often left out when it comes to envisioning solutions to the obstacles that confront them.

In this chapter, we describe the somewhat serendipitous discovery of the storyboard as a specific drawing text, and we describe its use in a participatory visual methodologies workshop that addressed poverty in rural contexts. We chose to focus on the work of a group of 60 adults within the larger international workshop setting. We have also followed a similar procedure with young people, parents, teachers, and healthcare workers in rural South Africa and university lecturers teaching and researching in agriculture in Ethiopia. We discuss some of the key themes and issues that we saw in the storyboards that were produced in the Kigali workshop and also reflect on some of the challenges, strengths, and opportunities of storyboards. We conclude with a discussion of how researchers might incorporate the storyboard into the repertoires of visual data possibilities, particularly in relation to working in an area where 'every voice counts'.

SETTING THE SCENE

Signatory nation states have committed themselves, in terms of the MDGs, to a range of goals, from ensuring the eradication of extreme poverty and hunger (MDG 1) by 2015 to improving gender equality and promoting the empowerment of women (MDG 3) as well as improving maternal health (MDG 5). In particular, MDG 1 requires nation states to achieve three targets by 2015: Target 1 aims to "halve the proportion of people whose income is less than $1 a day", Target 2 aims to "achieve full and productive employment and decent work for all, including women and young people", and Target 3 aims to "halve, between 1990 and 2015, the proportion of people who suffer from hunger". Regarding gender equality, the United Nations Convention on the Elimination of All Forms of Discrimination

L. Theron et al. (eds.), Picturing Research: Drawing as Visual Methodology, 219–231.

against Women (CEDAW) has committed member states to ensuring that legislation and interventions are put in place to prevent any form of discrimination against women. In this context, regional policies and treaties have been developed to address local contexts and to make certain that there is close monitoring and evaluation of member states' progress towards achieving these targets. For example, the Southern African Development Community (SADC), of which South Africa is a member, has put in place a policy framework that considers gender and gender equality as key to effective development interventions in the region. Adopted by member states in 1997, the "SADC Declaration on Gender and Development" has committed heads of states to ensuring the eradication of all gender inequalities in the region. It notes that gender equality is a fundamental human right and commits to "the integration and mainstreaming of gender issues into the SADC Programme of Action and Community Building Initiative as a strategy towards sustainable development in the region" (SADC, 1997, point B).

In the context of these international policy frameworks and the concomitant national policies on gender equality, significant inroads have been made towards gender parity and equality in Africa over the past decade, particularly in the social and political spheres. As has been highlighted internationally, there has been a great deal of progress made in the establishment of gender-responsive legislation and reforms, allowing greater political representation of women. For instance, women in Rwanda have achieved the highest political representation of any country in the world. Liberia has elected the first female president of the African continent, Ellen Johnson-Sirleaf. South Africa is not far behind, boasting one of the highest number of women cabinet ministers of any African country in 2009 (42%), albeit down from previous post-1994 parliaments (Mbola, 2009).

However, the positive outcomes of these improvements in political gender inequities often fail to translate into improved quality of life for the majority of women and children, particularly rural African girls and women. This is in spite of the various poverty reduction programmes that have been implemented in South Africa, including, for example, the Expanded Public Works Programme (EPWP) of the national Department of Public Works, the Integrated Sustainable Rural Development Programme (ISRDP), the Urban Renewal Programme (URP), and the Department of Social Development's Food and Emergency Relief Programme (Public Service Commission, 2007). There is growing evidence in South Africa that the number of women living in poverty has increased disproportionately to that of men (Africa Partnership Forum [APF] Support Unit & the New Partnership for Africa's Development [NEPAD] Secretariat, 2007). The 2000 measurement of poverty by Statistics South Africa indicated that "35% of the total population, or 14.3 million South Africans are vulnerable to food insecurity" (South African National Department of Agriculture, 2002, p. 22). Among the most vulnerable in this group were women, children, and the elderly. The gendered aspect of poverty is evidenced by data suggesting that during the period from 2002 to 2006, the percentage of children who went hungry was substantially higher in female-headed households than in male-headed households. In 2006, children in 3.4% of female-headed households went hungry as compared to 1.6% in male-headed households

(Lehohla, 2007). Furthermore, a recent study carried out by Amnesty International (2008) on the high incidence of HIV and AIDS among rural women in South Africa identifies the co-existence of HIV and sexual violence, noting that inequality and poverty play a key role.

Similarly, elsewhere on the African continent, research from Ethiopia suggests that girls and women are being marginalised in the country's rural sector. This is at odds with the National Women's Policy, which has sought, in recent years, to address and support the role of women in agriculture. Federal and Regional Family Laws, Women's Policy, and special constitutional provisions are just some of the gender-sensitive policies and development strategies introduced in recent years by the Ethiopian government with the support of donors (International Livestock Research Institute [ILRI], 2004). The Ethiopian Bureau of Agriculture, under the Women's Policy, has officially introduced extension services for female-linked agricultural activities. It has encouraged women-headed households to participate in programs and facilitated the provision of credit and other resources to rural women. However, despite the appearance of policy support, other data indicates that these national and regional-level guidelines and provisions have not been adequately implemented. For example, even after the introduction of guidelines for increasing availability of agricultural extension services to women, 2001 data shows that only 3% of the 14% of farmers who received such services were female. Furthermore, over 95% of female recipients were given support for home economics projects rather than livestock activities (a focus that was non-existent among male recipients) (Buchy & Basaznew, 2005). At the same time, a key component of Ethiopia's National Action Plan for Gender Equality ("Unleashing the potential of women") seeks to assist women to achieve gender equality through active and empowered participation in all development programs. The MDGs also serve as a key instrument to help women achieve equality. The 2004 MDG report for Ethiopia calls for the need to focus on women in rural areas, noting the necessity for women to have equal access to assets such as land and livestock within families (The Ministry of Finance and Economic Development [MOFED] & United Nations Country Team, 2003).

A critical gap remains in understanding the lived experiences of girls and women—particularly in rural areas—where these do not neatly divide into the health sector, education sector, or agriculture sector. As we highlight in this chapter, the idea of envisioning solutions must start with the story itself—the story of the lived experiences of women. We therefore explore how solutions can be envisaged through the drawing of a storyboard.

DRAWING OURSELVES INTO THE STORY

The fieldwork described in this chapter is situated in Rwanda, set against the backdrop of the good intentions of various national and international policies addressing the needs of girls and women. The fieldwork is also framed by the many barriers to the socio-economic empowerment of girls and women. In the three countries—South Africa, Ethiopia[i], and Rwanda—where we have worked,

221

we have focused our research on what De Lange et al. have termed an 'every voice counts' framework.[ii] Such a framework acknowledges the significance of participation and engagement, drawing on methodologies such as community-based participatory video in which participants themselves construct narratives of social change at various levels (see also Mitchell & De Lange, 2011; Moletsane et al., 2009). Our focus in this chapter is on storyboarding, as a drawing-into-social-change activity, and the examples referred to come, as we have noted above, from an intervention in Rwanda. However, we also note the contributions of this work to settings in South Africa and Ethiopia.

The use of drawings revolves around the place of the storyboard as a key component of our work in community-based participatory video. Our idea of community-based participatory video, as we describe elsewhere (Mitchell & De Lange, 2011; Moletsane et al., 2009) is based on the idea that 'any community group can make a video in a day'. In such an approach, community participants go from identifying which issues are important in their lives and choosing a topic to focus on for a video to planning out a short video (through the use of storyboarding) and shooting and screening it—all in one session. Drawing the images in a storyboard is just one piece of the process. A storyboard, stated very simply, is a visual outline or skeleton made up of a series of drawings or sketches. In the case of our 'video in a day' approach, each sketch or drawing represents one camera shot. For us, it is a planning device that participants use to discuss their video production—what it is meant to do and the sequence of shots. Although there are a number of digital programs that professional filmmakers might use to plan out their shots (see, for example, Oliver, 2009), we have always used a very 'low tech' storyboard. Such a storyboard relies on a set of eight or 10 frames of a rectangular shape (much like a succession of comic book frames) within which a small group can sketch out the basic sequence of events of their story. The storyboard consists of a title, shot 1, shot 2, shot 3, and so on through to the credits at the end. Creating the storyboard is just one step in the process and something that prepares each group for shooting its video. However, as we describe here, the storyboarding process of planning (through drawing) the shots in a short video on a specific theme can also constitute a visual text in and of itself.

VIDEO PRODUCTION FOR 60 PARTICIPANTS ... A SOLUTION

Our process usually begins with an introduction to the field in which we are working, such as HIV and AIDS, gender-based violence, poverty alleviation, and so on. The participants are given a clear and specific prompt like the following: *"Explore issues that are important to you and that affect your professional lives as teachers."* The participants then brainstorm the 'issues', which are written up on a large sheet of paper. Each participant attaches coloured dots (stickers) next to the 'issues' that he or she thinks are the most important. By tallying up the dots, it becomes clear which issues the group deems most important and what the theme for the video could be about.

The team then facilitates the writing of a short storyboard, which depicts graphically the group's story by encapsulating the chosen 'issue' and by presenting some solutions to the problem. The participants are then introduced to the technicalities of working a video camera and to the basics of taking short video clips (shots). For example, they are told not to shoot into the light or not to shoot in a windy location where their voices might not be picked up by the camera's microphone. A No-Editing-Required approach follows, which requires them to take 8–10 shots of 10–30 seconds each, one after the other, providing a seamless transition between shoots. Once they have filmed their stories, the groups gather to watch all the participatory videos that have been created.

Figure 16.1. N-E-R approach to participatory video.

Often, as researchers, we are enthusiastic to share our visual participatory methodology skills with other researchers, especially where research with a social change agenda (Schratz & Walker, 1995) could possibly make a difference. In the international workshop on participatory methodologies for working with rural girls and women, we set out to introduce a group of approximately 60 participants (both men and women) to participatory video. The task involved explaining and showing what participatory video is, how it can be used to initiate change, and how the participants themselves can use it in their own context to generate solutions for alleviating poverty. The large size of the group presented challenges for engaging the participants in developing a participatory video. There was a need for some improvisation on our part. As described in the next section, we sought to engage in the process without necessarily using video cameras.

The Process

In the workshop in Rwanda, the participants were provided with a brief introduction to participatory video, as previously described. After this, the facilitators showed two South African participatory video productions to the

223

participants: *Seeing for Ourselves* and *Masenze Umehluko*: *Together We Can Make a Difference*. In this way, the participants were given a clear picture of what was expected of them and how the process of participatory video production works.

The two South African videos illustrate how groups of between 8 and 35 participants can successfully engage in participatory video work. The aim of the participatory video productions was not only to identify problems, but, more importantly, to reflect on possible solutions in order to enable the participants to take action in their communities. The workshop in which *Seeing for Ourselves* was produced involved a group of 35 parents, teachers, community healthcare workers, and learners who were asked to identify issues that affect their daily lives. They came up with issues such as poverty, HIV and AIDS, gender-based violence, teenage pregnancy, crime, and so on (De Lange, 2008; Moletsane et al., 2009). In *Masenze Umehluko*, the 8 teachers were asked to identify issues that are important to them and that affect their professional lives as teachers. They identified a variety of issues but chose to work with two: lack of parental involvement and poverty (De Lange, Olivier, & Wood, 2008). Showing *Masenze Umehluko* to the 60 participants in Rwanda allowed them not only to see the final video *products* made by the participants but also the *process*—including the storyboard—used when doing participatory video work.

In the Rwanda workshop, instead of working through the whole process of planning and filming with a large group of participants, we could pick up only on the power of discussion around the making of the storyboard in the 90 minutes allocated to us. The storyboard became the product. We placed the participants in 10 groups of 6 each, gave each group a blank storyboard, and provided the following prompt to generate a narrative text: "*Identify one challenge related to the social and economic empowerment of rural girls and women in Rwanda.*" The groups were required to develop a story in 6 to 8 scenes, which would clearly show the issue and the solution. For the groups to identify one out of the many challenges they face required some debate: We witnessed this as we moved around the groups that were working on their storyboards. Similarly, to reach consensus about a solution to depict on the storyboard also required discussion and careful thinking about the best or most appropriate solution.

We allowed 30 minutes for the creation of the storyboard (discussion, drawing, and writing), but with the high level of engagement, the groups were reluctant to stop working! We are convinced that they could have sustained their interest and engagement for much longer and perhaps even more nuanced analyses of the issues and solutions would have been achieved. In future workshops, more time could be allocated, especially when we are working with large groups such as this and where the process does not include the participatory video as the final process/product. To allow others to actually see the participatory video work, we usually show the short videos to the whole group, but here we allowed each group to explain briefly their identified problem and their envisaged solution so that all 60 participants could hear what each group identified as the most important issue. In choosing to focus on only the storyboard, we showed how we might, without cameras and lights, and in only a short period of time, still draw on the power of participatory video.

The Product: Our Reading of the Storyboards

The workshop in Rwanda yielded 10 storyboards instead of the usual 10 short videos. However, as we documented elsewhere (Moletsane et al., 2009) and as Weber & Mitchell (2007) have shown, visual narratives, in whatever form, lend themselves to close readings. In the case of the 10 storyboards produced in the Rwanda workshop, there is clearly a fascinating range of 'treatments' of the topic: *"challenges and solutions to addressing the social and economic empowerment of rural girls and women"*. Given the important role of the storyboard as a planning device in video production, we saw firsthand the potential for communities to engage with the issues through the storyboarding process—by drawing themselves into the issues.

First, participants identified very different issues on which to focus. We see this in their choice of working titles, which is an important stage in the storyboarding (and also the video-making process). In the case of the 10 storyboards, the working titles (and issues) indicated many social challenges: "Family Dilemma: HIV/AIDS in the Family—A Contaminated Husband and Non-Contaminated Wife", "Lack of Self-Confidence Among Rural Girls", "Girls Can Make It", "Coming Together: Reducing Effects of Poverty on Girls Dropping out of Schools", "Socio-Psychological Impact of Family-Based Violence", and "Parents' Attitudes to Girls' Education". Thematically, the storyboards can be read as visual representations of some of the many key issues in girls' education more broadly: poverty, gender inequality, HIV and AIDS, violence, and the lack of awareness of girls' rights. Interestingly, several of the storyboards make the same point that Brown and Gilligan (1992) made close to 2 decades ago: We cannot look at the lives of girls without looking at the lives of women. In the "Coming Together" storyboard, for example, it is the women who make it possible for girls to go to school. It is the community sensitisation in the storyboard "Girls Can Make It" that helps men and women see the value of girls' education.

Second, a critical point in the storyboarding process, as we have framed it, is that the 'producers' (who are also the participants) must come to some sort of resolution in addressing the issue that they have identified. Indeed, one of the tensions that we often see in small group work is a type of perseveration: Participants simply come up with an endless list of all the problems and then spend little time on finding solutions. Although this might be resolved by directed facilitation and allocating more time to the group work activity, we believe storyboarding (and participatory video making) offers a more efficient means of identifying solutions to the issues. In the storyboarding activity, participants have only seven to nine frames in which to tell the story and resolve it. This does not mean that the storyboard has to have a happy ending, but it does mean that there has to be some type of definitive ending. In the case of the "Coming Together" storyboard, the girls are shown working in the fields while the boys go to school. A group of rural women then start a co-operative and engage in a number of activities, including educating the village on children's rights and gender equality. They also teach women how to make better use of their land. The women go to other villages to teach what they have learned. In addition, because the women in these communities are so successful, they are now able to send both sons and daughters to school. In "Girls Can Make It", the girls are shown burdened with domestic chores and therefore unable to go to school. Rose, the protagonist, has not gone to school at all. However, through a district sensitisation program, parents start discussing the issues, and Rose gets to attend school. Not only that, she scores the highest marks in the district and eventually becomes the Minister of Education.

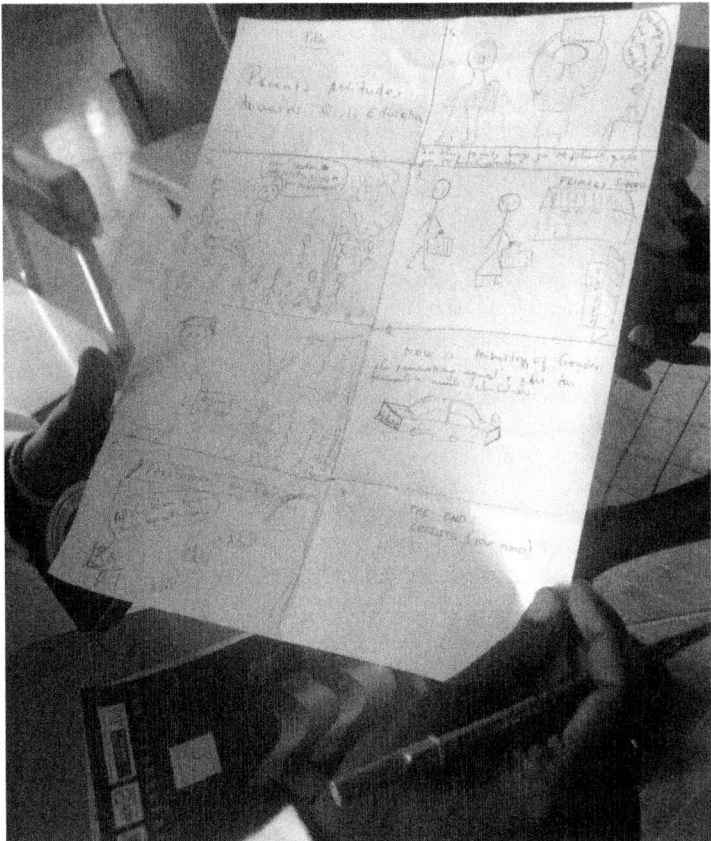

Figure 16.2. The storyboard for "Parents' Attitudes to Girls' Education".

Third, it is interesting to notice the differences in the styles of drawing and important to discuss whether this affects the messages in the storyboards. Some of the storyboards (as in Figure 16.1) were made up of very simple stick figures whereas the storyboard "Socio-Psychological Impact of Family-Based Violence" (see Figure 16.2) was made up of more sophisticated drawings that show more complex relationships between the characters. As Oliver (2009) observed, storyboards can, of course, be artistic works in and of themselves, but, as can be seen in the examples from the workshop, it is the process of sequencing, filling in of the detail, and coming to some sort of resolution that is the point here.

We might also think of these storyboards as a type of cartoon (see Chapter 15 in this volume) or as a manifestation of a comic book or graphic novel. We include the complete storyboard of "Socio-Psychological Impact of Family-Based Violence" (see Figure 16.2) as a way of showing the full product, and also to highlight, in this case, its meta-element—the reference to a drawing in the storyboard. The storyboard starts with the portrayal of a little girl who is clearly doing poorly in school. The teacher notices this and asks the little girl to draw any picture. The little girl draws a picture of a father threatening his children: "I will kill you" and "Forgive us Dad". The teacher takes on the responsibility of visiting the family and offering counselling. At the same time, the little girl flees the household and goes to stay with her stepmother. She eventually returns to school and engages actively in the class: "Every classmate is amazed about her." In the final square are the credits—the names of the authors/artists.

Finally, notwithstanding the sheer economy of effort of small groups identifying issues and seeking resolutions, we were interested in the actual engagement and ownership of the problems. The very simple feature of listing the credits contributes to this sense of ownership. Although there were no video products to show, when we asked each group to at least report to the whole group of 60 participants on its chosen title and the issue being highlighted, we were interested in the engagement process. Seeing the value of each group's work, the program of the day was adjusted to allow more time for further engagement by asking each group to choose 5 minutes from its storyboard and to act it out for the whole group. Although we think that the storyboarding process was useful for tackling certain burning issues, the dramatisations were clearly an effective way of engaging participants further and for putting into action some of their creativity. More than anything else, it highlighted for us the blurring of boundaries between visual genres and, hence, the significance of multi-modalities. By this, we mean that work represented though one mode often translates into other modes of expression, something highlighted by researchers working in the area of arts-based methodologies (see, for example, Knowles & Cole, 2008). In this case, the 'drawing-into-performance' helped us see the overlaps.

Figure 16.3. The storyboard of "Socio-Psychological Impact of Family-Based Violence".

REFLECTING ON THE PROCESS OF STORYBOARDING

In reflecting on the process, we see that there are a number of challenges to this type of 'group draw' activity. Perhaps the most difficult was simply to have the participants 'get something down on paper'. This may in part be because adult participants appear to be reluctant to draw. In this case, the process relied on one or two group members doing the drawing and the others doing the directing. It may be even more intimidating to draw on behalf of a group. And given the delay in starting the drawing, there was a great flurry of activity towards the end of the process in order to accommodate the time constraints. This points to the importance of the workshop facilitators' allocation of time for the beginning, middle, and end of the storyboard process. However, perhaps it is important to place less emphasis on process–product issues since it is the discussion and creativity behind the scenes that is important and not the quality of the drawings. This was something we, as facilitators, emphasised.

There are, nonetheless, a number of strengths to the storyboarding process. As noted in the previous section, the production of the storyboard is itself a way to go deeply in a discussion, but is also a way to contain it, since at a certain point in time the group has to have a beginning, middle, and end to the story. Critically, there is also something to show, and even though flip-chart brainstorming activities may also offer a product at their end, they are more often than not long lists of ideas that are not necessarily 'constructed' into something. We think that the idea of the concrete story (or interview or other type of narrative) somehow takes very abstract concepts such as 'poverty', 'socio-economic development', and 'gender' and puts them into very concrete line drawings. Taken as a whole, these drawings, which tell a story through eight or so squares, provide yet another take on drawings as visual data, and as researchers, we might see opportunities to develop new approaches to interpreting drawing. As noted in the section on our reading of the storyboards, the types of stories being told, the approaches to drawing, and the use of words and drawings—to name only some of the variations—offer raw material for new insights. On further reflection of the strengths of such work, we see the participants having a product—a storyboard about a problem and some envisaged solutions—that they can take back to 'enact' in their community, as the provision of an entry point for engaging with possible solutions to the problem.

Gender Inequalities

The storyboards produced by the young people, teachers, and healthcare workers in South Africa (Moletsane et al., 2009), by the lecturers in an agricultural faculty in Ethiopia, and by workshop participants in Rwanda (as described in this chapter) as part of a video-making process, contribute to deepening an understanding of gender inequalities. As for the obstacles facing rural girls and women in Rwanda, South Africa, Ethiopia, and other parts of Africa, gender inequalities not only prevent them from benefiting from efforts to combat poverty and to empower women but also impede them from contributing directly to addressing the challenges they face. The result is often that girls' and women's choices and capacities are usually not adequately taken into account when responses to health, sanitation, or agricultural challenges, including rural innovations and related micro credit opportunities, are being designed. Community participation is enshrined in social and legal frameworks, particularly in relation to the commitment of South Africa and Rwanda to decentralisation and local governance. However, decentralisation remains an ideal rather than a practice commonly applied in the everyday lives of citizens. For girls and women, there are added barriers to participation by virtue of their low status in the community (as demonstrated, for example, by the disproportionate number of girls and women who are victims of gender violence). For rural girls and women, these barriers are accentuated by geographic isolation. Although many of these barriers are acknowledged by various organisations, there are relatively few structures that work with girls and women. Few place 'giving a voice' at the centre of programming, even in programmes in which the issues are addressed by the community at large and often even more so when the issues are addressed by girls and women themselves.

CONCLUSION

As fascinating as it was to go back over the storyboarding narratives, we are also interested in locating this work in a broader framework of cultural production and social change. We see the storyboarding activity as part of what Henry Jenkins (2006) referred to as a participatory culture. Each of the storyboards was co-created by a group, and although we had no clear sense of the group dynamics, we did manage to get a bird's eye view of group process in action. This was especially significant when the groups were given an opportunity to perform small segments of their productions. More than anything, we see that this kind of work calls for some greater convergence in how visual researchers talk about the various visual forms. Thus, as important as it is not to collapse all visual methodologies into one, as Jon Prosser (2010) pointed out, we should not lose sight of their value within a narrative framework. As we noted above, the storyboarding activity drew attention to the significance of multiple modalities in representation. Our interest initially was primarily in the area of participatory video, and yet, the result of the workshop was a set of 10 storyboards, each one offering a complete narrative, followed by short performance pieces. When the groups began working on their storyboards, they were not informed that they might be performing these pieces. The performance was an adaptation—or, perhaps, in the language of Henry Jenkins (2006), we were seeing a convergence of media forms: drawing-video-storytelling.

NOTES

[i] Claudia Mitchell, Ann Smith, and Naydene de Lange facilitated a workshop titled "Visual Participatory Methodologies in Teaching and Research: Gender and HIV & AIDS" with staff of Jimma University College of Agriculture and Veterinarian Medicine in Jimma, Ethiopia, from February 1–6, 2010.

[ii] De Lange, N. et al. (2007–2011). *Every voice counts: Teacher development and rural education in the age of AIDS.* National Research Foundation proposal.

REFERENCES

Africa Partnership Forum (APF) Support Unit & The New Partnership for Africa's Development (NEPAD) Secretariat. (2007). *Gender and economic empowerment in Africa.* Retrieved from the Organisation for Economic Co-operation and Development website: http://www.oecd.org/dataoecd/57/53/38666728.pdf

Amnesty International. (2008). *'I am the lowest end of all': Rural women living with HIV face human rights abuses in South Africa.* London, England: Author. Retrieved from http://www.amnesty.org.

Brown, L. M., & Gilligan, C. (1992). *Meeting at the crossroads: Women's psychology and girls' development.* New York, NY: Ballantine Books.

Buchy, M., & Basaznew. F. (2005). Gender-blind organizations deliver gender-biased services: The case of Awasa Bureau of Agriculture in southern Ethiopia. *Gender, Technology and Development, 9*(2), 235–251. doi:10.1177/097185240500900204.

De Lange, N. (2008). Women and community-based video: Communication in the age of AIDS. *Agenda, 77*, 19–31.

De Lange, N., Olivier, T., & Wood, L. (2008). Participatory video documentary: Just for whom? *Education as Change, 12*(2), 109–122. doi:10.1080/16823200809487210.

International Livestock Research Institute (ILRI). (2004). *What ILRI is doing to address gender in Ethiopia.* Retrieved November 10, 2010, from http://www.ilri.org.

Jenkins, H. (2006). *Convergence culture: Where old and new media collide.* New York: New York University Press.

Knowles, J. G., & Cole, A. L. (2008). *Handbook of the arts in qualitative research: Perspectives, methodologies, examples, and issues.* Thousand Oaks, CA: Sage.

Lehohla, P. (2007, August 23). Women's month reminds us of struggles past, and future challenges. *Statistics South Africa.* Retrieved from http://www.statssa.gov.za/news_archive/ 23August2007_1.asp

Mbola, B. (2009, May 10). South Africa: More women make up new cabinet. *BuaNews.* Retrieved from http://allafrica.com/stories/200905100035.html.

The Ministry of Finance and Economic Development (MOFED) of the Federal Democratic Republic of Ethiopia & United Nations Country Team. (2003). *Millenium Development Goals report: Challenges and prospects for Ethiopia.* Addis Ababa, Ethiopia: Author. Retrieved from www.unmillenniumproject.org/documents/ethiopia_mdgreport.doc.

Mitchell, C., & De Lange, N. (2011). Community-based participatory video and social action in rural South Africa. In E. Margolis & L. Pauwels (Eds.), *The SAGE handbook of visual research methods.* London, England: Sage.

Moletsane, R., Mitchell, C., De Lange, N., Stuart, J., Buthelezi, T., & Taylor, M. (2009). What can a woman do with a camera? Turning the female gaze on poverty and HIV and AIDS in rural South Africa. *International Journal of Qualitative Studies in Education, 22*(3), 315–331. doi:10.1080/ 09518390902835454.

Oliver, K. (2009). *Storyboards ... An unauthorized biography.* Retrieved from the Event Videographer's Resource website: http://www.eventdv.net.

Prosser, J. (2010, March). *Visual ethics.* Proceedings from Digital Futures Symposium: Participatory Archives in the Age of AIDS, Howick, South Africa.

Public Service Commission. (2007). *Report on an audit of government's poverty reduction programmes and projects.* Pretoria, South Africa: Author. Retrieved from http://www.psc.gov.za.

Schratz, M., & Walker, R. (1995). *Research as social change: New opportunities for qualitative research.* New York, NY: Routledge.

South African National Department of Agriculture. (2002). *The integrated food security strategy for South Africa.* Pretoria, South Africa: Author. Retrieved from the Food and Agriculture Organization of the United Nations website: http://www.fao.org/righttofood/inaction/countrylist/SouthAfrica/ IntegratedFoodSecurityStrategy_2002.pdf.

Southern African Development Community (SADC). (1997). *Declaration on gender and development.* Retrieved from http://www.sadc.int/index/browse/page/174.

Weber, S., & Mitchell, C. (2007). Imaging, keyboarding, and posting identities: Young people and new media technologies. In D. Buckingham (Ed.), *Youth, identity, and digital media* (pp. 25–47). Cambridge, MA: MIT Press.

LIST OF CONTRIBUTORS

ABOUT THE EDITORS

CLAUDIA MITCHELL is a James McGill Professor in the Faculty of Education of McGill University, Canada, and an honorary professor in the School of Language, Literacies, Media and Drama Education at the University of KwaZulu-Natal, South Africa, where she is a co-founder of the Centre for Visual Methodologies for Social Change. Her research looks at youth and sexuality in the age of AIDS, children's popular culture, rurality, girlhood, teacher identity, participatory visual and other arts-based methodologies, and strategic areas of gender and HIV and AIDS in social development contexts. She is the co-founder and co-editor of *Girlhood Studies: An Interdisciplinary Journal*.

ANN SMITH has a PhD in Feminist Literary Theory from the University of the Witwatersrand, South Africa, where she currently supervises PhD students working in queer theory and in English literature. She teaches Business Communication and Business Writing skills at the Wits Business School and is an adjunct professor at McGill University where she lectures in literary theory. She is also a visiting lecturer at the University of Pretoria, South Africa, where she supervises doctoral students working in English literature. Ann is the co-author of *Methodologies for Mapping a Southern African Girlhood in the Age of Aids* and the managing editor of *Girlhood Studies: An Interdisciplinary Journal*.

JEAN STUART is discipline head of Media in Language Education and a co-director of the Centre for Visual Methodologies for Social Change in the Faculty of Education at the University of KwaZulu-Natal, South Africa. In her doctoral study, she looked at how visual arts-based approaches can be put in practice by preservice teachers to address HIV and AIDS. Her research interests include using participatory and arts-based approaches that position participants as cultural producers to engage with socio-cultural aspects of health issues. She is a co-author and co-editor of the book *Putting People in the Picture: Visual Methodologies for Social Change*.

LINDA THERON is a professor in the School of Education Sciences, Faculty of Humanities, North-West University, Vaal Triangle Campus, South Africa, and a practising educational psychologist. Her research focuses on understanding the resilience of South African youth and on exploring how teachers affected by HIV and AIDS can be supported towards resilience in the face of the pandemic's multiple challenges. .She is currently involved in the international, ICURA-funded Pathways to Resilience project (under the leadership of Dr. Michael Ungar, Dalhousie University, Canada) and she holds grants from the National Research Foundation and South Africa-Netherlands Research Programme on Alternatives in Development for related resilience-focused research.

ABOUT THE AUTHORS

LARA BOBER is a PhD student in the Department of Integrated Studies in Education at McGill University, Canada. She has worked for several years as an early childhood educator in creative arts programs. Her research is focusing on the political economy of migration, community arts and education, and children's participation in refugee and migrant justice movements.

CATHERINE ANN CAMERON is an honorary professor in the Department of Psychology at the University of British Columbia, Canada, and Emerita and Honorary Research Professor at the University of New Brunswick, Canada. A developmental psychologist, she conducts cultural research with resilient children and youth in communities around the globe using visual methodologies to afford young people a voice in collaboratively seeking to comprehend their experiences. Professor Cameron also examines cross-cultural differences in children's knowledge and moral judgments of verbal deception; stress reactivity of children, youths, and their parents, and parent-child telephone mediated communications, and she evaluates community-based violence prevention interventions.

ZACHARIAH CAMPBELL is a Montreal-based artist and illustrator. He holds BFA degrees in Studio Arts from Nova Scotia College of Art and Design, and in Film Production from Concordia University. He is currently a graduate student in Film Studies at Concordia's Mel Hoppenheim School of Cinema. His interests include transcultural visual media and the interaction between cinema and other fine arts traditions.

NAYDENE DE LANGE is a professor and holds the newly established HIV & AIDS Research Chair at the Nelson Mandela Metropolitan University, Port Elizabeth, South Africa. Her research focuses on visual participatory methodologies in addressing gender and HIV and AIDS. She publishes in international and national journals and has headed up and collaborates with various funded research projects. She was the lead editor of the book *Putting People in the Picture: Visual Methodologies for Social Change* and co-author of the book *Picturing Hope*. She is a National Research Foundation rated researcher.

LIESEL EBERSÖHN is Director of the Unit for Education Research in AIDS and full professor in the Department of Educational Psychology, University of Pretoria. She interrogates resilience within low-resource education environments. Her research acumen has been acknowledged with several research awards in Education and Educational Psychology, multiple invited presentations and lectures globally and regionally, her role as principal- or co-investigator in numerous international and local studies, her position in national- and international education research associations, as well as her prolific publications, and supervision of postgraduate students. She serves on the council of the World Education Research Association (2010–2013) and is incoming editor of the *South African Journal of Education.*

RONÉL FERREIRA is head of the Department of Educational Psychology at the University of Pretoria, South Africa. She acted as coordinator of the MEd

(Educational Psychology) course from 2001 to 2008. She is involved in various research projects, some of which involve international affiliations. Her research focus areas are HIV and AIDS, psychosocial support within the context of vulnerability, asset-based psychosocial coping, and the use of action research in combination with intervention-based studies that could improve community-based coping. Her research accomplishment is signified, in particular, by having received the Samuel Henry Prince Dissertation Award (on disaster research) of the International Sociological Association.

ELIZA M. GOVENDER is a lecturer for the Centre for Communication, Media and Society (CCMS) at the University of KwaZulu-Natal, South Africa. She is also the programme manager for the CCMS Communication for Participatory Development teaching and research track, funded by Johns Hopkins Health and Education in South Africa.

MATHABO KHAU holds a PhD in Gender and Education from the University of KwaZulu-Natal, South Africa. Her doctoral study employed participatory visual methodologies to explore women teachers' experiences of teaching sexuality education in rural schools in the age of HIV and AIDS. She has been a postdoctoral fellow at Linköping University and Örebro University's Centre of Gender Excellence in Sweden (Gendering Excellence (GEXcel): Towards a European Centre of Excellence in Transnational and Transdisciplinary Studies of Changing Gender Relations, Intersectionalities and Embodiment). Currently she is a postdoctoral fellow at Nelson Mandela Metropolitan University under the HIV&AIDS Research Chair. Mathabo's research interest is in sexualities, sexual health and reproduction, sexual pleasure, gender, and HIV in education.

KATIE MACENTEE is a doctoral student in the Department of Integrated Studies in Education at McGill University, Canada, where she is studying the development and integration of assessment strategies into participatory arts-based sexual health initiatives in South Africa and in Canada. This topic follows from her MA research: "Where Are We Now? Qualitative Evaluation of Participatory Arts-Based Sex Education in Canada". She also has experience facilitating collage workshops, working internationally with youth to address the topics of HIV and AIDS, sexuality, and risk.

MONICA MAK is a documentary filmmaker and communications studies scholar. She has been a postdoctoral fellow at the Centre for Visual Methodologies for Social Change at the University of Kwazulu-Natal, South Africa, where she conducted research on participatory video making and its function as a catalyst for self-empowerment and creative self-expression among youth. She directed the award-winning educational short video *Unwanted Images* (2001) while a researcher at the Canada-South Africa Education Management Program. Her PhD, completed at McGill University, focused on the democratizing aspects of digital film technology. She has recently completed *Tiara*, a documentary about Asian-

Canadian women and body image in the context of ethnic beauty pageantry in North America.

MACALANE MALINDI is a senior lecturer in the School of Educational Sciences, Faculty of Humanities, North-West University, Vaal Triangle Campus, South Africa. He completed his PhD in 2009 and has retained the focus of his doctoral study (i.e., resilience in street youth) as his current research focus. He is a collaborating researcher in the international, ICURA-funded Pathways to Resilience project led by Dr. Michael Ungar, Dalhousie University, Canada.

BATHSHEBA MBONGWE is a lecturer of educational psychology at the University of Botswana. Her research interests encompass learning, power, and partnerships. In this regard, her doctoral work at the University of Pretoria, South Africa, investigates power relations in participatory research. She is a graduate of the University at Albany (State University of New York) where she received her Master of Science degree in Educational Psychology and Methodology.

RELEBOHILE MOLETSANE is a professor and the JL Dube Chair in Rural Education in the Faculty of Education at the University of KwaZulu-Natal, South Africa. She has extensive experience in the areas of curriculum studies and gender and education (including gender-based violence and its links to HIV and AIDS and AIDS-related stigma), body politics, and girlhood studies in Southern African contexts. Her interests include the use of participatory visual methodologies in doing research and development work with marginalized groups. She is the co-author (with Claudia Mitchell, Ann Smith, and Linda Chisholm) of the book *Methodologies for Mapping a Southern African Girlhood in the Age of Aids* (Rotterdam: Sense).

KATHLEEN PITHOUSE is a senior lecturer in Teacher Education and Professional Development at the University of KwaZulu-Natal, South Africa. She recently completed a postdoctoral fellowship in the Faculty of Education at McGill University. Her PhD, conducted at the University of KwaZulu-Natal, explored self-study as a research methodology and as a pedagogic approach in teacher education. Kathleen's research interests include teacher development; HIV&AIDS education; collaborative scholarship; memory work; and creative, self-reflexive, and participatory approaches in education and research. She is lead editor of an interdisciplinary book on self-study titled *Making Connections: Self-Study & Social Action* (Pithouse, Mitchell, & Moletsane, 2009) and co-editor of the books *Teaching and HIV & AIDS* (Mitchell & Pithouse, 2009) and *Memory and Pedagogy* (Mitchell, Strong-Wilson, Pithouse, & Allnutt, 2011).

SERTANYA REDDY is a graduate of the Centre for Communication, Media and Society at the University of KwaZulu-Natal, South Africa. She is currently an editorial coordinator and research assistant at the Centre.

LINDA VAN LAREN is a senior lecturer in the School of Science, Mathematics and Technology Education, Faculty of Education, University of KwaZulu-Natal, South

Africa. She is a Mathematics Education lecturer and specializes in the teaching of modules that are designed for primary school teachers. Her research interests lie in assessment in mathematics, multicultural and anti-racist education, self-study methodology, and HIV&AIDS teacher education in mathematics. She earned her PhD from the University of KwaZulu-Natal where she focused on addressing HIV and AIDS in mathematics education with beginning teachers.

INDEX